Better Homes and Gardens®

CREATIVE AMERICAN QUILTING

© Copyright 1989 by Meredith Corporation, Des Moines, Iowa.
All Rights Reserved. Printed in the United States of America.
First Edition. Printing Number and Year: 5   99 98 97 96 95
Library of Congress Catalog Card Number: 88-62167
ISBN: 0-696-01800-4 (hard cover)
ISBN: 0-696-20517-3 (trade paperback)

BETTER HOMES AND GARDENS® BOOKS

Editor: Gerald M. Knox
Art Director: Ernest Shelton
Managing Editor: David A. Kirchner
Editorial Project Managers: Elizabeth Anderson, James D. Blume,
   Marsha Jahns, Rosanne Weber Mattson

Crafts Editor: Joan Cravens
Senior Crafts Editors: Beverly Rivers, Sara Jane Treinen

Associate Art Directors: Neoma Thomas, Linda Ford Vermie, Randall Yontz
Assistant Art Directors: Lynda Haupert, Harijs Priekulis, Tom Wegner
Graphic Designers: Mary Schlueter Bendgen, Mike Burns, Brian Wignall
Art Production: Director, John Berg; Associate, Joe Heuer;
   Office Manager, Michaela Lester

President, Book Group: Jeramy Lanigan
Vice President, Retail Marketing: Jamie L. Martin
Vice President, Administrative Services: Rick Rundall

BETTER HOMES AND GARDENS® MAGAZINE
President, Magazine Group: James A. Autry
Editorial Director: Doris Eby
Editorial Services Director: Duane L. Gregg

MEREDITH CORPORATION OFFICERS
Chairman of the Executive Committee: E. T. Meredith III
Chairman of the Board: Robert A. Burnett
President: Jack D. Rehm

Creative American Quilting
Editor: Joan Cravens
Contributing Editors: Gary Boling, Elizabeth Porter
Editorial Project Manager: Rosanne Weber Mattson
Graphic Designer: Mike Burns
Contributing Illustrators: Chris Neubauer, Lyne Neymeyer
Electronic Text Processor: Paula Forest

Cover project: See page 199.

❖ ❖ ❖

In recent years, Americans have discovered that the art of quilting is one of our country's own craft specialties. The rich history of quilting in our country and the fresh and imaginative expressions of today's quilters have established an artistic legacy for future generations to enjoy and cherish. In *Creative American Quilting,* you'll find spectacular quilts that represent not only some of the finest efforts of quilters from decades past, but dazzling contemporary designs to delight and inspire you as well.

CONTENTS

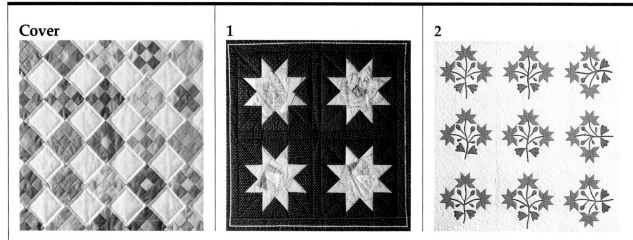

Cover   **1**   **2**

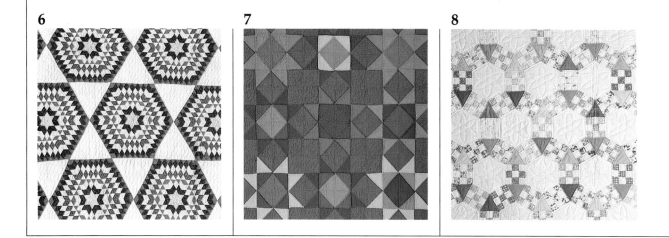

6   **7**   **8**

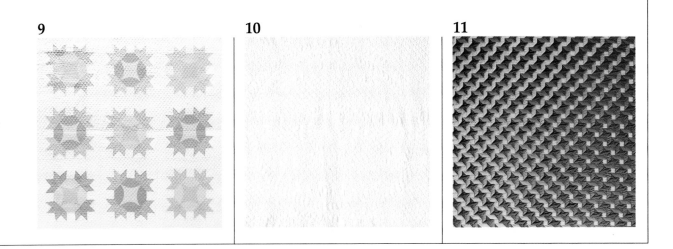

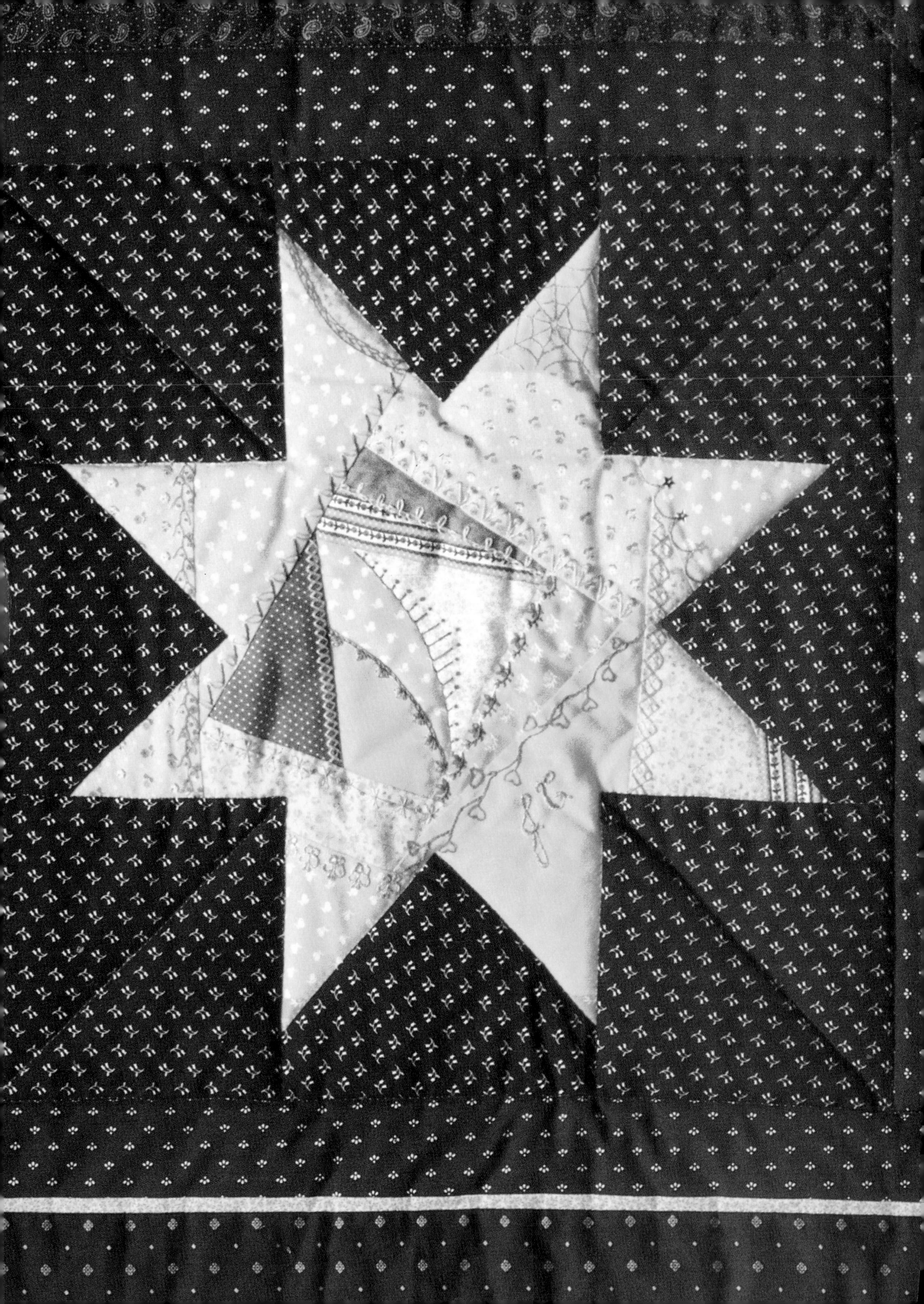

TODAY'S QUILTERS— MASTERING THE CRAFT, EXPLORING THE ART

The fresh and innovative work of our country's quilters is a sure sign that America's quilting tradition continues to flourish. Meet two quilters, a pair of quilting experts, and a hardworking quilt group who represent some of our country's best talent.

RUTH HEYSER

Challenged and inspired by the rugged terrain of northern California, Ruth Heyser relies on quilting as a means of self-expression.

Although Ruth Heyser has dabbled with a number of creative pursuits over the years, nothing has captured her imagination like quilting.

After years of meeting the daily demands of family and suburban life, she turned to quilting when she was in her forties. A stitcher since childhood, she discovered that excellent quilting calls for creativity and imagination as much as technical expertise. Today, after many baby quilts and wall hangings, Ruth continues her delight in and experimentation with color and design.

One of Ruth's design ideas is the crazy-patch quilt, *opposite.* Each block was stitched by members of Ruth's quilting group, the Pine Tree Quilt Guild, and demonstrates Ruth's concept of giving a shape to crazy quilting. She first creates a square of crazy patchwork and then adds an overlay of plain fabric to outline the design. For another example of Ruth's overlay technique, see the Star Banner on page 72.

LENDA DUBOSE

Nashville's Lenda DuBose has indulged a life-long infatuation with color. Each of her beautiful quilts resembles a mosaic, with all the components thoughtfully and artfully set into place.

Lenda DuBose began her craft pursuits with cross-stitching. Initially, she was intrigued by all aspects of color, especially how to achieve certain effects solely by the judicious selection and juxtaposition of subtle shades. One of her cross-stitch designs, *below left,* was an effort to duplicate the soft, often mottled look of worn Oriental carpets. She achieved this by combining several thread colors in the individual stitches.

Lenda turned to patchwork partly because she could work on a larger scale, and because she could work more quickly. Currently, Lenda works full-time as a quilter in her home with her husband Lucius, a printmaker. Working for the most part with squares, triangles, and other simple geometric shapes, she designs, creates, and sells her own patchwork pieces as well as executing commissioned works.

Lenda works in a studio, *left* and *opposite,* that anyone who quilts would envy. Fabrics, in a rainbow of solid colors and tiny, monochromatic prints, are not only stored, but also prominently displayed, in the room.

Because many of Lenda's designs rely on subtle variations in color, she shops for cottons everywhere. She cuts much of the fabric into strips, arranges it into color groups, and organizes it so she can cut it quickly into squares to be sewn into her quilts. One wall of Lenda's studio is marked into a grid so she can pin fabric pieces in place, make adjustments in the overall design, and have a pattern in plain view while she works.

Look for more of Lenda's work on the cover of this book and on pages 120, 178–179, and 199.

LIZ PORTER AND MARIANNE FONS

The mutual love for quilting that these two women share has spawned quilting classes, workshops, books, and a firm friendship.

One segment of today's generation of stitchers, self-named "new-wave" quilters, didn't learn the craft from their mothers. Instead, their knowledge of quilting comes from sharing information with their peers.

Liz Porter and Marianne Fons, *above right,* are two such quilters, and their combined interest in and devotion to this craft have led to nationwide recognition. Through quilting books, classes, and lectures, they have taught skills to thousands who didn't learn to piece quilts for necessity, perhaps, but for pleasure.

Liz and Marianne, who live close to each other in rural southwestern Iowa, each began quilting about 12 years ago, when the nation's bicentennial revived interest in crafts and folk art. Her quilt curiosity piqued, Marianne asked her county extension service about the possibility of offering quilting classes. When one was made available, both she and Liz signed up.

With much in common, including a rural life-style, three children apiece, and the inclination toward a worthwhile pastime, Liz and Marianne developed their skills.

Their goal in putting together their first book on quilted vest patterns and instructions was to create the kind of book that they themselves would buy. A second book on basket patterns followed.

Today, Liz and Marianne are sought-after instructors at workshops and quilting seminars, where quilters produce fine examples of traditional quilting like those *opposite.*

Some of each woman's work is included in this book, including Marianne's nursery design, pages 88–89, and the Delectable Mountains crib quilt, page 118. Liz designed several projects in this book and, as a contributing editor, worked with quilt instructions and patterns.

THE MONDAY QUILTERS

The Winterset quilters approach their craft with unbridled enthusiasm. Talented and dedicated, these women are typical of stitchers in groups across the country today.

Winterset, Iowa, is home to this quilting group. And although it is scarcely three years old, this assembly of prolific craftswomen produces some remarkable quilts.

Traditional patchwork patterns remain favorites of the members, and each design is complemented with quilting in simple, but expertly done, designs. As evident in the group's work, *opposite,* the members are not only adept at executing full-size quilts, but are interested as well in miniature designs like the one Donna Brayman is quilting, *above right.*

Unlike many groups, the Monday Quilters are not concerned with the structure of their club. Only the time and place of their meetings remain constant—for four hours each week at the Winterset Art Center, a former residence turned into a community facility. In a farming town where seasonal work might override time available for hobbies, weekly attendance varies from four or five members to more than 15.

Most important, the order of business for each get-together is the sharing of quilting knowledge, whether by passing around a new pattern, exchanging fabrics, or offering a timesaving hint.

INSPIRATIONS FROM AMERICA'S CLASSIC QUILTS

So much of
America's extraordinary quilting
legacy remains for us to enjoy that
many of today's quilters have
turned to these treasured antiques
for inspiration.

Magnificent patterns—for piecing,
appliqué, and quilting—in
treasured antique quilts can be
rewarding sources of inspiration
for new patchwork projects or gifts
and accessories in other crafts
techniques. Or, stitch a one-patch
design (see page 28), lavishing all
your creative energy on a stunning,
imaginative color arrangement.

Flower basket quilt designs are among the patterns that combine both piecing and appliqué, providing a showcase for the full range of a quilter's skill. They achieved widespread popularity during the 19th century, and quilters delighted in creating new and individual variations on this theme.

In this Grandmother's Basket Quilt, the pattern's familiar elements have been given a delightfully personal interpretation. The basket blocks are turned to the center of the quilt, so the design is attractive from all directions.

More of the quilt maker's touch is evident in the tiny baskets appliquéd on the corner blocks of the sashings and in the random-looking but carefully planned arrangement of leaves, vines, and flowers in the border. The result is a gracefully balanced and strikingly original overall design.

This 74x86-inch coverlet was presented to A. S. Barker by his mother, Mrs. H. M. Barker, in 1866, as noted in the inscription in the border. Projects based on the patchwork and quilting motifs of this quilt appear on the next four pages. Patterns and instructions for them, and for the quilt itself, begin on page 30.

Elements from the Grandmother's Basket Quilt enhance the pillows and sewing box shown here (see page 17 for a front view of the box). Careful study of your favorite quilts will develop your creative flair—and suggest dozens of new ways you can use the designs.

Every quilter loves to collect fabrics. The sewing basket *below* and on page 17 is a beautiful way to display a collection of prints, solids, and stripes. It's also a handy sewing accessory that will keep threads, notions, and sewing equipment within easy reach.

The basket ends are cut from 1-inch pine; the base is shaped like the quilt block's basket, and the top is gracefully curved. Use a woodburning tool to make outlines of the triangles and flower shapes. Then paint the designs with a wash of acrylic paints. Add woodburned details to the sides, as shown *below.*

The appliquéd wreath from the border is one of the quilt's many design elements that can stand alone. The pillow, *opposite,* is one adaptation of this sweetly simple motif.

As with the original quilt, the center of the wreath begs for an inscription, and the cross-stitched "Home Sweet Home" looks just right. Work the stitches over waste canvas—a piece of canvas that's basted over the background fabric and removed when the stitching's complete—using embroidery floss.

Piece the complementary pillow from scraps, using the triangle pattern from the quilt block. Making the zigzags is easy when you join right-angle triangles in contrasting colors.

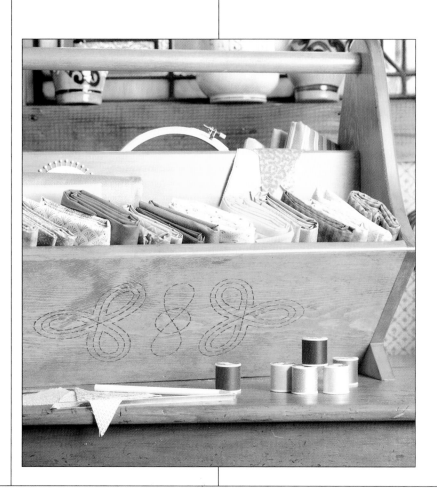

❖ ❖ ❖

When looking at patterns in antique quilts, don't pass up minor shapes or quilting motifs that can be translated into appliqué. Here are two small designs that are no less charming than the larger ones in the Grandmother's Basket Quilt.

The tiny baskets at the intersections of the sashing strips of the Grandmother's Basket Quilt are perfectly sized for the doll's coverlet, *opposite.* All of the baskets except the corner baskets are set on point. As with the larger quilt, the baskets are positioned to look right from any direction.

The Doll Quilt is actually one large piece of fabric, appliquéd and quilted to look like alternating patterned and plain blocks. But the "plain blocks" are quilted with the same heart that is quilted into the pattern blocks in the larger quilt.

The source for the appliquéd mat in the comb-painted frame, *below,* is the vine motif quilted into the sashing strips on the full-size quilt. Sized here exactly as it is on the quilt, the design could be altered easily for a smaller or larger picture.

❖ ❖ ❖

Like the basket quilt on the preceding pages, this handsome Peony Quilt is both pieced and appliquéd, and blocks are turned toward the center. The quilting, however, is singular. The quilt maker incorporated an abundance of graceful designs into the blocks and borders of this bedcover.

Dating from the second quarter of the 19th century, this Peony Quilt is thought to be the creation of Fanny Hoyt Wilson or her mother, Betsy Hoyt Wilson, of Deerfield, Massachusetts. This dazzling 101-inch-square design is just one of a small but choice collection of quilts from the Pocumtuck Valley area on permanent display at the Memorial Hall Museum in Deerfield.

Derived from the older Tulip pattern, the Peony block is a stunning example of pieced blossoms and appliquéd foliage. As with the Grandmother's Basket Quilt, blocks on this quilt are positioned to be viewed from several angles.

This quilt also is rich with quilting patterns. The plain setting squares, *above,* are quilted with an eight-petaled flower and an unusual crosshatch motif. The exquisite quilted border—a lyrical confection of vines, blossoms, leaves, and birds—is unexpected and unique. Among the most charming elements in the border is the outline of a winged dove with a heart stitched upon its breast—a graceful motif that would enhance any patchwork project.

❖ ❖ ❖

Quilting designs, which so often go unnoticed on vintage quilts, take center stage here. These motifs from the Peony Quilt are quilted to show off the original design or are worked in colorful appliqué.

The border on the Peony Quilt features a stunning arrangement of quilting motifs that translate beautifully into appliqué. Stitch the design onto a square tablecloth, then drape the cloth over a skirted round table. (The border is 8 inches deep; the finished cloth is 58 inches square.) Fusible webbing and machine-appliqué simplify sewing.

The trio of throw pillows, *right,* shows off several of the quilting motifs from the quilt. The square design features the flower from the setting squares and four small leaf clusters from the border. The handsome triangular pillow design is embellished with three oak leaves—the quilting motif found in the plain triangles set into the edges of the quilt top. A single dove graces the heart-shaped pillow; fill the background with a traditional grid pattern, a quilter's favorite.

❖ ❖ ❖

One-patch patterns present special challenges to quilters because the success of the design relies heavily on selecting the fabrics and positioning the patches. These Thousand Pyramids quilts—one is old and the other is new—beautifully illustrate this approach.

One way to begin piecing a one-patch quilt is to sketch a few possible combinations before stitching any patches together. Or, cut several triangles from fabric and lay them out on the floor in varying combinations.

The Thousand Pyramids Quilt at *right* shows an easy way to create an interesting pattern. Just divide the fabric triangles into a light group and a dark group. When making the quilt top, arrange all of the dark triangles with the points in one direction and all of the light triangles with the points in the opposite direction.

Use a more sophisticated color value scheme for the Thousand Pyramids Quilt *opposite*. Divide the group of triangles into three groups—light, medium, and dark colors. Join the triangles so that light and medium shades make up larger triangles, contrasting with triangles made of medium and dark shades.

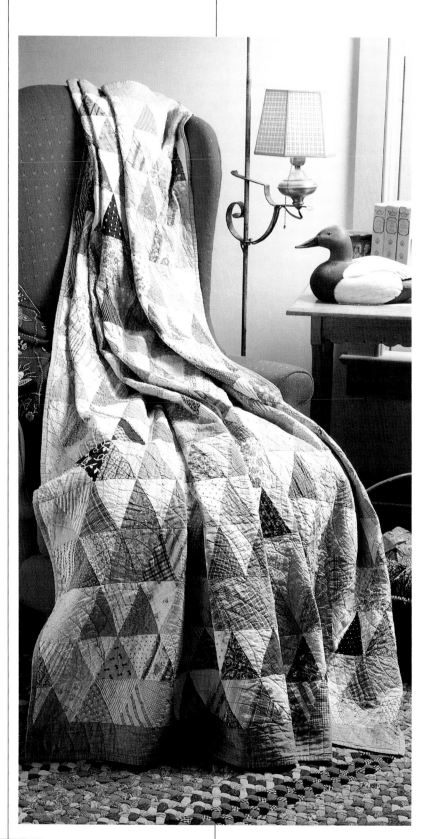

GRANDMOTHER'S BASKET QUILT

PAGE 18

Finished block is 11 inches.
Finished size is 74¼ x 85¾ inches.

Materials

2 yards of green fabric (small-basket-flower stems, leaves, and border vine)

5½ yards of muslin (background of basket blocks, borders, setting squares, binding, and piecing for lower quilt corners)

1¾ yards of red print (basket patchwork, basket handles, and lower quilt corners)

1¾ yards of pink print (sashing strips and outer squares, upper corners, some flowers)

¾ yard of white print (basket patchwork and lower corners)

½ yard of red fabric (block and border flowers)

¼ yard of orange fabric (border flowers)

¼ yard of dark pink print (small baskets in sashing squares)

5½ yards of backing fabric

Quilt batting

Cardboard or plastic for templates

Instructions

Trace and make templates for the patterns, pages 32–33. Patterns are finished size; add ¼-inch-wide seam allowances to pieces before cutting from fabric.

To cut the pieces: Cut borders from yardage *before* cutting pieces for patchwork. Measurements for borders *include* seam allowances and are longer than necessary. Trim borders to correct size when sewing them to the inner quilt top.

After cutting border strips, cut pieces for the quilt top, using templates. The numbers of pieces given below are for the entire quilt; numbers for a single basket block are in parentheses.

From muslin, cut:

2 border strips, each 8½ x62 inches

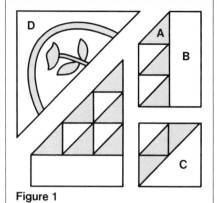

Figure 1

2 border strips, each 8½ x90 inches

26 D triangles (1). (For D pieces, make a right-angle triangle with 8⅕-inch legs. Use 5- or 10-squares-to-the-inch graph paper. Position triangle with legs along fabric's straight grain; add ¼-inch seam allowances.)

15 C pieces (1)

30 B pieces for basket blocks (2)

2 E pieces for lower corners

15 H pieces for sashing squares

340 inches of 1-inch-wide binding

From green fabric, cut:

52 J pieces (small leaves) for basket blocks and half-blocks (2); cut about 120 additional leaves for the border

8 P pieces (oak leaves) for border

12 O pieces (large leaves) for border

Approximately 360 inches of 1-inch-wide (finished width) bias for border vine (see tips, *opposite,* before cutting bias)

Approximately 120 inches of ⅝-inch-wide (finished width) bias for corner wreath vines

Approximately 120 inches of ⅜-inch-wide (finished width) bias for flower stems

60 inches of scant ¼-inch-wide (finished width) bias for small basket handles

From pink print, cut:

42 sashing strips, each 3¼ x11½ inches (measurement includes seam allowances)

11 H pieces (outer sashing squares); trim squares to triangles when you add borders

2 G pieces (upper corners)

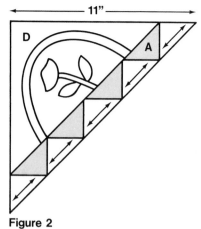

Figure 2

From red print fabric, cut:

26 bias strips, each approximately 1x13 inches, for handles for large baskets (1)

224 A pieces for 15 basket blocks and 11 half-blocks (12)

6 A pieces for lower corners; place long side on straight grain

2 F pieces for lower corners

From white print fabric, cut:

90 A pieces for 15 basket blocks (6); place short sides on straight grain

63 A pieces for 11 half-blocks and lower corners; place long side on straight grain

2 F pieces for lower corners

From red solid fabric, cut:

26 I pieces (flowers) for basket blocks and half-blocks (1). (The quilt shown has some flowers cut from pink sashing print.)

12 M pieces (posies) for lower-right and upper-left corners of quilt and border

5 Q pieces (tulips) for border

6 L pieces (centers of orange posies)

From orange fabric, cut:

6 M pieces (posies) for lower-left and upper-right border corners

3 Q pieces (tulips) for border

16 N pieces (pods), to group for 8 border flowers

12 L pieces (centers of red posies)

From dark pink print fabric, cut:

15 K pieces (small appliqué baskets)

To piece the basket blocks: Stitch patchwork portion of block following Figure 1, *above left.*

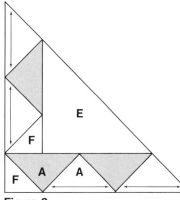

Figure 3

Next, appliqué the basket handles to the D pieces. See tip, *right.*

Appliqué the stem, flower (I), and leaves (J) in place. Stems are ⅜-inch-wide bias (finished size) and about 3 inches long.

Stitch the top (handle) portion of the block to the bottom (pieced) portion.

To assemble the inner top: Stitch 15 basket blocks and 11 half-blocks. See Figure 2, *opposite,* for half-blocks.

Appliqué K pieces to 15 H pieces. Use about 4 inches of the narrowest bias for each handle.

Lay out blocks and half-blocks according to Figure 4, page 34. Sew blocks and half-blocks into diagonal rows, with pink print sashing strips between the blocks.

Referring to Figure 4, piece the long sashes to go between the rows, alternating pink strips and muslin squares. Be sure the small baskets on the muslin squares are turned in the right direction. Begin and end each row with a pink print sashing square (H); trim the square into a triangle after joining borders to the quilt.

Add pink print G pieces to sashing strips at upper corners. Piece lower corner units following Figure 3, *above.* Add lower corner units to lower corners of the quilt.

The inner quilt top, excluding the borders, should measure 58¾x68¼ inches, including seam allowances.

To add borders: Stitch 8½x62-inch muslin borders to short sides of the top; trim. Trim excess fabric from pink print sashing squares.

(Continued)

STITCHING SYMMETRICAL BASKET HANDLES

Graceful and uniformly shaped curves are one of the hallmarks of expert appliqué stitchery. Try this method to appliqué bias strips in a consistent manner.

Cut a paper triangle the exact finished size of the top (handle portion) of the basket block. For Grandmother's Basket, this will be piece D. See Figure 1, *below.*

Figure 1   **Figure 2**

Fold the paper triangle in half; see Figure 2, *above.* Draw a handle shape on one half of the folded triangle. Trace the handle shape on the other half of the triangle. Hold the paper next to the top edge of the pieced basket portion of a block to be sure the handle will fit attractively on the basket. The drawn line will be the inside edge of the handle; check for placement of appliqués.

With the paper triangle folded, cut along the drawn line. Open the paper (see Figure 3, *below left*); try the handle shape on the basket again. When you are pleased with the shape, use the paper template and a water-erasable marker, chalk, or a needle to mark a placement line on each fabric triangle; see Figure 4, *below right.*

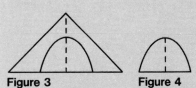

Figure 3   **Figure 4**

Fold and steam-press bias strips in thirds. (For Grandmother's Basket, use 1-inch-wide red print bias strips.)

Press one third of the bias to the wrong side along the length of the strip. Press the remaining third to

---

the wrong side; the raw edge should fall just short of the first fold. Turn the strip over and press on the right side.

Next, baste a handle along the marked line on each fabric triangle, allowing extra length at the ends of the handle to sew into the seam across the long side of the triangle.

For a smooth handle, sew the inner curved edge of the handles first, then the outer curved edge. If the outer handle edge won't lie flat, lightly steam-press the handle to shape it into the curve.

❖

CUTTING AND PRESSING BIAS STRIPS

For attractive stems and vines on quilts and smaller projects, cut bias strips approximately three times wider than the finished width, then fold the strips lengthwise in thirds. Bias strips cut this way will be easy to handle and pleasingly raised when sewn in place. After appliquéing, quilt along each side of the strips to enhance their rounded look.

For 1-inch-wide bias, cut strips 2¾ inches wide. For ⅝-inch-wide bias, cut strips 1¾ inches wide. For ⅜-inch-wide bias, cut strips 1 inch wide. For ¼-inch-wide bias, cut strips ⅝ inch wide.

To turn under raw edges, use a hot steam iron and press about one-third of the width of the bias toward the wrong side along the length of strip. Then press the opposite raw edge to the wrong side, making sure this edge falls just short of the first fold.

Turn the strip over and press it gently on the right side. If you use high-quality cotton, the creases will hold and you won't need to baste the layers together. Store prepared bias by wrapping it around a cardboard tube. To appliqué the strips, pin or baste them to the background.

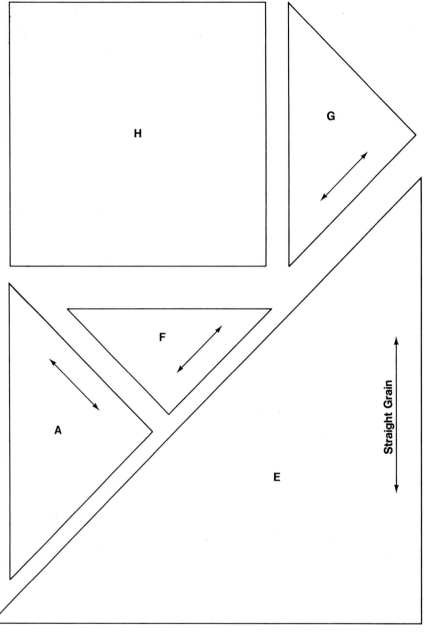

Stitch 8½x90-inch muslin borders to long sides of quilt top; trim excess. Also trim excess fabric from pink print sashing squares.

Make bias for border vine. Baste vines in position, using Figure 4, page 34, as a guide. Baste corner circle vines in place, each 7½ inches in diameter, measuring from outer edge of vine.

Appliqué leaves and flowers, using Figure 4 as a guide. Flowers on wreath in lower-right and upper-left corners are red. Remaining wreath flowers are orange. Flowers along borders alternate in color. Use ⅜-inch-wide bias (finished width) for flower stems.

Mark quilting designs. Place heart in piece C, figure eight with circle in piece B, vine and leaf motif in sashing strips, and remaining pattern in center of corner wreaths.

Finishing: Divide backing fabric into two 2¾-yard lengths. Cut or tear one length in half lengthwise. Sew one narrow panel to each side of the wide panel. Match the selvages; use a ½-inch seam. Trim the seams to ¼ inch; press to one side.

Layer quilt top, batting, and backing. Baste thoroughly.

In addition to marked designs, outline-quilt pieced and appliquéd pieces ¼ inch from seams.

Piece muslin strips; bind edges.

(Continued)

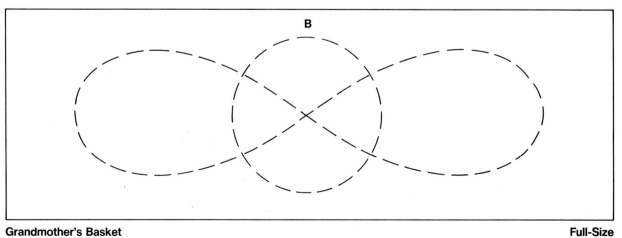

Grandmother's Basket

Full-Size

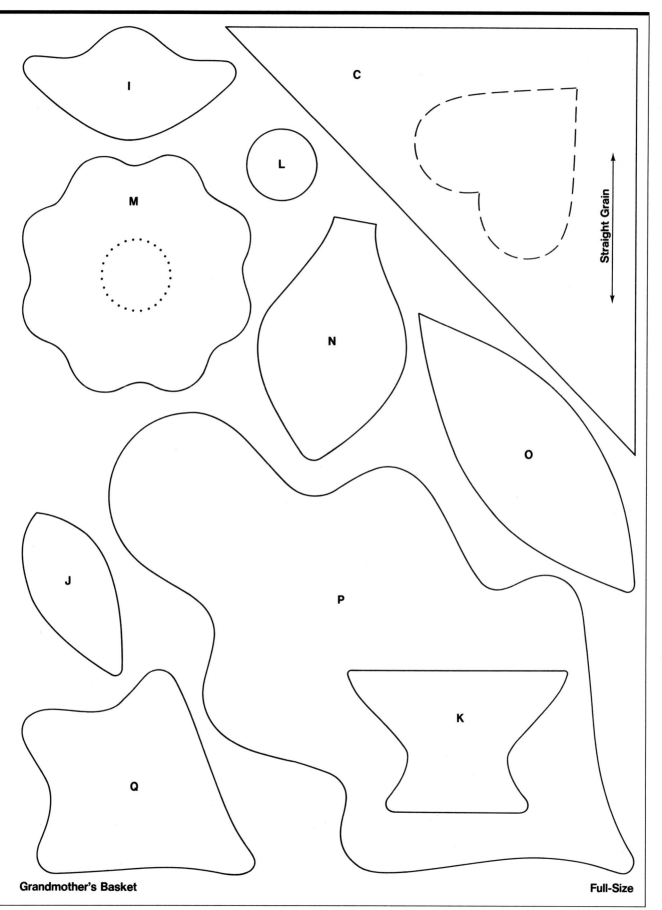

I

C

L

M

N

O

J

P

K

Q

Straight Grain

Grandmother's Basket

Full-Size

Overall Size: 74¼ x 83¾" Finished Block Size: 11"

DOLL QUILT AND PILLOWS
PAGE 22
Finished quilt is 20x20 inches.

Materials
¾ yard of ecru cotton
21x21-inch piece of quilt batting
Scraps of print fabrics for baskets, and batiste for basket linings
Bias tape for basket handles
Red embroidery floss; needle
Two 3-yard lengths (in complementary colors and patterns) of 2-inch-wide fabric strips for borders on quilt top and back

Instructions
For the coverlet: Cut ecru fabric into two 17½x17½-inch pieces, for the quilt top and back.

On the diagonal, mark 2½-inch squares on one ecru piece (there will be triangles on the edges)—5 squares across and 5 down. Treat each square as if it were a quilt block. You'll have 25 blocks to be appliquéd, 16 blocks between (to be quilted), 4 half-blocks (triangles) along each side, and a quarter-block in each corner.

Half- and quarter-blocks will be left plain. Using the heart quilting design on page 33, mark hearts in 16 blocks (see photograph on page 22).

Using pattern piece K on page 33, trace 25 baskets on wrong sides of the print scraps. Do not cut the baskets out.

With right sides of basket fabric and a scrap of batiste lining together, machine-sew on drawn lines. Cut out baskets, leaving a scant ¼-inch seam allowance. Clip curves, make a small slit in batiste backing only, and turn baskets right side out. Press.

Arrange baskets on remaining squares of quilt top, turning baskets as shown in the photograph. Baste and stitch, leaving tops open for handles.

Following tips on page 31, trim and press bias tape to make ¼-inch-wide (finished width) han-

dles. Tuck ends of handles under basket tops; baste and appliqué. Complete stitching of baskets.

For the borders, divide each 3-yard strip into four equal lengths. Sew border strips from one fabric to quilt top, mitering corners. Sew other border strips to the quilt back, mitering corners.

Pin the quilt top and quilt back, right sides facing and raw edges matching, atop the batting. Sew around the quilt, leaving an opening for turning. Trim excess batting, clip, and turn. Slipstitch the opening closed.

Using ecru quilting thread, quilt the diagonal grid. Using a single strand of red embroidery floss, quilt the hearts.

For the pillows: Appliqué basket flower to a 5¼x9-inch piece of ecru fabric, positioning stem ½ inch above edge of short side. Add 1¾ inches of fabric, ribbon, or lace trims to one long side, as shown in the photograph. Fold fabric in half (to 7x4½ inches), right sides facing; sew into a pillow. Sew an inner pillow of scraps; stuff, and insert in pillowcase. Make second pillow plain or the same as first one.

PILLOWS TO PIECE, APPLIQUÉ, AND CROSS-STITCH
PAGE 21

Materials
For appliquéd pillow
½ yard of ecru fabric for pillow front and back
Scraps of red, yellow, and green fabrics for appliqués
18x18 inches of muslin to back patchwork
Yellow piping
¼ yard of solid red fabric for ruffle
⅜ yard of green and white print fabric for ruffle
Red embroidery floss
Sharp embroidery needle
7x7 inches of 10-count waste canvas for embroidery
Quilt batting; fiberfill for stuffing

For pieced pillow
Scraps of olive, peach, red, yellow, light green, and pink fabrics
13x13 inches of backing fabric
1½ yards of yellow piping
Fiberfill for stuffing

Instructions
For the appliquéd and cross-stitched pillow: Wash and press all of the fabrics to shrink them and remove the sizing. Cut ecru fabric into two 18-inch-square pieces for the pillow front and back; set one piece (back) aside.

Baste waste canvas, centered, atop the remaining piece. Then, using three strands of red embroidery floss threaded into a sharp needle, cross-stitch "Home Sweet Home," centered, atop the pillow front. (Before stitching, find the vertical and horizontal centers of the chart, page 36, and the waste canvas; mark both with sewing thread. Use the center lines as reference points while you are stitching the design.)

After completing the embroidery, dampen the waste canvas with water and carefully slide the canvas threads, one at a time, from beneath the stitches. Press the fabric on the wrong side.

Next, cut approximately 28 inches of green 1¼-inch-wide bias, fold in thirds lengthwise, and appliqué in a ring approximately 7½ inches in diameter (inner dimension) around the cross-stitch motto. (*Note:* For easy positioning of the bias wreath, see tips for marking basket handles, page 31. Treat the wreath as if it were two semicircular handles joined at the ends.)

Using quilt pattern pieces M, L, and J, page 33, and adding ¼-inch seam allowances all around, cut three flowers, three flower centers, and six leaves from red, yellow, and green fabrics. Turn under raw edges on the appliqués; baste in place. Press the appliqués, then pin and baste the flowers and leaves around the wreath, as shown in the photograph.

(Continued)

Appliqué the flowers and leaves to the background fabric. Carefully trim ecru fabric from *beneath* the flowers, leaving a scant ¼ inch of ecru fabric beyond the seam line.

Sew the flower centers in place, then trim the red fabric from beneath each flower center, leaving a scant ¼ inch of fabric beyond the stitched line. (Trimming the excess fabric beneath the flowers and flower centers makes quilting easier.)

Back the appliquéd pillow front with a square of batting and the 18-inch square of muslin. Pin and baste the layers together, then quilt along the seams and within the flower shapes as shown in the photograph.

With the design centered, cut the pillow front into a 15-inch-diameter circle. Cut the pillow backing fabric to match the front. Baste yellow piping to the pillow front, ½ inch from the edge.

For ruffles, cut and piece a 4-inch-wide strip of red fabric and a 5-inch-wide strip of green and white print, each approximately 88 inches long. Join short ends of each strip in a ¼-inch-wide seam, forming a loop. Then fold each strip in half lengthwise, wrong sides facing; press. Run a gathering thread along the raw edge. To distribute the ruffle evenly on the pillow front, divide the ruffle and the pillow front into quarters. Gather one quarter of the ruffle to each quarter of the pillow front.

Baste the red ruffle to the pillow front along the seam line, then baste the print ruffle atop the red one.

With right sides facing, sew the pillow back to the front (tuck the ruffles inside). Leave an opening for turning. Clip the curves, turn the pillow right side out, and press. Stuff the pillow, then blindstitch the opening closed.

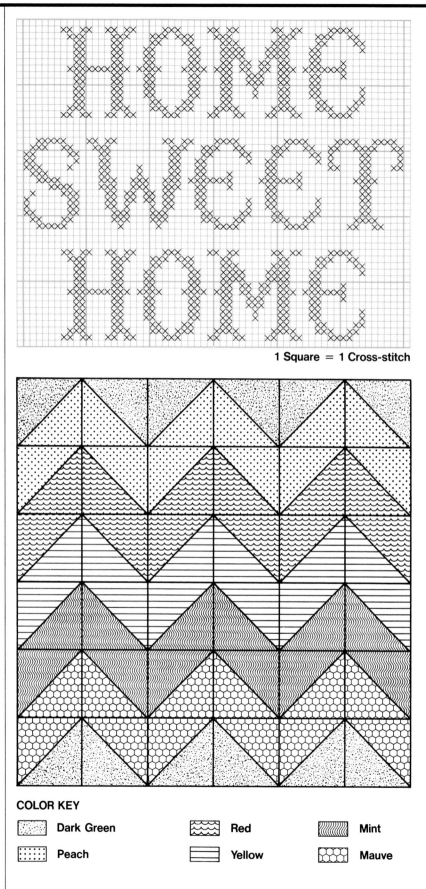

1 Square = 1 Cross-stitch

COLOR KEY

	Dark Green		Red		Mint
	Peach		Yellow		Mauve

For the pieced pillow: Using pattern piece A (from the basket block) and adding ¼-inch-wide seam allowances, cut pieces for the pillow front. See diagram, *opposite, below,* for colors and numbers of each triangle required for the pillow.

Following the position diagram, *opposite, below,* assemble triangles into squares; press seams to one side. Sew squares into rows, then join rows into the completed pillow top.

Sew piping to the front of the pillow, ¼ inch from edge.

With right sides facing, sew the pillow back to the front, leaving an opening for turning. Clip corners, turn right side out, and stuff with fiberfill. Blindstitch the opening closed.

❖

WOODEN SEWING BASKET
PAGES 17 and 20

Materials
1-inch-thick pine lumber: 2 A pieces, each 12x16 inches (join two 16-inch lengths of 1x8s with dowel or spline joints); 1 C piece, 8¾x18 inches; 1 D piece, 8½x18 inches; and 1 E piece, 8x18 inches (see diagram, *above right*)

22 inches of 1-inch-diameter dowel (B)

12x16-inch piece of paper

Woodburning tool; sandpaper; nails; glue; varnish; paintbrushes

Acrylic paints in red and green, or colors of your choice; graphite paper or carbon paper

Instructions
On a 12x16-inch piece of paper, enlarge the pattern, *right,* to make a pattern for the basket ends. As you construct the basket, refer to the diagram, *above right,* for dimensions and placement of the individual pieces of wood.

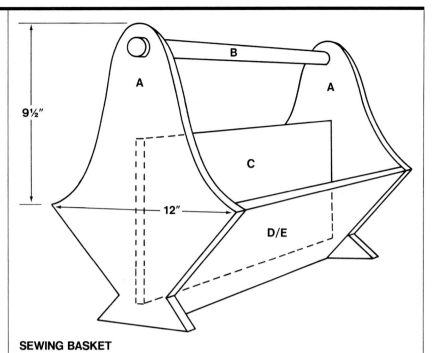

SEWING BASKET

To embellish the basket: Sand the wood. Using a router or rasp, round all the edges of all the pieces for the basket, except those edges that butt against other pieces when the basket is finally assembled.

Then, using graphite or carbon paper, transfer the outline of the ends of the basket from your master pattern to the wood A pieces; cut out. Sand A pieces; round the edges. Wood-burn triangles and flowers. Dilute acrylics with water, then paint the designs, referring to the photograph for colors (or using colors that match your own decor).

With the A pieces clamped together, drill a 1-inch-diameter hole (for the dowel handle) through both pieces; see your master pattern for placement.

On the *inside* of each end piece, mark placement of piece C; the top of C will be about 5⅜ inches below the top of the end piece (see assembly diagram).

Using graphite or carbon paper, transfer the quilting motifs for Piece B on page 32 onto the sides of the box (pieces D and E). (See photograph, *page 17.*) To simulate quilting stitches, wood-burn dashed lines along design lines.

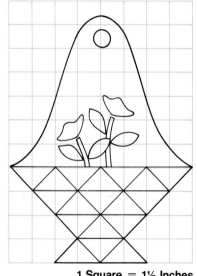

1 Square = 1½ Inches

Finishing: Nail and glue the basket together (see diagram). Begin by fitting Piece D to one end panel. Insert dowel; add remaining end panel. Add E, positioning it so base is flush with side of D. Fit C in place.

Using lacquer thinner or another solvent, remove any residue on the wood from the graphite or carbon paper. Stain the wood, including the design area, a light brown color. When stain is dry, seal the basket with two coats of varnish, sanding between coats.

(Continued)

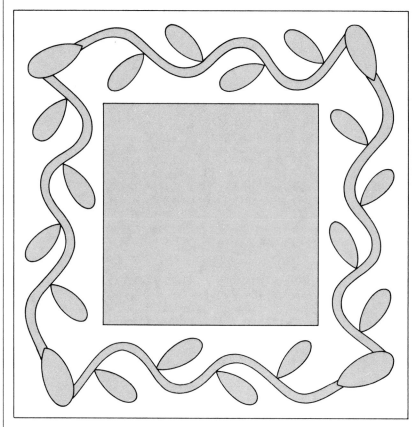

APPLIQUÉD PICTURE MAT
PAGE 23

Materials

½ yard of ecru cotton
Scraps of light green and olive
  cotton fabrics
18x18 inches of quilt batting
¼-inch hardboard, 14x14 inches,
  or size to fit in your picture
  frame
Picture frame
11x11-inch piece of paper

Instructions

The sashing strips for Grand-mother's Basket and the outer edges of the fabric matting for the picture are 11 inches long. Both are 2½ inches wide, making a 6-inch-square opening for the picture. For a larger opening, or a rectangular one, simply extend the design area on two or more sides. Work out the pattern on 2½-inch-wide strips of paper before you begin, so the vines meet gracefully in the corners.

To make the master pattern: Refer to the diagram, *above right.* On an 11x11-inch piece of paper, mark a 6-inch square in the center. Then mark the vine in the borders. Using the leaf patterns, *right,* add large leaves in the corners and add smaller leaves along the sides. Adjust the length of the vine to fit comfortably and attractively in the space available. This will be your master pattern.

To cut out the appliqué pieces: From light green fabric, cut approximately 40 inches of 1-inch-wide bias strips to use for stems. Fold bias in thirds lengthwise; press.

Next, trace the leaf at the top of the quilting design and one of the leaves along the vine to use as patterns for the appliqués. (The leaf at the top of the vine is larger than the other leaves.) Transfer these patterns to plastic.

Trace leaf patterns onto light green and olive fabrics; add ¼-inch seam allowances, and cut out

as many leaves as necessary for your design (we used six olive leaves and 14 light green leaves, including the larger ones).

Turn under raw edges of all leaves; baste.

To stitch the design: Transfer the master pattern, centered, to one 18-inch square of ecru fabric. Baste folded bias strips in place for stems, then baste leaves in position. Appliqué stems and leaves, using thread to match fabrics.

Sandwich batting between the appliquéd mat and the remaining piece of ecru fabric. Baste layers together. Machine-baste outline of 6-inch square in the center of the fabric. Outline-quilt stem and leaves.

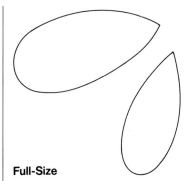

Full-Size

Finishing: Cut a 6-inch square in the center of the hardboard. Next, carefully cut an X in the 6-inch square in the center of the fabric, cutting *almost but not quite to* the corners. Stretch quilted fabric around hardboard, taping and then stapling raw edges to the back. Trim excess fabric and mount it in a frame over your picture, mirror, or paper cutout.

Peony Quilt

PAGE 25

Finished size is 101 inches square.
Quilt block is 15 inches square.

Materials

10 yards of muslin (borders, blocks, and binding)
2 yards of red-orange print (flower patchwork, buds)
1½ yards of green print (stems, leaves)
9 yards of backing fabric
Quilt batting larger than 101 inches square
Water-erasable pen
2 pieces of cardboard or template plastic, 1 piece at least 15½ inches square and 1 piece 8 inches square

Instructions

Trace and make templates for patterns A, B, C, D, F, G, and H, page 42. For the E piece, cut a 7½-inch square template. Patterns are full-size; add ¼-inch-wide seam allowances to pattern pieces before cutting them from fabric.

For the setting squares and triangles, cut a 15-inch square template from cardboard or plastic.

To cut the pieces: The number of pieces to cut for the entire quilt is listed first; the number to cut for one block follows in parentheses.

Adding ¼-inch seam allowances, use the 15-inch square template to mark and cut 9 setting squares—the cut square will measure 15½ inches. Set the squares aside.

For the setting triangles, draw a diagonal line between opposite corners of the template used for marking the setting squares. Draw a second diagonal line in the *opposite* direction, through the lower section of the template (see Figure 1, *above right*).

Cut on the drawn lines to form templates X and Z.

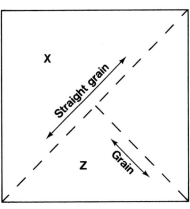

Figure 1

Using template X, mark 12 setting triangles on muslin with the *long* side of the triangle on straight grain. Adding ¼-inch seam allowances, cut out the triangles.

Next, using template Z, mark four corner-setting triangles on the muslin, with the legs of the triangle template on the straight grain. Adding seam allowances, cut out the triangles. Set the X and Z triangles aside.

(The cutting dimensions for the borders *include* ¼-inch seam allowances.) Measurements for the borders are 3 to 4 inches longer than necessary; trim excess after sewing borders in place.

From muslin, reserve ¾ yard for binding; then cut:
4 border strips, each 8½ × 104 inches
144 B pieces (9)
144 C pieces (9)
48 D pieces (3)
16 E pieces (1)

From red-orange print, cut:
288 A pieces (18)
32 F pieces—buds (2)

When cutting buds, trace template onto right side of fabric, add seam allowance, and cut out.

From green print, cut:
32 G pieces—large leaves (2)
32 F pieces—small leaves (2)
32 H pieces—bud stems (2)
1-inch-wide bias strips for stems

Each block requires approximately 30 inches of bias—about 16 inches for the center flower, and approximately 7 inches for each side flower. Finished width of the stems is about ⅜ inch. For tips on cutting and folding bias strips for stems, see instructions for the Grandmother's Basket Quilt, page 30.)

To make one block: The starlike flowers that make up most of the peony block are pieced. Because the muslin squares and triangles in these areas must be set in, hand piecing is recommended. (Stitch from seam line to seam line, rather than to raw edges.)

Referring to Figure 2, *below,* sew diamonds into pairs; make three pairs. Join the pairs to make six-diamond flowers. Make three six-diamond flowers for each block.

Next, set three B squares and three C triangles into each section (see Figure 2). When joining the C pieces that fit into the bases of the flowers, leave the seams open at the corner, so the stem can be tucked in later.

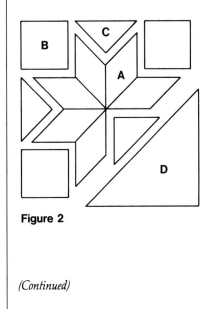

Figure 2

(Continued)

Sew D pieces to each flower section. Join flower sections and E piece to complete the piecing of each block (see Figure 3).

Prepare bias strips, following tip instructions, page 31.

For appliquéd leaves, turn under seam allowances; baste along fold lines. At ends of bud stems, trim seam allowance to 1/8 inch.

Referring to peony block diagram, Figure 3, *right*, for placement, add stems, buds, and leaves. Using matching thread, appliqué center flower stem first, leaving openings for leaves and side stems. After tucking stems under flower diamonds, sew openings closed. For bud ends, first appliqué bud. Use the end of the needle to turn back seams of the bud covering as you appliqué it over each bud.

Make 16 peony blocks.

To set the quilt top: Use quilting designs on page 43 and a water-erasable pen to mark designs on muslin squares and triangles (see Figures 4, 5, and 6, *right* and *opposite*). Fold and lightly press the muslin pieces in half or in quarters; creases form the placement guidelines.

Stitch the pieced and plain blocks together in diagonal rows, turning the pieced blocks along the sides of the quilt toward the center. See Figure 7, *opposite*. The quilt top, without borders, should measure 85½ inches square, including the seam allowances.

Cut border strips to exact size and stitch them to the inner quilt, mitering corners.

Finishing: Using the quilting patterns, pages 43–45, and referring to Figure 8, page 41, mark the border designs with a water-erasable pen, chalk, or marker. For placement of motifs in the border, see Figure 8.

(Continued)

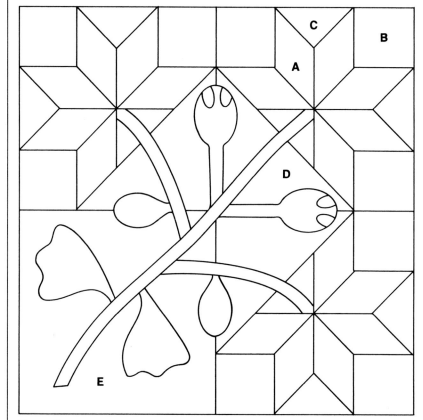

Figure 3

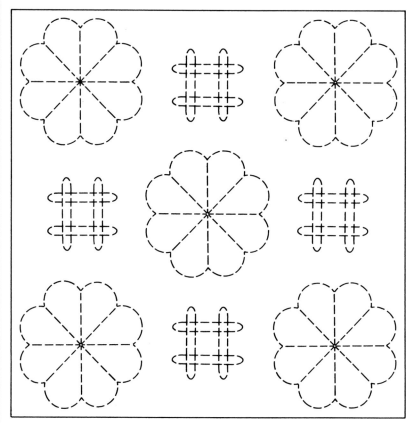

Figure 4

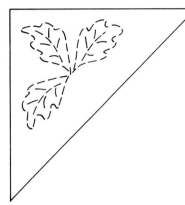

Figure 5

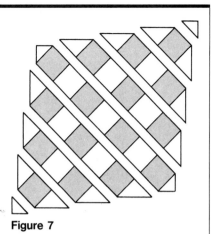

Figure 6

Figure 7

Figure 8

For backing, divide the fabric into three 3-yard lengths. Tear one length into a 24-inch-wide strip. Sew a full 3-yard length to each side of the 24-inch strip, using ½-inch seams. Cut off the selvages, leaving approximately ¼-inch-wide seam allowances. Press seams to one side.

Layer the backing (wrong side up), the batting (slightly larger than quilt top), and the quilt top (right side up). Baste the layers securely together.

Quilt all motifs along marked lines. Also quilt "in the ditch" (along seams) around each flower diamond, along the stems, around the leaves, along seams between quarter-block sections, and between whole blocks. In addition, quilt segments of the large leaves as shown in the photographs.

When quilting is complete, bind the outer edge of the quilt with bias strips of muslin. Finished binding on the quilt shown is approximately ¼ inch wide.

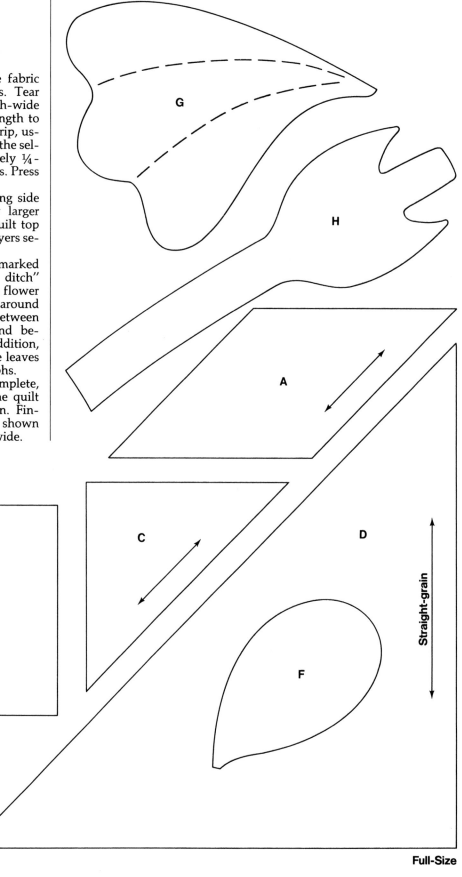

Peony

Full-Size

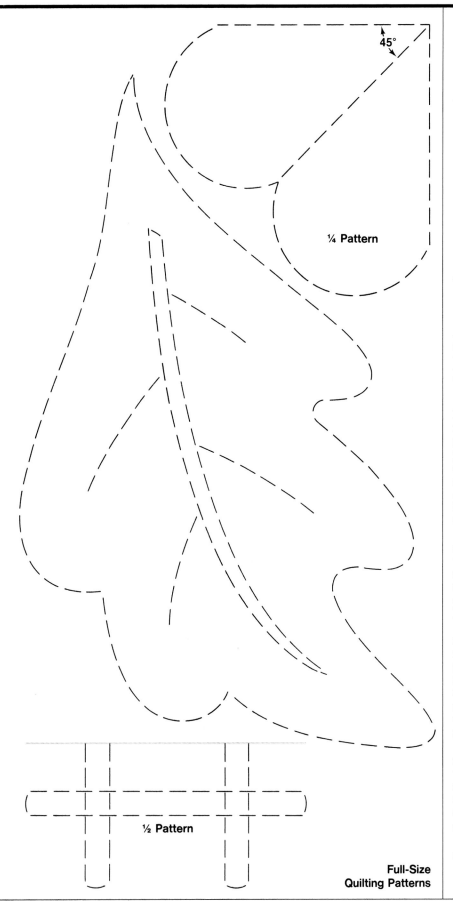

45°

¼ Pattern

½ Pattern

**Full-Size
Quilting Patterns**

❖

QUILTED PILLOWS
PAGE 27
*See instructions for finished sizes,
excluding ruffles.*

Materials
½ yard of fabric in *each* of the
following colors: peach solid,
peach print, rust print,
light green solid, light green
print, dark ecru, and
brown plaid
1 spool of quilting thread in
each of the following colors:
dark green, rust, reddish brown,
and ivory
4 yards narrow cording
Quilt batting and backing
Water-erasable pen
Polyester fiberfill

Instructions
For the square pillow: Mark a 13-
inch square (finished size) on solid peach fabric. Referring to the
photograph, page 27, and the
quilting patterns, *left,* transfer designs to fabric with a water-erasable pen. Layer the backing,
batting, and peach fabric; baste
together.
   Stitch the design using rust
quilting thread. After quilting,
trim the fabric to ½ inch past the
outline. Using 1-inch-wide bias
strips of rust fabric, cover sufficient cording to edge the pillow.
Baste cording to the outside edge.
   For the ruffle, cut three 6x45-
inch strips from peach print fabric. Sew the short ends together;
fold the strip in half lengthwise
(wrong sides together) and press.
Gather the ruffle along the raw
edge and baste it in place along
the cording. Sew ruffle and cording in place.
   To assemble, cut backing piece
from peach fabric to same size as
top. Sew back to front with right
sides facing, leaving an opening
for turning. Clip corners, trim
seams, and turn. Stuff with fiberfill; slip-stitch closed.

(Continued)

Peony Tablecloth

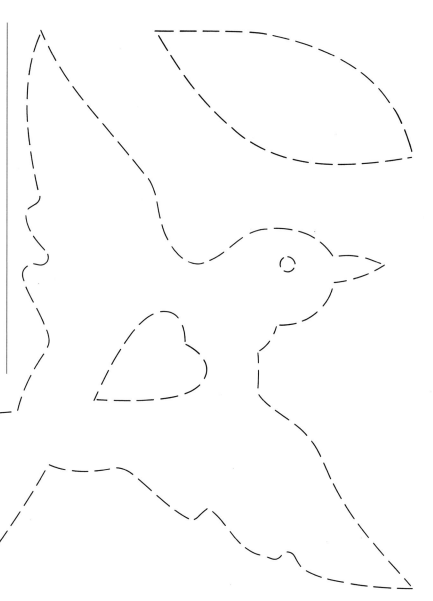

For heart-shaped pillow: On tracing paper, draw a heart 12 inches wide and 11½ inches high; transfer to dark ecru fabric. Trace bird, *below,* inside heart. Fill background with a grid of diagonal parallel lines (¾ inch apart).

Layer backing, batting, and top as for square pillow. Quilt the bird with reddish brown thread. Quilt the grid with ivory thread. Using brown plaid for ruffle and rust print for piping, complete as for square pillow.

For triangular pillow: On tracing paper, draw a right-angle triangle with 17-inch-long short legs. With the right angle at the top (forming a peak), draw three oak leaves, page 43, inside the triangle. Transfer design to light green fabric. Layer backing, batting, and top; baste. Quilt design with dark green thread. Using green print for ruffle and rust print for piping, complete as for square pillow.

Quilting Patterns   **Full-Size**

44

Position Guide

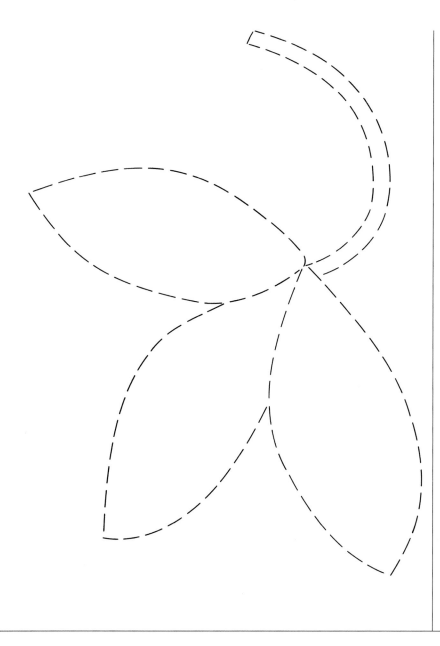

❖

PEONY TABLECLOTH
PAGE 26
Finished size is 58x58 inches.

Materials
1¼ yards of dark ecru fabric
1⅔ yards of light ecru fabric
1⅔ yards of backing fabric
1 yard of dark green print
¼ yard *each* of assorted print
   fabrics
Tracing paper, lightweight paper,
   lightweight cardboard, or
   template plastic
Water-erasable marking pen

Instructions
Note: Use ½-inch seams.
   Referring to the position diagram for the border, *above,* and using the full-size quilting designs, *opposite* and *left,* draw the tablecloth border pattern on tracing paper. The finished border measures 8 inches deep.
   Trace each of the appliqué shapes (birds, heart, oak leaf, and small and large leaves); cut the shapes from cardboard or template plastic.

(Continued)

To make the top: Cut a 43-inch square from dark ecru fabric for the center square. From light ecru fabric, cut two 9x43-inch border pieces and two 9x60-inch border pieces. Join the shorter borders to opposite sides of the dark ecru; join the longer border strips to the remaining edges.

Cut backing fabric to measure 59x59 inches; set aside.

Trace the design onto the border using a water-erasable pen.

From dark green print, cut ½-inch-wide bias strips for the vine, piecing the strips to make a total of 6⅞ yards. Baste the assembled strip to the border along the vine outline.

Cut appliqués from scraps, and baste them in place.

Using a medium-width zigzag stitch and thread that matches the color of the appliqués, machine satin-stitch around the shapes.

To prevent distortion of the appliqués as you stitch, insert a piece of lightweight paper between the throat plate on the sewing machine and the layers of fabric. Stitch through the paper, then gently tear away the paper when the stitching is complete.

Finishing: Place the backing fabric and the appliquéd top right sides together. Sew the edges, leaving an opening for turning. Clip corners and trim seams to ¼ inch. Turn, press, and slip-stitch the opening closed.

THOUSAND PYRAMIDS QUILT
PAGES 28 and 29
Finished triangle is 4 inches high.
Finished quilt is 70x70 inches.

Materials
Approximately 3½ yards of assorted light to medium-light fabric scraps
Approximately 3 yards of assorted medium-dark to dark fabric scraps; 1 pyramid can be cut from a 4½-inch square.
4¼ yards for the borders, quilt back, and self-binding
Quilt batting
Cardboard or plastic for templates

Instructions
The Thousand Pyramids Quilt shown on page 28 is pieced with all of the dark triangles pointing in one direction and all of the light triangles pointing in the opposite direction.

Trace and make a template for the triangle pattern, *below.* The pattern is finished size. Add ¼-inch seam allowances when cutting the pieces from the fabric.

To cut the pieces: From the backing fabric, cut two 3½x72-inch borders. Cut both on the lengthwise grain. Cut 336 triangles from light to medium-light fabric scraps and 336 triangles from medium-dark to dark fabric scraps. (Cut a total of 672 triangles.)

To make the pyramids: Piece the triangles into pyramids, larger triangles made from four small triangles.

To make an A pyramid, choose three dark triangles and one light triangle. Sew a dark triangle to each side of the light triangle, forming a larger triangle as shown in Figure 1, *below.* Make 84 A pyramids.

To make a B pyramid, choose three light triangles and one dark

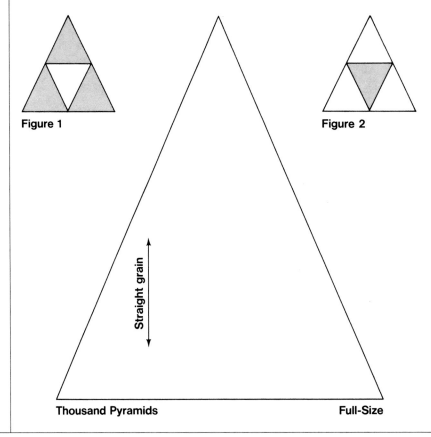

Figure 1

Figure 2

Straight grain

Thousand Pyramids　　　　　　　　**Full-Size**

triangle. Sew a light triangle to each side of dark triangle, forming larger triangle as shown in Figure 2, *opposite*. Make 84 B pyramids.

To make the quilt top: Piece the pyramids into eight horizontal rows. To make the first row and all odd rows, alternate 10 A pyramids and 11 B pyramids with the bases of the A pyramids down and the bases of the B pyramids up. Repeat to make a total of four rows.

To make the second row and all even rows, alternate 11 A pyramids and 10 B pyramids with the bases of the A pyramids down and the bases of the B pyramids up. Repeat to make a total of four rows.

Join the eight rows. Straighten the sides of the quilt by trimming the excess triangles.

Sew a border to the top and bottom of the quilt; trim excess border.

Finishing: To piece the quilt back, cut the remaining backing fabric into two equal lengths. Cut or tear one length in half lengthwise. Sew one narrow panel to each side of the wide panel. Match the selvages; use a ½-inch seam. Trim the seams to ¼ inch; press to one side.

Layer the backing, batting, and pieced top. Baste layers together; quilt as desired.

When quilting is complete, trim the excess batting even with the quilt top. Trim the quilt back so it is 1 inch larger all around than the quilt top. To form a self-binding, turn the quilt back under ½ inch to the wrong side of the backing fabric, then turn the fold to the quilt top, covering the raw edge. Stitch in place.

SELECTING AND PREPARING PATCHWORK AND QUILTING MATERIALS

Most of the beautiful 19th-century antique quilts that we see today were made entirely of cotton. Because family clothing was stitched of cotton, scraps were available, although extra yardage often was purchased for quilting. Cotton is still the recommended cloth for quilts. It is lightweight and easy to sew through. It takes a crease well, which makes it fold crisply for appliqué. It washes well, and, even when it fades, it remains attractive and appealing.

Choosing prints: When gathering fabrics for quilts, try to acquire a variety of print types. Small-, medium-, and large-scale prints, used with solids, add vitality and interest to a design. Also pay attention to color values. Including light-, medium-, and dark-value prints (and solids) in a quilt often results in a more pleasing finished project than safe, over-coordinated fabrics with little or no contrast between them.

Some print fabrics can be especially challenging to work with, so before buying them, study your patchwork pattern carefully. For example, a directional print featuring tiny trees printed in rows needs to be cut carefully to avoid upside-down trees in the quilt.

Stitching with striped fabrics also requires careful planning. You'll need to decide where in your design stripes can be used successfully. Also, when cutting pattern pieces of striped fabric, you may need to disregard suggested grain lines given on templates. If so, handle patchwork pieces carefully to avoid stretching them.

Wash fabrics before cutting: Fabric preparation includes washing, drying, and ironing *before* you mark and cut out pattern pieces.

Washing shrinks the fabric before cutting and eliminates the sizing, making the fabric easier to handle and softer to the touch.

If you plan to wash a finished quilt or other project in warm water, wash yardage the same way. Wash fabrics alone (darks with darks and lights with lights) or with the family laundry. Avoid fabric softeners; they often leave spots on new yardage. Machine- or line-dry fabrics.

Dark fabrics and intense colors may bleed. To test for colorfastness, wash your fabric, then place it in clean warm water in a sink or tub. If the color runs into the water, wash and test the fabric again. Avoid using fabrics that continue to bleed, unless the entire quilt will be made of similar fabrics.

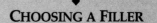

CHOOSING A FILLER

Batting—the filler used between the quilt top and backing—adds warmth and dimension to a quilt. Cotton and wool are the traditional fillers found in antique quilts. Because these natural-fiber fillers were not stabilized like today's battings are, they required extensive quilting to minimize shifting and bunching inside the quilt.

Most quilters today use polyester batting because it sews (or "needles") easily and washes well in the machine. It is available in packages sized appropriately to bed linen sizes or by the yard.

Choose good-quality batting that has been needle-punched, glazed, or bonded to prevent fibers from separating. The batting should be of uniform thickness and relatively thin if you plan to quilt by hand. Use high-loft batts for tied comforters.

Before assembling your quilt, lay the batting out and let it relax to remove deep creases and folds.

SCRAP QUILTS—
PRACTICAL
AND PRETTY

Combining snippets of many fabrics (often cut from remnants) in lively and imaginative ways is what separates American patchwork from other styles. The scrap tradition thrives today as quilters explore the challenges of working with color, pattern, and design.

Charm quilts, which were popular in the 1930s, are pieced so each fabric is used only once. Making a charm quilt is one way to add interest—and challenges—to scrap piecing. The two one-patch quilt designs shown here, each using a simple geometric shape, are good candidates for a charm quilt.

The pattern of the quilt on the bed, *left,* is aptly named Hit-and-Miss because the patches can be put together in the most random manner imaginable and the results are still striking. It's a good idea, however, to strive for a balance of lights and darks and an interesting mix of fabrics.

You also can vary the look of this quilt pattern by changing the direction of each row. After stitching the patches into rows, experiment by placing the rows together so the patches point in different directions. If you look closely at this quilt, you'll see that the quilter pieced exactly half of the quilt with uniform zigzags; the remainder of the quilt rows are joined haphazardly.

The quilt at the foot of the bed is a true charm quilt. When each trapezoid is cut from a print fabric as was done for this quilt, the design is called the Tumbler pattern. Stitching rows of these patches together creates slightly wavy—and very attractive—sides on the quilt.

Because both of these quilts are made with one shape repeated many times, it's easy to change the finished size of the quilt. Make fewer rows than directed for the quilt shown to fit on a twin-size bed. For larger beds, add more patches to each row for extra length, and make additional rows until the quilt is the necessary width.

Instructions begin on page 58.

With larger scraps, you can piece a block, or a large portion of a block, with just one fabric for more control over the quilt's color scheme and design.

Many times, a block assembled from numerous pieces enables you to use scraps to good advantage. The pattern pieces for the blocks of the Tipsy Star Quilt, *opposite,* are small, but the appearance of the finished block is bold and dynamic.

The inner square of this block is one of the many variations of the Ohio Star pattern. After you make the square, join four small triangles (two light ones, two dark) into a long, narrow right-angle triangle. Make four and sew one to each side of the center square. The long triangles nudge the star out of its conventional, upright position.

For the Morning Star Quilt, *above,* join sets of four small diamonds to make eight large diamonds. If your scraps allow for matching, make half of the large points from identical fabrics. To duplicate the look of the quilt shown, use one color for the background of half of the blocks and another color for the remaining half. Then, when joining the blocks, position the like-colored backgrounds in diagonal rows.

Dating from the 1930s
and 1940s, these two
quilts are thrifty creations
indeed. Tiny pieces of
prints and solids were
used for the patches. The
large amounts of white
fabric probably came from
worn sheets.

Another variation of the classic eight-point star, the Tiny Le-Moyne Star Quilt, *far left* and *opposite,* is an ideal choice for scrap piecing. Make each of the colorful stars from two fabrics, alternating a solid-color diamond with a print diamond.

When blocks of the Snowball Quilt, *near left* and *above,* are joined, white octagons form between the points. Make this quilt as shown with two contrasting prints per block. You also could use a print and a solid fabric for alternating points or even four different fabrics for each block.

Flower motifs always rank high with quilters. Here's an appliquéd flower design that's perfectly charming when stitched with scraps.

Consistent elements in each block of the Friendship Dahlia Quilt, *left,* unify this cheerful design. Use the same fabric for the flower centers, stems, and the sashing strips. To make this quilt a group effort, send each participant a template for the petal pieces, a fabric center and stem, and a background square with the flower outline drawn in place with a water-erasable marker.

The pattern of the Baby Bunting Quilt, *below* and on pages 48–49, looks intricate, but the design consists of only one fan shape. Make 16 fan units for each block and position them carefully.

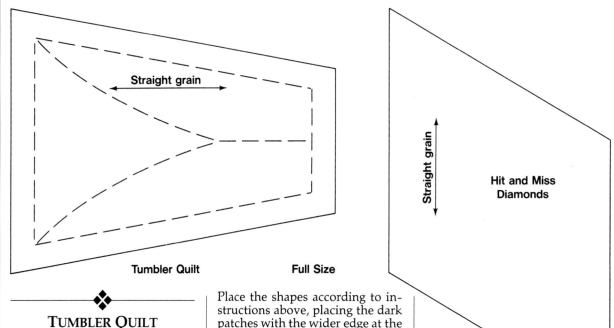

Tumbler Quilt   Full Size   Hit and Miss Diamonds

❖

TUMBLER QUILT
PAGE 50
Finished row is 3½ x 86 inches.
Finished size is approximately
86 x 94½ inches.

Materials
Approximately 10 yards of
assorted fabrics. (A scrap as
small as 3x4 inches is sufficient
for one patch; 1 yard of fabric
yields 144 patches.)
1 yard of binding fabric
5½ yards of backing fabric
Quilt batting
Cardboard or plastic for template

Instructions
Trace and make template for the
pattern, *above.* Pattern is finished
size; add ¼-inch seam allowances
when cutting the pieces from the
fabric.

To make the quilt top: Cut 1,053
tumbler shapes from fabrics.

To create horizontal rows, place
one patch with long edge at top.
Position next patch adjacent with
long edge at bottom. Position
third patch with long edge at top.
See photograph, page 50. Continue in manner until a row contains
39 patches.

For the first row, choose 20
dark patches and 19 light patches,
beginning with a dark patch.

Place the shapes according to instructions above, placing the dark
patches with the wider edge at the
top and the light patches with the
wider edge at the bottom. For the
second row, choose 20 light
patches and 19 dark patches, beginning with a light patch.

Repeat this joining sequence;
make a total of 27 rows.

Stitch rows together to make
quilt, matching short and long
edges of each patch.

Finishing: To piece the quilt back,
cut fabric into two equal lengths.
Cut or tear one length in half
lengthwise. Sew one narrow panel
to each side of the wide panel.
Match the selvages; use a ½-inch
seam. Trim the seams to ¼ inch;
press to one side.

Layer the back, batting, and
pieced top. Baste the layers together; quilt each piece as indicated on the pattern piece.

Cut binding fabric into 2-inch-
wide bias strips; join short ends,
making a single strip. Fold strip
in half lengthwise (wrong sides together) to make a 1-inch-wide
strip.

Sew raw edges of strip to top of
quilt with ¼-inch seam, following the zigzag edges along two
sides. Turn folded edge to back
and hand-stitch in place.

60°

❖

HIT-AND-MISS QUILT
PAGE 50
Finished size is 71 x 81 inches.

Materials
Approximately 9 yards of
assorted fabrics. (A scrap as
small as 3x5 inches is sufficient
for one diamond; 1 yard of
fabric yields 96 diamonds.)
5 yards of backing fabric
Quilt batting
Cardboard or plastic for templates

Instructions
Trace and make template for the
pattern, *above.* Pattern is finished
size; add ¼-inch seam allowances
when cutting the pieces from the
fabric.

To make the quilt top: Cut 930
diamonds from scraps.

Top is pieced in 30 vertical rows
with 31 diamonds in each row.

Join diamonds in rows so that
all angles are parallel. Then join
the rows together, alternating the
direction of the angles randomly.

When all rows have been
joined, trim the top and bottom to
make a straight edge.

Finishing: To piece the quilt back, cut fabric into two equal lengths. Cut or tear one length in half lengthwise. Sew one narrow panel to each side of the wide panel. Match the selvages; use a ½-inch seam. Trim the seams to ¼ inch; press to one side.

Splice the binding strips together at 45-degree angles. Trim, fold in half lengthwise, and press.

Layer the back, batting, and pieced top. Baste the layers together and quilt.

When quilting is complete, trim batting to same size as quilt top. Trim backing ½ inch larger than top and backing. Turn raw edges of backing under ¼ inch; bring folded edge around to front and hand-stitch in place.

❖

MORNING STAR QUILT
PAGE 53
Finished block is 11 inches square.
Finished quilt is 71x88 inches.

Materials
4 yards of tan fabric (plain blocks, borders, and binding)
1 yard of deep red fabric
1 yard of rose fabric
3½ yards of fabric scraps (approximately ⅛ yard per block)
5½ yards of backing fabric
Quilt batting
Cardboard or plastic for templates

Instructions
Trace and make templates for the patterns, *right.* Patterns are finished size; add ¼-inch seam allowances when cutting the pieces from the fabric. Label pieces A, B, and C.

To cut the pieces: The number of pieces to cut for the entire quilt is listed first; the number to cut for one block follows in parentheses.

Cut triangle B pieces with longest side on straight grain.

Take care when handling the A diamonds; two sides are on the bias and may stretch.

Borders are longer than needed; trim them after stitching.

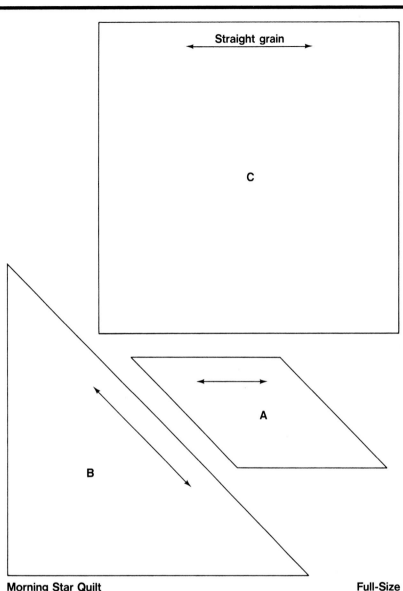

Morning Star Quilt   **Full-Size**

From tan fabric, cut:
Two 3x90-inch border strips
24 11½-inch squares; this measurement includes seam allowance
10 2½-inch strips (binding)

From deep red fabric, cut:
48 B triangles (4)
48 C squares (4)

From rose fabric, cut:
48 B triangles (4)
48 C squares (4)

From scraps, cut:
768 A diamonds (32)

To piece the blocks: Make 48 sets of four identical large diamonds (each pieced from four small A di-

amonds). Make a total of 192 large diamonds.

Choose two sets of four large diamonds for each block. Lay out diamonds, alternating matching large diamonds.

Using ¼-inch seams, stitch the diamonds together in pairs; stitch the pairs together to form a large diamond.

Refer to the instructions for assembling an eight-point star, pages 70–73, to stitch the large diamonds together. Set in deep red B and C pieces for half of the blocks and rose B and C pieces for the remaining blocks. Make 24 blocks.

(Continued)

59

To make the quilt top: Lay out quilt blocks. Alternate a pieced block with a tan block, placing deep red and rose pieced blocks in diagonal rows. Make eight rows of six blocks.

Sew eight blocks into six rows; stitch rows together.

Sew border strips to long sides; trim excess fabric.

Finishing: To piece the quilt back, cut fabric into equal lengths. Cut or tear one length in half lengthwise. Sew narrow panel to each side of wide panel. Match the selvages; use a ½-inch seam. Trim the seams to ¼ inch; press to one side.

Layer quilt top, batting, and backing. Baste layers together. Quilt shown is quilted in parallel diagonal rows 1 inch apart.

Sew the binding strips together into one long piece with diagonal seams. Fold binding in half lengthwise, wrong sides together, and press.

When quilting is complete, trim away excess batting and backing so that edges are even with the quilt top. Sew the binding to the right side of the quilt, raw edges together. Turn the folded edge to the back; hand-stitch in place.

TIPSY STAR QUILT
PAGE 52
Finished block is 9 inches square.
Finished size is 64x64 inches.

Materials
2½ yards of muslin
3½ yards of assorted fabric scraps
4 yards of backing fabric
Quilt batting
Plastic or cardboard for templates

Instructions
Trace and make templates for the patterns, *above right.* Patterns are finished size. Add ¼-inch seam allowances when cutting the pieces from the fabric.

For the setting squares and triangles, make a 9-inch square template from cardboard or plastic.

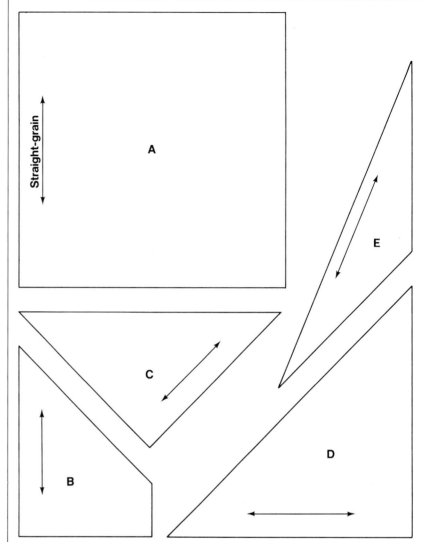

Tipsy Star Quilt   Full-Size

To cut the pieces: The number of pieces to cut for the entire quilt is listed first; the number to cut for one block follows in parentheses.

Adding ¼-inch seam allowances, use the 9-inch square template to mark and cut 16 setting squares from muslin (The cut square will measure 9½ inches square.) Set the squares aside.

For the setting triangles, draw a diagonal line between opposite corners of the template used for marking the setting squares. Draw a second diagonal line in the *opposite* direction, through the lower section of the template (see Figure 1, *opposite*).

Cut on the drawn lines to form templates X and Z.

Using Template X, mark 16 setting triangles on muslin with the triangle's *long* side on the straight

grain. Adding ¼-inch seam allowances, cut out the triangles.

Next, using Template Z, mark four corner-setting triangles on the muslin, with the legs of the triangle template on the straight grain. Adding seam allowances, cut out the triangles. Set the X and Z triangles aside.

From muslin, cut:
200 triangles from template C (8)
200 triangles from template E (8)
Six 2½-inch-wide strips across the fabric width (binding)

From print or solid fabrics, cut:
25 pieces from template A (1)
100 pieces from template B (4)
100 pieces from template B/r (4)
200 pieces from template C (8)
100 pieces from template D (4)

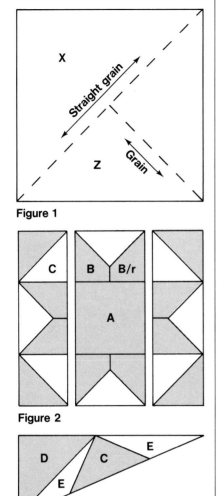

Figure 1

Figure 2

Figure 3

Note: Place straight grain parallel with a side of the triangle.

To piece one block: Refer to Figure 2, *above.* Begin by joining a muslin C triangle with B and B/r. Make four units. Join two B/C units to opposite sides of piece A.

Combine a muslin C triangle with a print C triangle to make a square; make four squares. Add a C/C square to each side of B/C unit to form two rectangles.

Join two rectangles to piece A assembly.

Seam the long side of a D triangle to the long side of an E piece. Add a dark C triangle to the side of the E patch. Then add another E piece. See Figure 3, *above.* Make four of these units.

(Continued)

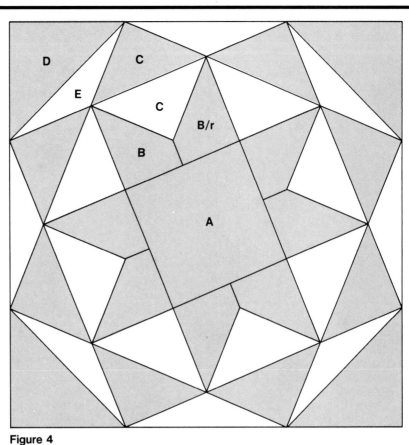

Figure 4

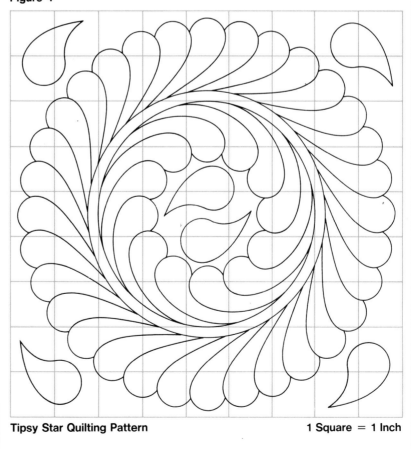

Tipsy Star Quilting Pattern   **1 Square = 1 Inch**

Stitch one of these pieced triangles to each side of the center star assembly. See Figure 4, page 61.

To make the quilt top: Piece 25 Tipsy Star blocks. Note that the quilt top is pieced in diagonal rows, with muslin squares between the pieced blocks; all blocks are turned on point. If desired, transfer the quilting pattern to the muslin squares and setting triangles before assembly; see finishing instructions, below.

Join the blocks as follows: Join five pieced blocks with alternating muslin squares for the center row; add one Z triangle to each end. Join four pieced blocks with alternating muslin squares for the adjacent rows; add one X triangle to each end.

Continue in this manner, working from the center row outward, and using one less pieced block per row. Add remaining Z triangles to complete corners. Stitch rows together to complete the top.

Finishing: To piece the quilt back, cut fabric into two equal lengths. Cut or tear one length in half lengthwise. Sew one narrow panel to each side of the wide panel. Match the selvages; use a ½-inch seam. Trim the seams to ¼ inch; press to one side.

Enlarge the quilting pattern on page 61, and transfer the design to each of the muslin squares. Divide the pattern into halves and quarters and transfer designs to the X and Z triangles.

Splice the binding strips together at 45-degree angles. Trim seams, fold in half lengthwise (wrong sides together), and press.

Layer the back, batting, and pieced top. Baste the layers together and quilt.

When quilting is complete, trim away excess batting and backing so that all edges are even with the quilt top. Sew the binding to the right side of the quilt, raw edges together. Turn the folded edge to the back; hand-stitch in place.

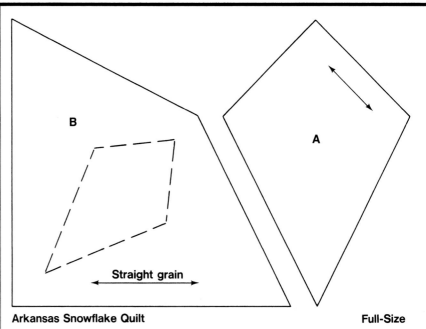

Straight grain

Arkansas Snowflake Quilt   Full-Size

❖

SNOWBALL QUILT
PAGE 55
Finished block is 6 inches.
Finished size is 72x78 inches.

Materials
4 yards of assorted scraps for A pieces (a 5-inch square scrap is sufficient for two A patches)
6½ yards of muslin for B pieces and binding
8½ yards of prepared muslin bias (binding)
5 yards of backing fabric
Quilt batting
Cardboard or plastic for templates

Instructions
Trace and make templates for the patterns A and B, *above.* Patterns are finished size; add ¼-inch seam allowances when cutting the pieces from the fabric.

To cut the pieces: The number of pieces to cut for the entire quilt is listed first; the number to cut for one block follows in parentheses.

From scraps, cut:
312 *pairs* of A diamonds (4)

From muslin, cut:
624 B pieces (4)

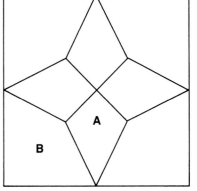

Figure 1

To piece one block: Referring to Figure 1, *above,* stitch four A diamonds together to form a star. Be sure that opposite points of the star are cut from the same fabric.

Set in the four corner (B) pieces. Press seams toward the star. Make 156 blocks.

To piece the quilt top: Lay out the finished blocks in 12 rows of 13 blocks each. Move the blocks around, if necessary, to achieve a balance of colors and values.

Using ¼-inch seams, stitch the blocks together to make rows. Join the rows together.

Finishing: To piece the quilt back, cut fabric into two equal lengths. Piece together.

Outline-quilt each A and B piece, stitching ⅛ inch inside the seam; transfer remaining quilting design from pattern to each B piece.

Layer backing, batting, and top; baste together. Quilt.

Trim excess backing and batting even with quilt top.

From remaining muslin, cut and piece 8½ yards of 2½-inch-wide bias-cut strips. Fold in half lengthwise, wrong sides together, and press.

Sew the binding to the right side of the quilt, raw edges together. Turn the folded edge to the back; hand-stitch in place.

❖

TINY LeMOYNE STAR QUILT
PAGE 54
Finished block is 4½ inches.
Finished size is 74x87½ inches.

Materials
¼ yard of *each* of the following pastel solids: green, pink, rose, red, gold, yellow, light purple, lavender, and blue
2½ yards of assorted scraps to coordinate with pastels
4¾ yards of muslin (plain blocks, pieced blocks, and binding)
3½ yards of muslin (borders)
5½ yards of backing fabric
Quilt batting
Cardboard or template material

Instructions
Trace and make templates for pattern pieces A, B, and C, *above right.* The patterns are finished size. Add ¼-inch seam allowances when cutting the pieces from the fabric.

To cut the pieces: The number of pieces to cut for the entire quilt is listed first; the number to cut for one block follows in parentheses.

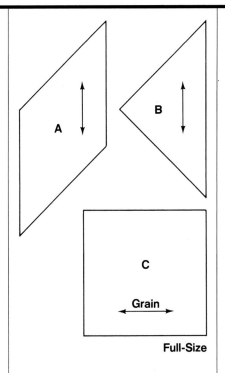

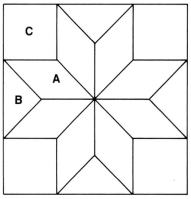

Grain

Full-Size

From border muslin, cut:
4 10½-inch-wide border strips, each 3½ yards long

From solid fabrics, cut:
360 A diamonds (4); cut four of the same color for each block. The fabric amount given should yield 56 diamonds; you may choose to vary the amounts of one color or group of colors.

From print scraps, cut:
360 A diamonds (4); cut in sets of four, with each set coordinating with a set of solid fabric diamonds

From remaining muslin, cut:
90 5-inch squares; this measurement includes seam allowances
360 B pieces (4)
360 C squares (4)

To piece one block: Referring to Figure 1, *below,* and referring to directions for piecing a LeMoyne Star, pages 70–73, assemble block. Make sure that diamonds are solid fabrics alternating with a coordinating print.

Make 90 blocks.

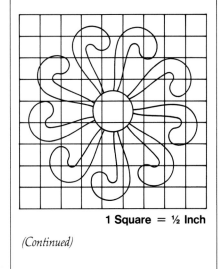

Figure 1

To make the quilt top: Lay out blocks alternately with plain muslin squares. Make 12 rows of 15 blocks each.

Using ¼-inch seams, stitch blocks together to form rows. Stitch rows together.

Enlarge block quilting pattern, *below.* Transfer to plain blocks.

Stitch border strips to quilt top, mitering corners. Mark the center of each side.

1 Square = ½ Inch

(Continued)

Enlarge scallop and quilting pattern, *below.* Beginning at center of each long side, trace three quilt pattern repeats in each direction toward corner (a total of six per side). For top and bottom border, center a single quilt pattern repeat along border; add two repeats in each direction toward corner (a total of five per each top and bottom border).

Round one corner, adjusting it slightly to make a smooth edge. Repeat for remaining corners. Complete quilting design within corners.

Finishing: To piece the quilt back, cut fabric into two equal lengths. Cut or tear one length in half lengthwise. Sew one narrow panel to each side of the wide panel. Match the selvages; use a ½-inch seam. Trim the seams to ¼ inch; press to one side.

From remaining muslin, cut 10 yards of 2-inch-wide bias strips. Join. Fold in half lengthwise, wrong sides together, and press.

Layer the back, batting, and pieced top. Baste layers together.

Quilt along marked lines. Outline-quilt pieced blocks.

When quilting is complete, trim away excess batting and backing about ½ inch from border quilting to create scallops and rounded corners. Sew the binding to the right side of the quilt, raw edges together. Turn the folded edge to the back; hand-stitch in place.

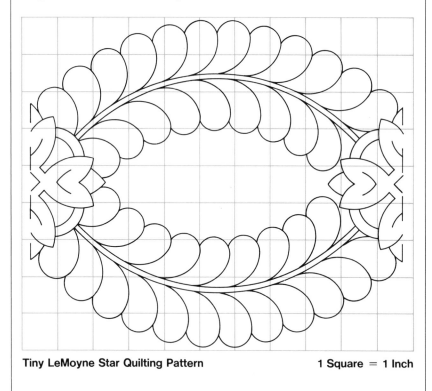

Tiny LeMoyne Star Quilting Pattern

1 Square = 1 Inch

❖

FRIENDSHIP DAHLIA QUILT

PAGES 56–57
Finished block is 12 inches.
Finished size is 72½ x88 inches.

Materials

5 yards of muslin (background squares, outer borders, and binding)

2½ yards of yellow fabric (sashing and flower centers)

2 yards of assorted prints and solids (petals) (a scrap as small as 3x5 inches is sufficient for one petal)

¼ yard of green fabric (stems)

5¼ yards of backing fabric

Quilt batting

Cardboard or plastic for templates

Water-erasable marker

Instructions

Trace and make templates for pieces A, B, and C, *opposite.* The patterns are finished size. Add ¼-inch seam allowances when cutting the pieces from the fabric.

On tracing paper, draw a 12-inch square. Referring to Figure 1, *below,* use templates to draw flower pattern inside square. Use this as a guide for appliqué.

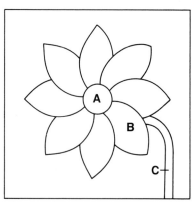

Figure 1

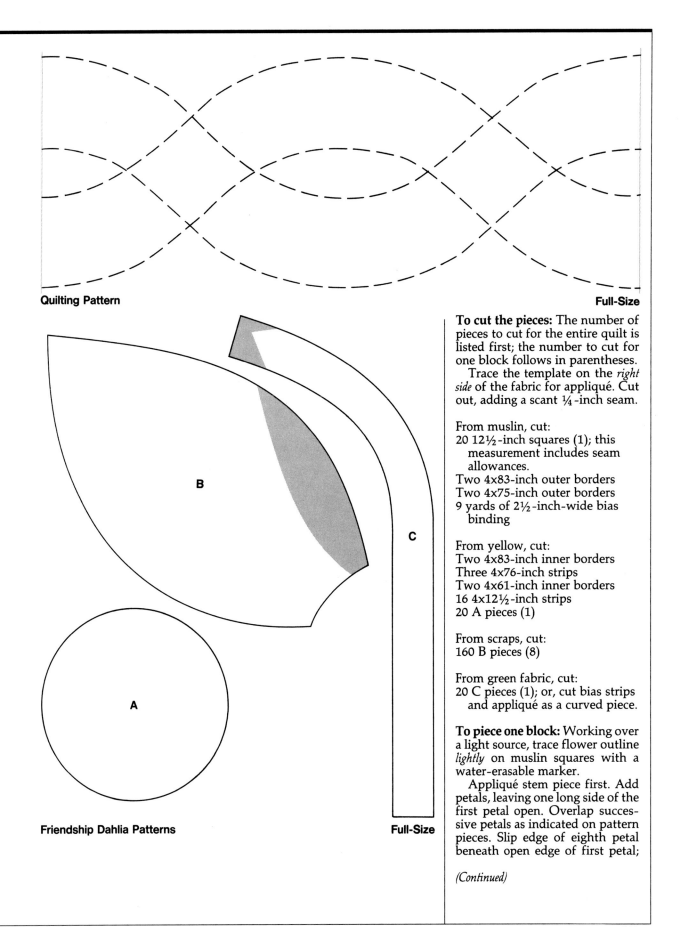

Quilting Pattern

Full-Size

B

C

A

Friendship Dahlia Patterns

Full-Size

To cut the pieces: The number of pieces to cut for the entire quilt is listed first; the number to cut for one block follows in parentheses.

Trace the template on the *right side* of the fabric for appliqué. Cut out, adding a scant ¼-inch seam.

From muslin, cut:
20 12½-inch squares (1); this measurement includes seam allowances.
Two 4x83-inch outer borders
Two 4x75-inch outer borders
9 yards of 2½-inch-wide bias binding

From yellow, cut:
Two 4x83-inch inner borders
Three 4x76-inch strips
Two 4x61-inch inner borders
16 4x12½-inch strips
20 A pieces (1)

From scraps, cut:
160 B pieces (8)

From green fabric, cut:
20 C pieces (1); or, cut bias strips and appliqué as a curved piece.

To piece one block: Working over a light source, trace flower outline *lightly* on muslin squares with a water-erasable marker.

Appliqué stem piece first. Add petals, leaving one long side of the first petal open. Overlap successive petals as indicated on pattern pieces. Slip edge of eighth petal beneath open edge of first petal;

(Continued)

65

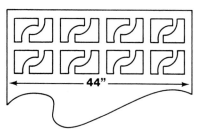

Cutting Diagram

complete stitching. Add piece A. (*Note:* To hand-appliqué, fold under raw edge to seam line marked on face of fabric; baste. Position on background and sew in place using tiny invisible stitches.)

To piece the quilt top: Join five blocks in a vertical row with 4x12½-inch sashing strips between blocks. Make four rows.

Lay out the rows, placing a 4x76-inch yellow strip between each row. Stitch these rows and strips together, lining up the blocks and pressing the sashing horizontally at the block seams to make placement guides for the blocks in the next row.

To add the yellow borders, stitch the two 4x61-inch strips across the top and bottom, trimming any excess fabric on the center sashing strips. Next, sew two 4x83-inch strips to sides of quilt. Trim as needed and press.

To add the muslin borders, sew the 4x83-inch borders to the sides, then sew the 4x75-inch borders to the top and bottom. Trim the borders; extra fabric is allowed for sashing strips and borders for slight variations in seam allowances and cutting.

Finishing: To piece the quilt back, cut fabric into two 2½-yard lengths. Cut or tear one piece in half lengthwise. Sew one narrow panel to each side of the wide panel. Match the selvages; use a ½-inch seam. Trim the seams to ¼ inch; press to one side.

Layer the back, batting, and pieced top. Baste layers together.

Mark the cable quilting design, page 65, on the sashing strips and borders. Mark a grid of 1-inch squares on the background of the flower appliqués. Outline-quilt around each shape; quilt the grid.

Splice binding strips with diagonal seams. Fold in half lengthwise, wrong sides together; press.

When quilting is complete, trim excess batting and backing even with the quilt top. Sew the binding to the quilt, raw edges together. Turn the folded edge to the back; hand-stitch in place.

BABY BUNTING QUILT
PAGES 48–49 and 57
Finished fan unit is 5 inches square.
Finished block is 20 inches square.
Finished quilt is 80 inches square.

Materials
4½ yards of muslin
2 yards of yellow fabric
Approximately 5 yards of assorted scraps for B pieces (a scrap as small as 2x3 inches is sufficient for one patch)
5 yards of backing fabric
Quilt batting
Cardboard or plastic for templates

Instructions
Trace and make templates for A, B, and C pieces, *opposite.* The patterns are finished size; add ¼-inch seam allowances when cutting the pieces from the fabric.

To cut the pieces: The number of pieces to cut for the entire quilt is listed first; the number to cut for one block follows in parentheses. Match grain lines on patterns to grain of fabric.

From muslin, cut:
256 C pieces (16); see instructions below for cutting these pieces

From yellow fabric, cut:
256 A pieces (16)
9½ yards of 2½-inch-wide bias binding

From scraps, cut:
1,280 B pieces (80)

When cutting C pieces, *carefully* transfer the dot mark on the C template center to seam allowances on C muslin pieces. Lay out the pieces according to the cutting diagram, *above right,* for best use of fabric. Because of the unusual shape of this piece and the necessarily wasted fabric, extra yardage is included in the materials' list to ensure a sufficient amount.

To piece one fan unit: Each block is made from 16 small fan units; see Figure 1, *below.* Using ¼-inch seams, sew five B pieces together to form an arc. Fold the arc in half to find the center of the middle B piece; press lightly.

Join an A piece and a C piece to each arc, matching center dots to the press line of the B arc.

Make 256 fan units.

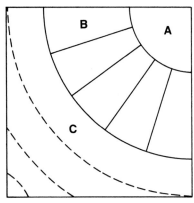

Figure 1

To piece one block: Referring to Figure 2, *opposite,* arrange 16 fan units. Sew together four units in rows; sew the four rows together.

Make 16 blocks.

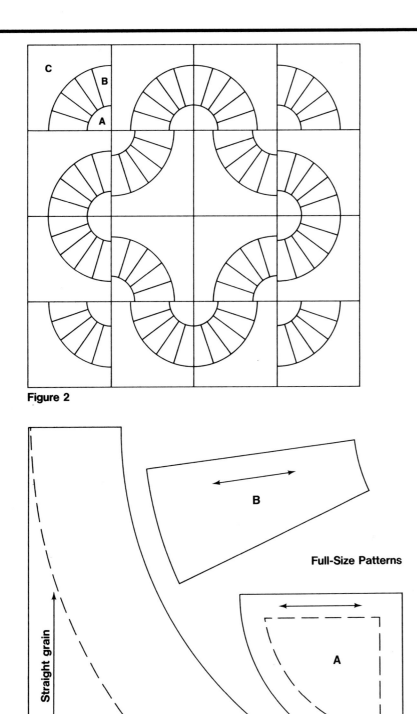

Figure 2

Full-Size Patterns

Straight grain

To piece the quilt top: Arrange the blocks in four rows; each row should have four blocks. Sew together each row; join the rows.

Finishing: To piece the quilt back, cut fabric into two 2½-yard lengths. Cut or tear one length in half lengthwise. Sew one narrow panel to each side of the wide panel. Match the selvages; use a ½-inch seam. Trim the seams to ¼ inch; press to one side.

Layer the back, batting, and pieced top. Baste layers together. Quilt as desired, or according to the quilting lines indicated on the A and C pattern pieces.

To make the binding, splice the bias-cut strips together with diagonal seams into one long strip. Fold in half lengthwise, wrong sides together, and press.

When quilting is complete, trim away excess batting and backing so that all edges are even with the quilt top. Sew the binding to the right side of the quilt, raw edges together. Turn the folded edge to the back; hand-stitch in place.

STITCHING WITH STRINGS AND RANDOM PATCHES

In American patchwork, stitchers have often joined small pieces of fabric to make a larger pattern piece. In this chapter, you'll explore some new ways of duplicating the haphazard—but often dynamic—appearance of old quilts. We show you how to eliminate tedious piecing and yet create patchwork that is delightfully spontaneous.

PIECING FABRIC STRIPS

Using a rotary cutter lets you turn out dozens of precise fabric strips quickly and easily.

To a quilter, a "string" is simply a long strip of fabric. Quilters have used strings, alone and in combination, for many beautiful designs. A prime example is the String Star Quilt, *above*, a variation of the LeMoyne Star pattern.

For best results when cutting strings, cut across full widths of fabric so you can combine strings freely and consistently.

Instructions begin on page 78.

1

2

3

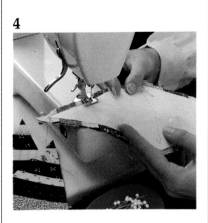

4

5

6

7

❖

1 Cut assorted fabrics across the fabric width into strips ranging from ¾ to 2 inches wide.

To speed the cutting, cut the fabrics using a rotary cutter, cutting mat, and a heavy plastic ruler. Fold a fabric piece into fourths along the lengthwise grain, so the folded piece is approximately 11 inches wide. Using the ruler and cutter, square off one cut edge. *Note:* Hold the ruler firmly down on the fabric with one hand. With the other hand, roll the cutter along the ruler *away* from yourself, pressing firmly to cut through the fabric. (See the photo *opposite, below.*)

2 Using ¼-inch seams, sew the strings together in a pleasing arrangement of colors to create a fabric piece 42–45 inches wide and 13–14 inches deep. Piece short strings to achieve needed length. Press all seams to one side.

3 Using the pattern for the String Star on page 78, draw eight diamonds on plastic-coated freezer paper; transfer the arrow on the pattern to the paper diamonds. Cut out each paper diamond.

Place the *coated* side of the eight paper diamonds on the wrong side of the pieced fabric, placing the diamonds so the fabric seams run parallel to the arrow on the diamonds. Space the diamonds at least ½ inch apart to allow for ¼-inch seam allowances around the diamonds. Using a warm, dry iron, press the diamonds to the pieced fabric. Cut out the diamonds ¼ inch larger than the paper diamonds to make seam allowances.

4 Repeat steps 1–3 to make a second set of eight diamonds. You will have 16 diamonds, enough to make two stars.

To make a star, choose four diamonds from each set to give the star variety and to avoid a bull's-eye effect in the center.

Sew sets of two diamonds together to form four pairs of diamonds. For all steps of the star construction, stitch only on the sewing line (along the edge of the paper); **do not extend stitching into the seam allowances.** Backstitch at the beginning and end of all seams.

5 Sew pairs of diamonds together to create star halves.

6 Join the two star halves, taking care to match all the diamond points at the star center. Press the seam allowances to one side so they fan around the star.

7 To add the triangles and squares to complete the star, follow steps 5–7 for the Random Patch Star on page 73.

71

PIECING RANDOM PATCHES

Plastic-coated freezer paper makes a stable base for joining small patches. This technique works for crazy patchwork, too.

The LeMoyne Star pattern used for the String Star Quilt on the previous pages takes on a new look when assembled from randomly shaped patches.

To duplicate the look of the quilt, *left,* gather small pieces of fabric in one or two colors. Use these fabrics to piece each of the eight points for the star, following the instructions opposite. Set in muslin triangles and squares to complete the block and assemble the quilt top with alternating plain blocks in a contrasting color.

The colorful star banner, *left,* uses the same assembly technique. But start with a 16½-inch square of freezer paper, and stitch yellow patches on it to make the inset portion of each star block. Then reverse-appliqué navy squares and pentagons over the patchwork to complete the block. Make four blocks for the banner, and embellish each one with hand embroidery.

1

2

3

4

5

6

1 Make templates for the diamond, triangle, and square patterns for the Random-Pieced LeMoyne Star Quilt on page 79. Using the diamond template, draw eight diamonds on plastic-coated freezer paper; cut out the diamonds. Mark and cut out four triangles and four squares from muslin.

Using a warm iron, press the coated side of a paper diamond onto the wrong side of a fabric scrap, making sure the fabric extends at least ¼ inch beyond the sides of the diamond to allow for the seam allowances.

2 Choose a second fabric scrap; check to be sure the scrap will cover the paper diamond and allow for seam allowances after it is sewn. With raw edges even, pin the right side of the scrap to the scrap already on the diamond. Stitch the scraps together, sewing through the paper diamond.

Open out the fabric and press the second scrap to the paper diamond.

3 From the wrong side (paper side up), trim excess fabric, leaving ¼ inch for seam allowances around the diamond. Repeat steps 1–3 to make eight diamonds.

4 Referring to steps 4–6 for the String Star on page 73, stitch the diamonds into a star.

5 To set the muslin triangles into the openings along the star edge, pin a triangle along one side of a star point, matching corners and stitching lines. Sew the pinned seam, stitching only on the stitching line. Clip threads and remove work from the machine.

6 Pin the second side of the triangle to the adjacent diamond side, carefully matching points and sewing lines. Sew the pinned seam, again stitching only on the sewing line.

7

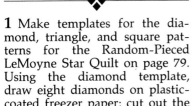
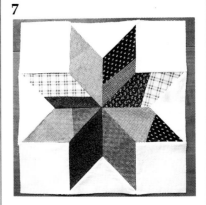

7 Set the three remaining triangles into openings between the star points. Following the same method, set squares into the four corners to complete the block.

❖ ❖ ❖

These three quilt designs incorporate the two easy piecing techniques described on the previous four pages.

The unusual quilt, *opposite,* is a random-patch variation of an all-time favorite pattern, the Double Wedding Ring. To assemble the patched arcs fast and accurately, make some rectangles of random-patched fabric and cut out the arcs after completing the piecing. Assemble the quilt conventionally.

Make random-patched rectangles in the same way for the Crumb Quilt, *above right.* Combine fabrics freely, paying attention to the position of lights and darks. Also strive for attractive balance, placement of color, and scale of prints. Use a rotary cutter to make quick work of cutting the sashing squares and rectangles.

Assemble strips of fabric for the Rail Fence Quilt, *below right,* as for the String Star Quilt on pages 70–71. Then simply cut the assemblies into squares. Join the squares together, alternating the direction of the strips, to make this lively quilt top.

❖ ❖ ❖

Perfect for quick-piecing, these table accessories also show how one basic block can be assembled in various ways.

Patchwork strings don't have to be the same width. To make the triangles for the Spool pattern blocks, combine strings ranging from ¾ to 1¼ inches wide. Stitch them to a wider strip of contrasting fabric (we used tan cotton with blue vines), and cut four triangles from these strips for each block.

Each of the place mats, *above,* requires six Spool blocks. Join the blocks so their striped portions align vertically, horizontally, or in alternating configurations.

The dynamic pattern of the table runner, *opposite,* results from the half-drop setting. Each of the outer rows of the runner is made from six blocks. The inner row is seven blocks long, with the end blocks trimmed away. When joining the rows, offset the center row so it falls midway between the outer rows.

❖

STRING STAR QUILT
PAGE 70
Finished block is 19 inches square.
Finished size is 69x82 inches.

Materials
4 yards muslin
Approximately 4½ yards of assorted print fabric scraps
5 yards backing fabric
Quilt batting
Plastic or cardboard for templates
Plastic-coated freezer paper

Instructions
Trace and make template for the diamond pattern, *right.* For Piece C, draw a 5-inch square on graph paper; bisect this square diagonally for Piece B. Make templates for Pieces B and C. Patterns are finished size; add ¼-inch seam allowances when cutting the pieces from the fabric.

To cut the pieces: The number of pieces to cut for the entire quilt is listed first, with the number to cut for one block following in parentheses. Border measurements include seam allowances and are longer than necessary. Trim borders to exact size when you sew them to the quilt top.

From muslin, cut:
2 borders, each 6½x78 inches
2 borders, each 3½x72 inches
48 triangles from template B (4)
48 squares from template C (4)

From freezer paper, cut:
96 diamonds from template A (8)

To make one block: Refer to pages 70–73 for instructions for making the diamonds and piecing the star blocks. You can cut eight diamonds, enough diamonds for one block, from a pieced strip. Use diamonds from several different strip sets for each star to give the stars a random appearance.

To make the quilt top: Make 12 blocks. Sew blocks into four horizontal rows with three blocks per row. Join the rows.

Sew the wide borders to the quilt sides; sew the narrow borders to the top and bottom. Trim excess border fabric.

Finishing: To piece the quilt back, cut fabric into two equal lengths. Cut or tear one length in half lengthwise. Sew a narrow panel to each side of the wide panel with a ½-inch seam. Trim seams to ¼ inch; press to one side.

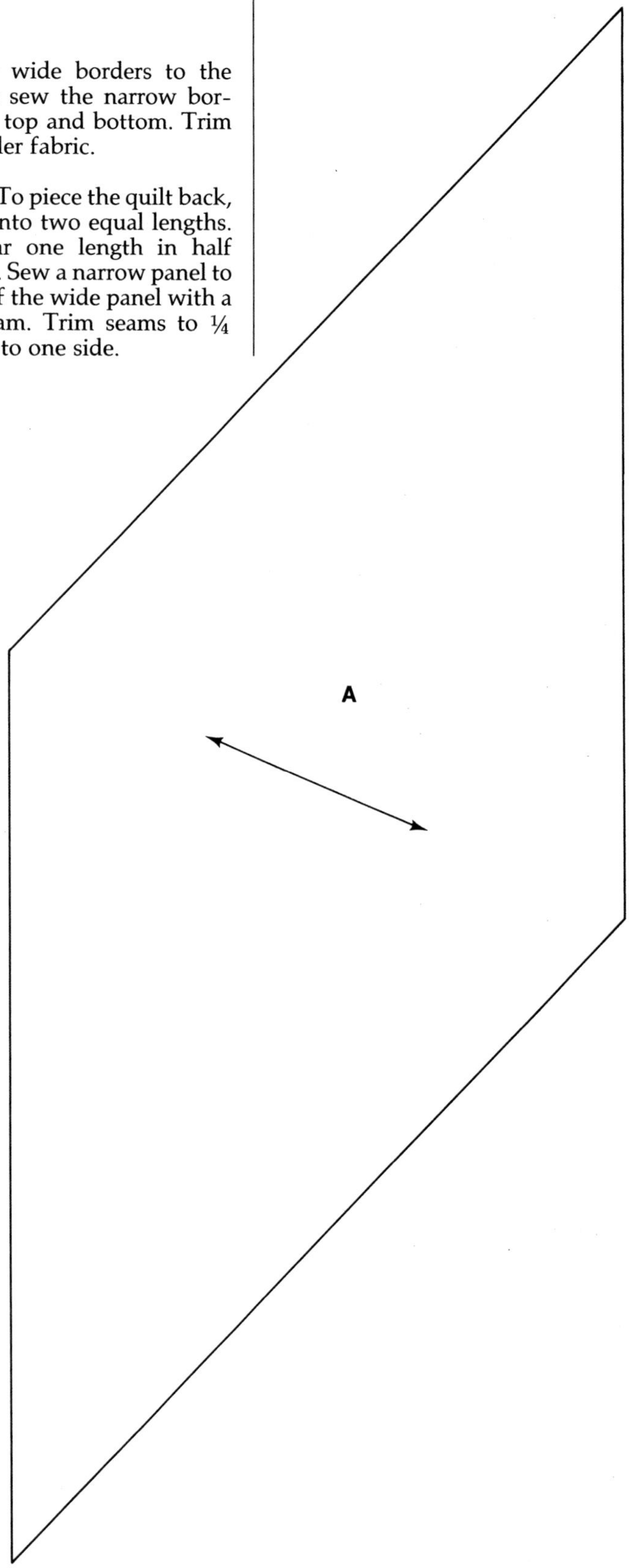

A

Layer the back, batting, and the pieced top. Baste layers together; quilt.

From the remaining muslin, cut 2½-inch-wide strips across the width of the fabric. Splice the strips together at 45-degree angles into a piece approximately 9½ yards long. Trim, fold in half lengthwise with wrong sides together, and press.

When quilting is complete, trim away excess batting and backing so all edges are even with the quilt top. Sew the binding to the right side of the quilt, raw edges together. Turn the folded edge to the back; hand-stitch in place.

❖❖❖

RANDOM-PIECED LEMOYNE STAR QUILT
PAGE 72
Finished block is 14 inches.
Finished size is 64x74 inches.

Materials
3 yards muslin
3 yards yellow print fabric
Approximately 2½ yards of assorted print fabric scraps
4½ yards backing fabric
Quilt batting
Plastic or cardboard for templates
Plastic-coated freezer paper

Instructions
Trace and make template for the diamond pattern, *right.* For Piece C, draw a 4⅛-inch square on graph paper; bisect this square diagonally for Piece B. Make templates for Pieces B and C. Patterns are finished size; add ¼-inch seam allowances when cutting the pieces from the fabric.

For setting squares and triangles, make a 14-inch square template from cardboard or plastic.

To cut the pieces: The number of pieces to cut for the entire quilt is listed first, with the number to cut for one block following in parentheses. Borders include seam allowances and are longer than necessary. Trim borders after sewing them to the quilt top.

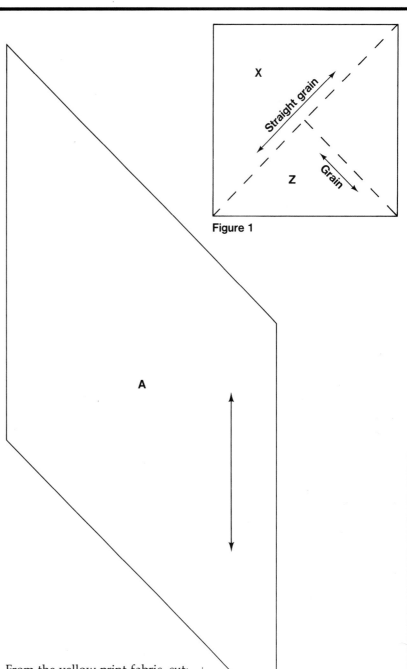

Figure 1

A

From the yellow print fabric, cut:
2 borders, each 2½x66 inches

Adding ¼-inch seam allowances, use the 14-inch square template to mark and cut 9 setting squares from yellow print fabric. (The cut square will measure 14½ inches square.) Set the squares aside.

For the setting triangles, draw a diagonal line between opposite corners of the template used for marking the setting squares. Draw a second diagonal line in the *opposite* direction, through the lower section of the template (see Figure 1, *above*).

Cut on the drawn lines to form templates X and Z.

Using template X, mark 12 setting triangles on the yellow print fabric with the *long* side of the triangle on the straight grain. Adding ¼-inch seam allowances, cut out the triangles.

(Continued)

STITCHING WITH STRINGS AND RANDOM PATCHES

Next, using Template Z, mark four corner-setting triangles on the yellow print fabric, with the legs of the triangle template on the straight grain. Adding seam allowances, cut out the triangles. Set the X and Z triangles aside.

From muslin, cut:
2 borders, each 3x66 inches
64 B triangles (4)
64 C squares (4)

From freezer paper, cut:
128 A diamonds (8)

To make one block: Refer to pages 70–71 for instructions for making the diamonds and stitching them together into a star. Refer to pages 72–73 for instructions for adding the triangles and squares to the star to complete the block.

To make the quilt top: Piece 16 Random-Pieced Lemoyne Star blocks. The quilt top is pieced in diagonal rows with yellow print squares between the pieced blocks; all blocks are turned on point.

Join the blocks as follows: Join four pieced blocks with alternating yellow print squares for the center row; add one Z triangle to each end. Join three pieced blocks with alternating yellow print squares for the adjacent rows; add one X triangle to each end. Continue in this manner, working from center row outward and using one fewer pieced block per row. Add remaining Z triangles to complete corners. Stitch rows together to complete the top.

Finishing: To piece the quilt back, cut fabric into two equal lengths. Cut or tear one length in half lengthwise. Sew one narrow panel to each side of the wide panel. Match the selvages; use a ½-inch seam. Trim the seams to ¼ inch; press to one side.

Layer the back, batting, and the pieced top. Baste layers together; quilt.

From the remaining muslin, cut 2½-inch-wide strips across the width of the fabric. Splice the binding strips together at 45-degree angles into a long piece approximately 8½ yards long. Trim, fold in half lengthwise with wrong sides together, and press.

When quilting is complete, trim away excess batting and backing so all edges are even with the quilt top. Sew the binding to the right side of the quilt, raw edges together. Turn the folded edge to the back; hand-stitch in place.

RANDOM-PATCH STAR BANNER
PAGE 72
Finished block is 16 inches.
Finished size is 45x45 inches.

Materials
½ yard *each* of five different navy print fabrics (prints A, B, C, D, and E)
1½ yards of a sixth navy print fabric (print F)
¼ yard of a yellow print fabric
Approximately 24 different print fabrics, each from ⅛ to ¼ yard; fabrics are predominately yellow, with accents of blue and green
1 yard muslin
2 yards backing fabric
Quilt batting
Embroidery floss
Cardboard or plastic for templates

Instructions
Referring to instructions for Random-Pieced LeMoyne Star Quilt, page 79, trace diamond pattern, page 79. Cut out a template of this shape. Tracing around template, make a 14-inch star pattern by repeating the pattern eight times. Draw a 16-inch square with this star in the center.

Cut out the star shape. Use this overlay as a guide when creating the crazy-patch blocks.

To make the crazy-patch blocks: Referring to the directions for piecing random patches, page 73, cut a 16½-inch square of plastic-coated freezer paper or muslin. Using scrap fabrics, cover muslin or freezer paper with patches.

Use a three- or five-sided patch near the center of the star area and work toward the edges. Place the overlay atop work periodically to check patch position and shape.

Make four blocks.

To cut the pieces: Using tissue overlay, make a pattern of the 5⅛-inch square and the five-sided piece that lies between the squares. Make templates of the square (Piece A) and the pentagon (Piece B). Patterns are full size and do not include seam allowances; add ¼-inch seam allowances when cutting the pieces from the fabric. Measurements for borders and sashing strips are the correct size, and include ¼-inch seam allowances.

From *each* of the A, B, C, and D navy prints, cut:
4 A squares
4 B pentagons

From the E navy print, cut:
4 2½x16½-inch sashing strips
2 2½x38½-inch inner borders
2 2½x40½-inch inner borders

From the F navy print, cut:
1 2½-inch square
2 5½x40½-inch outer borders
2 5½x45½-inch outer borders

To make the blocks: With a tailor's chalk, mark the seam lines on each set of A and B Pieces. Stitch a B Piece between a pair of A Pieces; then join two A/B sets with two additional B Pieces. Press seams to one side. Press under the seam allowances on remaining raw edges of star outline. Finished size of overlay should be 16½ inches square.

Hand-appliqué the overlay to the crazy-patch block. Use a quilter's or carpenter's square to line up the corner squares over the crazy-patch block.

Trim away the excess crazy-patch block to about ¼ inch.

Referring to hand-embroidery stitches, page 215, and using embroidery floss, add accent stitches.

Assembly: Lay out blocks to form a square. Lay the four sashing strips between the blocks and the F navy print square in the center.

Stitch the two right-hand blocks to one sashing strip; repeat for the two left-hand blocks. Stitch the square between the two remaining strips; stitch this long strip between the two sets of blocks.

Using ¼-inch seams, stitch the two shorter inner borders (cut from the E navy print) to the sides of the center panel. Stitch the two remaining inner borders to the top and bottoms of the center panel and ends of the side borders.

For piping, cut four 1x40½-inch strips from yellow print. Fold in half lengthwise with wrong sides together, and press.

Cut a 45-inch square of backing fabric, piecing if necessary. Cut a 45-inch square of quilt batting. Layer backing and batting; center quilt front atop batting and baste in place.

Aligning raw edges and using ¼-inch seams, stitch piping to quilt front. Stitch a length to each side and then to top and bottom.

Fold border strips (cut from the F navy print) in half lengthwise with wrong sides facing; press. Fold under seam allowance along one long edge; press.

With right sides together and aligning raw edges, stitch the shorter border piece to sides of front. Fold border strips to back of quilt; slip-stitch in place. Repeat with top border strips, except stitch short sides together before turning border to back side.

Using transparent nylon thread, machine-quilt in the ditch around each A and B Piece and along sashing strips. Quilt diagonal lines in each A Piece, radiating from center of star to corner of block. If star looks too puffy, tack crazy-patch to the backing.

From backing fabric, cut two 10x44-inch casings. Fold each in half lengthwise, right sides facing, to form a tube. Stitch each long side, turn, and press. Slip-stitch to top and bottom edges on backing.

RANDOM-PATCH DOUBLE WEDDING RING QUILT
PAGE 74
Finished block is 18 inches.
Finished quilt is 63x72 inches.

Materials
5½ yards beige fabric
½ yard red fabric
3¾ yards assorted print fabrics
4¼ yards backing fabric
1 yard binding fabric
Quilt batting
Plastic-coated freezer paper
Cardboard or plastic for templates

Instructions
Referring to full-size patterns, page 82, make pattern piece templates. Piece F (adjacent to Piece B) is to be repeated for a total of four times to create pattern Piece D and for a total of two times to create Piece E; see Figure 3, page 83. Patterns are finished size; add ¼-inch seam allowances when cutting the pieces from the fabric. Transfer all dots on the pattern pieces to *each* piece of fabric in the seam allowance. Matching these dots will increase the accuracy of the finished block.

To cut the pieces: The number of pieces to cut for the entire quilt is listed first; the number to cut for one block follows in parentheses.

From red fabric, cut:
56 A squares (4)

From beige fabric, cut:
56 A squares (4)
21 D Pieces (1)
13 E Pieces
2 F Pieces
46 C Pieces (4)

From freezer paper, cut:
112 B Pieces (8)

From binding fabric, cut:
7½ yards of 1½-inch-wide bias strips

To make the patched arcs: Referring to instructions for piecing

random patches, pages 72–73, stitch fabric scraps to paper shapes. Fabric should extend past paper at least ¼ inch for seams.

To piece a ring block: Join a B arc to one side of a C Piece; join a second B arc along the opposite side of the C Piece. Add one *beige* A Piece to one end of the arc units and one *red* A Piece to the opposite end of the arc units. See Figure 1, *below.*

Make four units for one block.

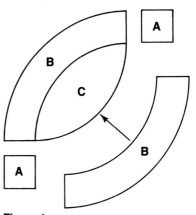

Figure 1

Join one arc unit to Piece D; join a second unit to the opposite side of Piece D. Add the two other arc units to the remaining edges of the D Piece. When joining arcs, match dots at the center of each curved piece. See Figure 2, *below.*

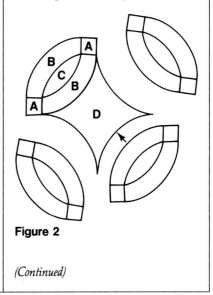

Figure 2

(Continued)

81

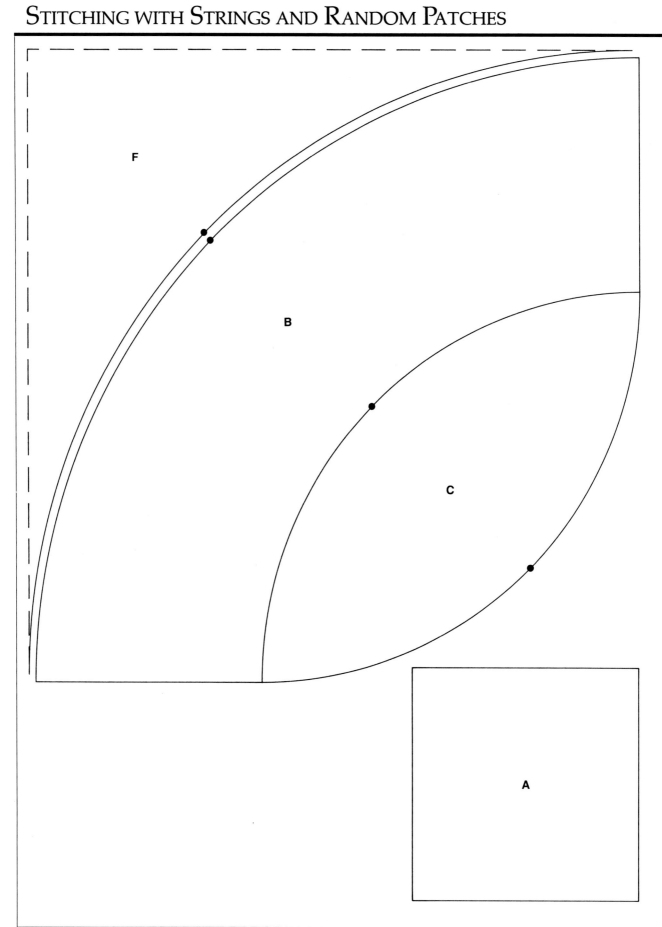

F

B

C

A

Figure 3

Make 12 circles in this manner. Set circles aside.

Make four half circles using piece E instead of piece D.

To make the quilt top: Lay out the pieced circles in four horizontal rows of three blocks; place the half circles along the right side. Join these rows by adding piece D between the circles. See Figure 3, *above.* Square off edges by setting in piece E along the top, bottom, and left side (the E pieces were sewn to the right side when the half-circle blocks were added).

Add an F piece to the upper- and lower-left corners to complete the quilt top.

Finishing: To piece the quilt back, cut fabric into two equal lengths. Cut or tear one length in half lengthwise. Sew one narrow panel to each side of the wide panel. Match the selvages; use a ½-inch seam. Trim the seams to ¼ inch; press to one side.

Transfer desired quilting patterns to quilt top.

Layer the back, batting, and the pieced top. Baste layers together; quilt.

When quilting is complete, trim away excess batting and backing so all edges are even with the quilt top.

Piece bias binding into one length, joining strips at 45-degree angles. Sew the binding to the right side of the quilt with right sides together and matching raw edges. Fold under ¼ inch on binding and turn to the back.

❖

RAIL FENCE QUILT
PAGE 75
Finished block is 3 ¼ inches.
Finished quilt is 65x71 ½ inches.

Materials
8 yards assorted fabric scraps in colors such as navy, burgundy, red, royal blue, black, tan, white, off-white, pink, and brown; this amount includes fabric for the binding
4½ yards backing fabric
Quilt batting

Instructions
To cut the pieces: Using a rotary cutter, heavy plastic ruler, and cutting mat, cut the fabric into 44- to 45-inch-long strips. Vary the widths of the strips from ½ to 1½ inches.

To piece the blocks: Divide the strips into groups of contrasting prints and colors. Using ¼-inch seams, assemble the strips into sets that are 3¾ inches wide. Make 40 strip sets.

Press seams to one side. Cut the strips into 3¾-inch squares; each strip should yield 11 squares.

Repeat these steps to make a total of 440 squares.

To make the quilt top: Lay out the squares, striving for a pleasing balance of lights and darks, and distributing all colors evenly. Referring to photograph, alternate the direction of each adjacent square. Make 22 rows with 20 squares per row.

Using ¼-inch seams, join the blocks to form a row; join rows.

(Continued)

Finishing: To piece the quilt back, cut fabric into two 2¼-yard lengths. Cut or tear one length in half lengthwise. Sew one narrow panel to each side of the wide panel. Match the selvages; use a ½-inch seam. Trim the seams to ¼ inch; press to one side.

Quilt as desired. Trim excess batting and backing even with the quilt top.

To make binding, cut 2½-inch-wide strips of varying lengths from assorted fabrics. Piece together to make a strip about 8 yards long. Fold binding in half lengthwise with wrong sides together and press so the binding is 1¼ inches wide. Stitch to right side of quilt top with raw edges even with edge of quilt, mitering corners. Turn folded edge to quilt back and hand-stitch in place.

CRUMB QUILT
PAGE 75
Finished block is 7½ x14½ inches.
Finished quilt is 69½ x86½ inches.

Materials
6 yards assorted print fabric scraps
2¼ yards yellow plaid fabric
½ yard blue print fabric
5½ yards of backing fabric
Plastic-coated freezer paper
Quilt batting

Instructions
To cut the pieces: Cutting measurements for the sashing strips and sashing squares include ¼-inch seam allowances.

From the yellow plaid fabric, cut:
35 sashing strips, each 4x15 inches
24 sashing strips, each 4x8 inches

From the blue print fabric, cut:
28 sashing squares, each 4 inches square

To piece one block: Cut 30 rectangles from freezer paper, each 7½x14½ inches.

Refer to the instructions for how to piece random patches, pages 72–73. Using this random-patchwork technique, cover the paper rectangles with patchwork, leaving ¼ inch of fabric around the paper for seam allowances.

To make the quilt top: Stitch five rows of blocks; piece together six blocks for each row with 4x15-inch sashing strips between the blocks and at the ends.

Stitch four rows pieced from six 4x8-inch sashing strips with blue sashing squares between the strips and at the ends.

Sew the rows together, alternating block rows and sashing rows, to complete the quilt top.

Finishing: To piece the quilt back, cut fabric into two equal lengths. Cut or tear one length in half lengthwise. Sew one narrow panel to each side of the wide panel. Match the selvages; use a ½-inch seam. Trim the seams to ¼ inch; press to one side.

From the remaining fabric scraps, cut 2½-inch-wide strips. Splice the binding strips together at 45-degree angles into a 9½-yard-long piece. Fold binding in half lengthwise with wrong sides together and press.

Layer the back, batting, and the pieced top. Baste layers together; quilt as desired.

When quilting is complete, trim away excess batting and backing so all edges are even with the quilt top. Sew the binding to the right side of the quilt, raw edges together. Turn the folded edge to the back; hand-stitch in place.

STRIP-PIECED TABLE ACCESSORIES
PAGES 76 and 77
Finished block is 6 inches.
Place mat is 12x18 inches.
Table runner is 18x36 inches.
Napkins are 16 inches square.

Materials
3 yards tan print fabric
2 yards backing fabric
¼ yard *each* of approximately 12 different print fabrics
½ yard contrasting fabric (piping)
11 yards piping cord
1½ yards fleece
1 yard muslin
Cardboard or plastic for template

Instructions
Note: Materials listed are sufficient for one table runner, four place mats, and four napkins.

Refer to the instructions for cutting and piecing strips, pages 70–71. Use a rotary cutter and heavy ruler to cut the strips, or mark the fabric with a ruler and cut strips with scissors.

On graph paper, draw a 7¼-inch square. Bisect the square diagonally in both directions to form four right-angle triangles. Use one of these triangles to make a template. This triangle *includes* ¼-inch seam allowances.

With a ruler, find the midpoint of each of the short sides. Mark these points and connect them with a straight line.

To make the triangles: Cut tan print fabric to 2½ inches wide. Cut strips from a variety of fabrics in 1¼-, 1-, and ¾-inch widths. Creating many different arrangements, stitch the narrow strips to the tan strip to make a strip that is exactly 5 inches wide, placing a strip that is at least 1 inch wide along the outer edge Placing a wider strip at the edge prevents a seam from falling into the seam allowance.

Cut triangles from the pieced strip, aligning the seam between the tan fabric and an adjacent print with the marked line on the template. Invert alternate triangles so half of the triangles have pieced strips at the point and half have pieced strips along the base.

One strip yields 10 or 11 triangles. Cut 76 triangles (38 of each type). Cut 96 triangles for the set of place mats (48 of each type).

To piece the blocks: Referring to Figure 1, *below,* arrange triangles to form blocks. Using ¼-inch seams, stitch the four triangles together to form a block.

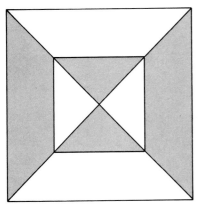

Figure 1

Make 19 blocks for the table runner and six blocks for each place mat.

To assemble runner and place mats: Referring to placement diagrams, *right,* arrange blocks.

Note half-drop set on table runner. Use seven blocks for the center strip of the runner.

Using ¼-inch seams, stitch the blocks into rows. Stitch the rows together. Trim center strip of runner even with adjacent rows.

Runner

Cut piping fabric into 1-inch-wide strips. Cover cord. Sew piping to the outside edges of the place mats and table runner.

Cut fleece to same size as patchwork; baste together. Quilt through patchwork and fleece.

Cut backing to same size as patchwork. Place patchwork and backing right sides together; stitch around piping line, leaving an opening for turning.

Turn and slip-stitch closed.

For the napkins: Cut four 16½-inch squares *each* of tan print and muslin. Cut eight ⅞-inch-wide strips from piping fabric. Fold piping in half lengthwise, wrong sides together; press. With right sides together, sew piping around the edge of the tan squares. With right sides together, sew the tan print squares to muslin squares, leaving an opening for turning. Turn and press, then slip-stitch opening closed.

Place Mats

CELEBRATIONS OF CHILDHOOD

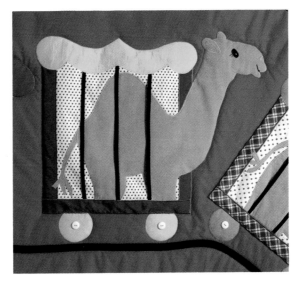

The lively
patchwork designs for kids' rooms
in this chapter are a charming mix
of contemporary appliqué motifs
and traditional patchwork patterns.
To involve your own kids in these
sewing projects, let them help
choose fabric colors or suggest
ways to personalize the designs.

Accessories for a nursery are among the most delightful items to make for baby. Here's a room brimming with projects based on a patchwork pieced triangle pattern and a tulip appliqué motif. With today's coordinating fabrics, you can duplicate this charming style.

Because the projects, *opposite,* were designed with a selection of sweet, small-scale prints in mind, you should plan on combining several fabrics to stitch them. Start with a color scheme, and then find a half dozen prints that you can mix and match freely.

Allow two fabrics to predominate by using them for both the bench pad and the crib quilt. The pattern for these designs is a simple repeat of two triangles. Refer to our hints (on pages 150–151) for piecing and cutting right-angle triangles.

Plan on piecing and cutting extra triangles to trim a set of curtains. For the matching valance, piece two fabric strips together and then add a garden of appliquéd tulips in clusters or standing alone. Measure across the top of the nursery window to determine curtain panel fullness and tulip placement—a panel twice the width of the window it covers is a good rule of thumb.

To add a ruffle and underskirt to a bassinet like this one, use the same formula to calculate the width of the fabric. Appliqué tulips to the ruffle, or make a border of triangle-squares as shown on the curtains and attach it to the lower edge.

As with many appliqué designs, the tulip motif can double as a stencil pattern. To decorate a toy box, cut stencils for the petals, stems and leaves. Choose paint colors to match the fabrics used in the window and bassinet projects. For contrast, add a two-color border of stenciled triangles.

Instructions begin on page 100.

Circuses—and their colorful clowns, animals, and festivities—are childhood favorites. These appliqué projects will make any youngster feel like a ringmaster.

A rollicking circus train is the subject for the bedspread and headboard, *opposite.* The bedspread is machine-appliquéd and is also machine-quilted during assembly. Use the clown-and-engine design to cover a padded headboard as shown here, or adapt the motif to create a wall hanging.

The same clown—this time astride a peaceful pachyderm—is front-and-center on a bag, *opposite,* that's a perfect catchall for laundry or pajamas. You also can make a banner for a child's room door by appliquéing any of the designs to a fabric panel.

The three-dimensional version of our happy clown, *below,* juggles a string of stars. Easy construction and shaping techniques speed his assembly.

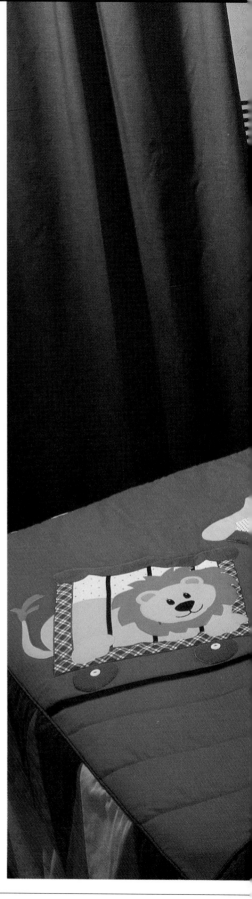

With these kids' room accessories, the fun is creating a pattern by repeating just one block. One of the many names for this design is Love Ring.

The first consideration when making the Love Ring bed linens, *right,* is the number of fabrics to combine. Here, we've used three floral and two geometric prints in a repeated sequence. You also could combine different colors of fabrics in prints, plaids, and solids, or use several fabric patterns in one shade.

The painted wooden puzzles, *below,* demonstrate the various ways the blocks of this quilt pattern can be assembled. Cut the pieces from lumber scraps and tint them with acrylic washes. Make the puzzle frames from ripped 1x2s and add a piece of hardboard for the backing.

❖   ❖   ❖

The small motifs used for the decorative accessories in this room are versatile, indeed. Use them for appliqué, stenciling, and embroidery.

To make a special window roller shade like the one *opposite,* appliqué motifs onto a piece of fabric that's the same width and length as the window. Then back the fabric with firm interfacing and attach it to a roller.

A roll of narrow white wall-covering provides an easy way to create a background for the stenciled wall border, *opposite.* You can stencil the strip before or after it's affixed to the walls.

The sweet flower on the embroidered pillow, *below,* is actually the heart motif from the shade and paper border. Using a simple outline stitch, position four hearts side by side to complete the flower pattern.

❖ ❖ ❖

Instructions for this handsome At the Depot Quilt include using a rotary cutter with quick-piecing methods and conventional assembly techniques.

Two plain blocks in contrasting prints and one block pieced from three strips are used to assemble the At the Depot Quilt, *opposite*. Look for a series of coordinating fabrics to duplicate the tailored look of this quilt.

Because of the nature of the design and the wear that this quilt will receive, it has been tuft-quilted. When making a tufted quilt, ask a clerk at a quilt shop for the best batting—a high-loft batting will result in a puffier quilt.

Small scraps of stripe, pindot, and plaid fabrics left over from the quilt are sufficient for the room accessories, *below*. The top of the throw pillow is composed of 16 striped squares, and the bottom of the laundry bag is trimmed with strips joined randomly. Make two kinds of pieced blocks to edge the pillowcase, and alternate each block (and the direction of the piecing) to make the trim.

To decorate a bulletin board, make stencils that are the same size as the squares, rectangles, and triangles used for this quilt. For detail, add stripes to the rectangles and spatter-paint some of the squares.

❖ ❖ ❖

A pattern like the At the Depot Quilt is versatile because its design elements can be broken into smaller units and used as repeat patterns.

Pieced blocks join with triangles to form an energetic trim that's just right for a pair of curtains, *above* and *opposite.* You also can use a strip like this one to trim a sheet or a blanket.

The same stencils used to trim the bulletin board on page 96 can be used for other furnishings like the blanket chest and seating cubes, *opposite.* These handsome and hardworking pieces work just as well in grown-up areas; for example living and family rooms or in a kitchen.

Make other stenciled projects, using the curtain trim and the pillowcase design as inspiration. These linear patterns are appropriate for trimming around a window or door, or along the tops of the walls.

With this kind of design, it's a good idea to have at least one accessory—either quilted or stenciled—with the allover pattern. Then select additional coordinating designs as accents.

98

CRIB QUILT
PAGE 89
Finished size is 25x34 inches.

Materials
1½ yards of light pink print fabric
½ yard of light teal print fabric
¼ yard of light teal fabric
Quilt batting
Embroidery floss
7 yards of cording
Plastic or cardboard for template

Instructions
To make pattern for blocks, draw a 3-inch square on graph paper. Draw a diagonal line to bisect the square into right-angle triangles. Make a template from cardboard or plastic. The patterns are finished size; add ¼-inch seam allowances when cutting pieces from the fabric.

Cutting instructions: The cutting measurements for the borders include seam allowances and are longer than is needed. The borders will be trimmed when added to the quilt top.

From light pink print fabric, cut:
One 27x36-inch quilt back
Two 4x36-inch borders
Two 4x26-inch borders
54 triangles

From light teal print fabric, cut:
54 triangles

From light teal fabric, cut:
1-inch-wide bias-cut strips

To piece the top: With right sides facing and using a ¼-inch seam, sew a light pink print triangle to a light teal print triangle along long edge. Press seams toward darker fabric. Repeat until all triangles are joined.

Keeping the position of the colors consistent, stitch nine squares together to form a strip. Make six strips. Sew the strips together.

Cover the cording with bias-cut strips of light teal fabric, joining the strips at 45-degree angles.

Stitch cord to edge of pieced panel; trim away excess fabric from cording.

Add borders to quilt top, mitering corners and trimming excess. Stitch a second round of cording to edge.

Finishing: Cut quilt back from remaining pink fabric; cut quilt batting to size of quilt back. Center and baste quilt top atop batting with wrong side of top to batting. Lay backing atop quilt top, right sides together. Stitch around edge, leaving an opening for turning. Trim excess quilt back. Turn and slip-stitch closed.

Using three plies of embroidery floss, tuft quilt at corners of each triangle.

Alternate quick-piecing method: Referring to the directions for quick-piecing right-angle triangles, pages 150–151, assemble 54 pieced squares. Complete as directed above.

BENCH PAD
PAGES 88–89

Materials
Light pink print fabric
Light teal print fabric
Cording; quilt batting
Cardboard or plastic for templates

Instructions
Plan finished size of pad according to dimensions of bench top. Finished size of triangle is 3 inches on short sides. Allow for at least a 1-inch-wide border around the center pieced squares.

Make template as for Crib Quilt (see instructions, *left*), and join triangles to make sufficient number of squares for pad. Sew squares into rows; sew rows together. Trim assembly with covered cording.

Add border as for Crib Quilt. Omitting outer round of covered cording, assemble and tuft as for Crib Quilt.

See alternate quick-piecing method, pages 150–151, for joining right-angle triangles.

CURTAINS WITH SAWTOOTH BORDER
PAGE 89

Materials
Light teal stripe fabric for curtain panels
Light teal print for triangles
Light pink pindot for triangles
White batiste (lining)

Instructions
Plan width of each curtain panel. For best results, make finished width a multiple of 3 inches. Add at least 2 inches to height of each panel for rod pocket.

Refer to the instructions for the Crib Quilt, *left,* to make sufficient pieced squares to fit along inside long edge and bottom of curtain panel. Keeping position of each print consistent for each triangle, stitch squares into a row for inside edge of border; stitch row to curtain edge. Repeat for the bottom border.

Make second curtain panel similarly, reversing position of triangles so that sawtooth borders are symmetrically reversed.

To line curtains, place pieced panels and batiste right sides facing. Stitch around, leaving top edge open for turning. Clip corners, turn, press, and topstitch opening closed. Fold over excess curtain at top; stitch to create rod pocket.

VALANCE WITH TULIP APPLIQUÉS
PAGE 89
Finished height of tulip motifs is 7½ inches.

Materials
Off-white fabric
Light teal fabric
Scraps of light teal pindot, light pink pindot, and pink fabrics
Cardboard or plastic for templates

Tulip Applique Motif

Full-Size

Instructions

Plan finished size of valance. Plan for about top two-thirds of the valance to have an off-white background; the bottom third portion is light teal.

Referring to the full-size patterns, *above,* make a tissue overlay of completed design. Use the three-tulip motif, single tulips, or any combination that fits the size of the window you have.

Preshrink and press off-white background. Mark positions of tulips on fabric, placing the bottom edges of the leaves ¼ inch from bottom edge of the fabric.

Make a template for each of the tulip petal shapes and for the leaf. Mark fabric, using light teal pindot for leaves, light pink pindot for outer petals, and pink fabric for inner petals. Cut ¾-inch-wide strips for stems from light teal fabric.

Cut out each shape ⅛ inch past outline. Beginning with the leaves, appliqué shapes to background. Add stems next; then add the inner petals and the outer petals. (*Note:* To appliqué by hand, press under raw edge ⅛ inch. Pin shape to background. Secure shape in place with tiny invisible stitches.)

Stitch off-white and teal sections together. Finish bottom and sides of valance; add a rod pocket to top edge, or hang as desired.

❖

BASSINET RUFFLE WITH TULIP APPLIQUÉS
PAGE 89

Materials
Light pink pindot fabric
Light teal print fabric
Scraps of light teal pindot, light
  teal, off-white, and rose fabrics
⅜-inch-wide elastic

Instructions
Measure around bassinet at top edge. Multiply this measurement by 1.5 to determine width of underskirt. Hem underskirt, join short edges, gather, and secure to bassinet.

For ruffle, plan finished depth; ruffle shown is 18½ inches deep and is the same width as skirt. Piece sufficient pindot fabric to make ruffle; fold over top edge and hem lower edge. Stitch a channel for elastic, positioned ¾ inch from top edge. Referring to instructions for Valance, *below left,* appliqué single tulips (see pattern, *left*) along bottom edge. Position tulips 1 inch from bottom edge of ruffle and space the stems 16 inches apart.

Thread elastic through channel, secure ends, sew channel closed, and hang on bassinet. Add other trims to bassinet as desired.

❖

TOY BOX
PAGES 88–89

Materials
Painting and stenciling supplies
Unfinished toy box
Light teal flat latex paint
Stencil paints; stencil material
Polyurethane varnish

Instructions
Paint toy box inside and out with two coats of latex paint, sanding lightly between coats.

Referring to full-size pattern for tulip motifs, *above left,* cut stencils for tulip stem, leaves, inner petals, and outer petals. To make stencil for triangles, draw a right-angle triangle with 3-inch short sides. Cut out and stencil. To plan stencil placement, make a tissue overlay of toy box; plan a row of triangles along the bottom edge and a row of tulips along the top edge of the triangles.

Refer to photograph, pages 88–89, for colors and stencil designs.

Seal box with two coats of polyurethane varnish.

101

CIRCUS TRAIN BEDSPREAD
PAGE 91
Finished size is 59x95 inches.

Materials

11 yards of red fabric (top and lining)
1¼ yards of blue fabric
1 yard of yellow fabric
½ yard *each* of green and tan fabrics
⅓ yard *each* of gray, red-on-white polka dot, and blue-on-white polka dot fabrics
¼ yard *each* of blue print, green plaid, and orange fabrics
Rust, black, and pink fabric scraps
5 yards of polyester fleece
6½ yards of purchased blue piping *or* cotton cording to make piping
3½ yards ¼-inch-wide black grosgrain ribbon
Extra-wide black double-fold bias tape
Black, white, and pink embroidery floss
Eight ⅝-inch-diameter white buttons
Fusible webbing
Compass; glue stick

Instructions

Note on assembly: This quilt is machine-quilted in stages. First, appliqué the train cars and animal figures to a fabric background. Layer top on fleece; machine-quilt around shapes. Then, stitch the border triangles together atop a piece of fleece. Stitch the border assembly to the center, adding piping along sides and bottom edge of center panel. Line the quilt; machine-quilt near piping.

To appliqué the top: Cut a 39½x85-inch piece of red fabric. Enlarge the car top and animal patterns, *opposite;* trace onto tissue paper to make a master pattern. Make a 2⅝-inch-diameter circle pattern for the wheels.

Referring to photograph, page 91, draw a curved line to represent train track. Lay car patterns along line; pin in place. Make any adjustments to track line.

For lion car, cut one 10x9¼-inch background piece from blue-on-white polka-dot fabric. From green plaid, cut one 12x1¼-inch car bottom and two 9¼x1¼-inch car sides. From green, cut car top and wheels, and from yellow, cut lion body, head, and tail. Cut orange mane and tail tip.

For camel car, cut one 10x10¾-inch background piece from blue-on-white polka-dot fabric. From blue, cut one 12x1¼-inch car bottom and two 10¾x1¼-inch car sides. From yellow, cut car top and wheels. Cut camel pieces from tan.

For elephant car, cut one 10x9½ inch background piece from red-on-white polka-dot fabric. From green plaid, cut car bottom and sides as for lion car. From pink, cut two wheels and one car top. Cut elephant pieces from gray.

For giraffe car, cut one 10x10¾-inch background piece from blue-on-white polka-dot fabric. From blue print, cut car bottom and sides as for camel car. From blue, cut car top and wheels. Cut one yellow giraffe. Cut two orange horns and rust spots.

Cut pink inner ears and black eyes for all animals. Cut lion's nose from black.

Cut fusible webbing to match each shape.

For each car, arrange the pieces atop the fabric. Secure in place with glue stick. Slightly overlap each car background piece with the sides and top. Then add the animals and the bars (cut from black grosgrain ribbon). Omitting the bars over the lion's face and elephant's ear, secure the bars at the tops and leave the bottoms free. Fuse in place. Machine-zigzag-stitch around each shape with matching thread. Before completing each car, add the car bottom and wheels, tucking the tops of the wheels and the lower ends of the bars slightly under the bottom piece. Complete zigzag stitching.

Embroider eyelashes with black and eye accents with white. Embroider pink noses on camel and giraffe.

Sew one button to the center of each wheel. Sew bias tape to track line.

To machine-quilt: Cut a 42x90-inch piece of fleece. Smooth top over a piece of fleece; baste together. Machine-quilt above and below track. Machine-quilt around each car and animal shape adjacent to zigzag stitches.

Make blue piping and sew along sides and bottom edge.

Border: To make pennant pattern, draw a triangle with a 6½-inch base and two 10½-inch sides.

For end triangle, draw another triangle to match pennant triangle; bisect it with a perpendicular line to form a right-angle triangle with a 3¼-inch base and a 10½-inch long side.

To make corner pattern, draw a triangle with a 5⅛-inch base and two 10½-inch sides.

Adding ¼-inch seam allowances to each border piece, cut 33 red pennant triangles, a total of 32 pennant triangles from blue, green, and yellow, and four red corner triangles. Cut out two red end triangles. Cut out four red corner triangles.

Cut two 10½x90-inch and one 10½x46-inch pieces of fleece for the border.

For each side border, alternate a red pennant (with point positioned to touch blue piping) with a contrasting pennant (with point touching outer edge); use 14 red pennants and 13 contrasting pennants along each side. Align 7 red pennants and 6 contrasting pennants for bottom border. Place a pair of red corner triangles at lower ends of side borders. Place one end triangle at top end of side borders.

To assemble border, place right sides of two triangles together, and then place on fleece. Using ¼-inch seams, stitch along one 10½-inch side, sewing through fleece.

(Continued)

Circus Train Bedspread

Fold

1 Square = 2 Inches

Open out triangle over seam; position right-hand side of the next triangle right sides together with triangle stitched to fleece and sew along next open side.

Continue in this way until all triangles are stitched to fleece.

Stitch borders to center panel along piping line.

To line the quilt: Trim all fleece even with fabric. Piece red fabric for quilt back. Place backing and top right sides facing; stitch around, leaving an opening along top edge for turning.

Turn. Smooth spread and close opening. Topstitch backing in place just inside piping.

With water-erasable marker, draw curved quilting lines to fill in the area below the train track. Machine-quilt along the lines.

CIRCUS TRAIN HEADBOARD
PAGE 91
Finished width is 39 inches.

Materials
¾ yard of yellow fabric
1¾ yards of blue fabric
⅓ yard of red fabric
¼ yard of green fabric
Polyester fleece
Scraps of orange, yellow, pink, peach, black, white, green stripe, green plaid, blue print, red polka-dot, and white print fabrics
¾ yard *each* of ⅜-inch-wide green and blue plaid ribbons
Six red star appliqués
Black, red, and white embroidery floss
Fusible webbing; quilt batting
¾-inch plywood; staple gun

Instructions
From the yellow fabric, cut one 21x38-inch rectangle.

Enlarge patterns of smoke, letters, and clown, *right,* and trace onto tissue paper.

For smoke, pin patterns to white fabric and cut out. Cut out oval behind letters from white; cut out letters from black fabric.

1 Square = 2 Inches

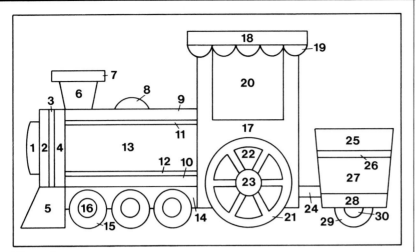

Figure 1

For clown, cut the motif into separate paper patterns. Cut the face and hands from peach and the hair from orange. Cut the hat from red and the hand band and pom-pom from green. Cut collar from yellow and sleeves from blue print. Cut eyes from black.

Beginning at engine front and using Figure 1, *above,* as a guide, cut out pieces as follows:

Piece 1 (light): Cut one orange 5x1¼-inch rectangle; trim one long side into curved shape.

Pieces 2–4 (vertical bars): Cut one green (Piece 2) and one green plaid rectangle (Piece 4), each 1x7 inches; cut one yellow ⅝x7-inch rectangle (Piece 3).

Piece 5 (cow catcher): Cut one blue 4¼-inch-wide by 3¾-inch-high rectangle, angle-cut so top measures 2⅝ inches.

Pieces 6–7 (smokestack): Cut one blue 3½-inch-wide by 2½-inch-high rectangle, angle-cut so base measures 2½ inches (Piece 6). Cut one blue 5x1-inch rectangle for top (Piece 7).

Piece 8 (bell): Cut one orange 3½-inch-wide by 1¼-inch-high rectangle; trim one long side into curved shape.

Pieces 9–14: (front of engine): Cut two red dotted 12¼x1-inch rectangles (Pieces 9 and 10); cut two 12¼-inch pieces of blue plaid ribbon (Pieces 11 and 12); cut one red 12¼x4¼-inch rectangle (Piece 13); cut one blue 12¼x2-inch rectangle.

Pieces 15–16 (small wheels): Cut three red 3⅝-inch-diameter circles (Piece 15) and three pink 1⅝-inch-diameter circles (Piece 16).

Pieces 17–18 (cab): Cut one red 14¾x9½-inch rectangle (Piece 17) and one red 11¼x1¼-inch rectangle (Piece 18).

Piece 19 (roof scallops): Cut one pink 11¼x1¼-inch rectangle. Mark one long side into five 2¼-inch sections and cut a curved edge at each section.

Piece 20 (window background): Cut a 6¾-inch white print square.

Pieces 21–23 (large wheel): Cut one green 8-inch-diameter circle. For wedge, cut a 5½-inch-diameter circle into six equal parts; cut six wedges from green stripe fabric. Cut one yellow 2½-inch-diameter circle.

Piece 24 (hitch): Cut one red 2¼x1-inch red rectangle.

Pieces 25–28 (car): Cut one green plaid 7¼x2-inch rectangle; cut one yellow 7¼x⅝-inch rectangle; cut one green 7¼x3¼-inch rectangle; cut one green plaid 7¼x1¼-inch rectangle. Align pieces from top to bottom; angle-cut each short edge to make a trapezoid shape that is 7¼ inches along the top and 6 inches wide at the bottom.

Pieces 29–30 (car wheel): Draw a 3-inch- and a 1½-inch-diameter circle; cut in half. Cut one large red half-circle and one small pink half-circle.

Piece 31 (balloons): Draw a 2⅝-inch-diameter circle; cut from blue, pink, green, red, and orange.

Appliqué assembly: Arrange the pieces onto yellow background fabric; see Figure 1, *left.* Fuse. Machine-satin-stitch around shapes with matching thread. Add five lengths of string to upper and lower sides of clown's left hand; tie strings into bows and tack under balloons. Trim.

Refer to instructions for Clown Doll, page 106, to embroider face.

Fuse stars in place. Tie the green ribbon into a bow and tack to collar. Sew one button to each small wheel.

Assembly: Cut two 11x63-inch and two 11x45-inch blue borders. Stitch to panel, mitering corners.

Cut plywood to 39 inches wide and to a height suitable for frame.

Cover portion of plywood that extends above bed with two layers of batting. Smooth fabric over batting; staple in place.

CLOWN DOLL
PAGE 90
Finished height is 24 inches.

Materials
½ yard *each* of pink (body) and red (hat) fabric
¼ yard of yellow fabric (collar)
½ yard *each* of red polka-dot and blue plaid fabric (suit)
17½x4-inch piece of green fabric (hat cuff)
Orange rug yarn (hair)
Three ¾-inch-diameter yellow buttons
3 yellow pom-poms
Black, red, and white embroidery floss
Red and blue double-fold bias tape
4 red star appliqués
1½ yards of ⅞-inch-wide green satin ribbon
1¼ yards of ⅜-inch-wide green satin ribbon
1½ yards of ⅛-inch-wide green satin ribbon
White string; round cord elastic
Polyester fiberfill
Dental floss *or* quilting thread

(Continued)

Instructions

Note: Body and costume measurements include ¼-inch seam allowances, unless noted otherwise.

Body: From pink fabric, cut two 7x5½-inch body pieces. Cut two 12x5-inch arm pieces. For the head, cut two 5-inch-diameter circles and one 16¼x1¾-inch strip. From red fabric, cut two 17½x6-inch legs.

Suit: From *both* red polka-dot and blue plaid, cut one 21½x18-inch torso/leg piece and one 14x14-inch sleeve. For the raglan seam line, make a paper triangle pattern with a 5-inch base and 3½-inch sides. Fold each sleeve in half. Pin the triangle pattern to one corner, matching sides of triangle to sides of corner; cut sleeve across base of triangle. Fold each torso/leg piece in half lengthwise. Pin the triangle pattern to corner of fold, matching sides of triangle to sides of fold and the cut edge; cut torso/leg piece across base of triangle.

Collar: Cut two 28x4¼-inch pieces from yellow fabric.

Hat: Cut one 17½x8¾-inch piece from red fabric.

Assembly: Arms: Fold each arm in half lengthwise. Stitch long edge; begin taper for pointed hand 2½ inches from end. Trim tapered edge; clip and turn. Stuff to within 2 inches of top. Center the seam and sew gathering stitches across top; pull up to measure 1 inch. Tie string twice around wrist; knot and trim. Repeat for elbow.

Legs: Fold each leg in half lengthwise. Stitch long edge; begin taper for pointed foot 4½ inches from end. Trim tapered edge; clip and turn. Stuff to within 2 inches of top. Center the seam and sew gathering stitches across top; pull up to measure 2½ inches. Tie string twice around ankle; knot and trim. Repeat for knee.

Body: Sew legs to one short edge of body—keeping raw edges even and with seams to back—with the legs meeting at the center and the outer edges of legs ¼ inch from sides of body. Machine-baste one arm to each body side—again keeping raw edges even and with seams to back—¼ inch from top of body. Pin body front to back; turn up ¼ inch at bottom. Extend legs and arms through bottom opening. Sew together along sides and top. Turn, stuff firmly, and sew the opening closed.

Head: Sew short ends of strip together to form a ring. Sew one side of ring around each circle, leaving an opening for turning along one side; clip curves. Turn, stuff firmly, and slip-stitch the opening closed. Pin the head atop body front, placing chin 1¼ inches below the top body seam. Stitch the head to the body with dental floss, joining chin and back of head to body.

Embroidery: Trace eyes, nose, and smile patterns from the appliqué clown, page 104, onto paper, adding ⅛ inch to each end of smile; cut out. Arrange onto face and pin. Trace around shapes with light pencil lines. Use two strands of floss to satin-stitch the nose and smile with red and the eyes with black. Add black straight stitches for eyelashes and white eye accents. Make black French knots at ends of eyelashes.

Hair: Wrap yarn 10 times around a 3½-inch length of cardboard. Slip from cardboard, tie around center, and cut each end. Tack to head. Repeat to cover head.

Suit sleeves: For casings, press under ½ inch along edge opposite raglan edge. Sew ¼ inch from the fold. Draw cord elastic through casing with a small safety pin. Pull elastic to fit wrist; sew across ends and trim. Sew sleeve seam; press open and turn. With ½-inch seams, sew to matching torso/leg piece along raglan seamline; pivot at underarms and leave ½ inch unstitched at each end. Press seam toward sleeve; clip underarm.

Torso/leg: To make casings, press under ½ inch along edge opposite the raglan edge. Sew ¼ inch from the fold. Draw cord elastic through casing with a small safety pin. Pull up elastic to fit ankle; sew across ends and trim. Sew 11½-inch inner leg seam. Sew center front seam of torso/leg pieces from top of inner leg seams. Press under ½ inch along neck edge. On wrong side of neck edge, sew atop cord elastic with wide-spaced zigzag stitches. Pull up elastic to fit neck; sew across ends and trim. Sew a 3-inch center back seam from top of inner leg seam.

Sew buttons to front of suit. Put suit on clown and sew the back opening closed. Tack the instep to the leg, sewing through the suit to make natural position for foot. Cut widest ribbon into two lengths and tie into bows around the ankles. Cut the ⅜-inch-wide ribbon into two lengths and tie into bows around the wrists.

Collar: Sew together short edges of collar pieces to form one long strip. Bind one long edge with blue bias tape. Topstitch the red bias tape 1 inch from the blue tape. Press under ½ inch along other long edge; sew ¼ inch from the fold. Draw cord elastic to fit neck; sew across ends and trim. Put collar on clown and sew the back seam together.

Hat: Fold green cuff in half lengthwise. Sew together long edges of cuff and hat. Fold cuff up over the seam and press. Fold hat in half, matching raw edges. For side seam, draw a curved line from top of cuff to top of fold on opposite side, leaving seam allowance at the top edge. Sew side seam, trim, and turn. Sew pompom to tip and tack hat to head.

Star string: Evenly space and tack star appliqués onto narrowest ribbon; tack to hands.

CLOWN PAJAMA BAG
PAGE 91
Finished size is 32½ x 18½ inches.

Materials
1½ yards of yellow fabric
½ yard of red fabric
Two 27½x4¼-inch pieces of white fabric
18x12-inch piece of gray fabric
9x6-inch piece of blue fabric
6x4-inch pieces *each* of red polka dot and red plaid fabric
Peach, pink, orange, red, green, blue-on-white pindot, and black fabric scraps
Fusible webbing
Black, red, and white embroidery floss
3½ yards of cotton cording
3 yards of ⅞-inch-wide green satin ribbon
4 red star appliqués
Red double-fold bias tape
Plastic clothes hanger
17¾x4¾-inch piece of heavy cardboard
Fabric glue stick

Instructions
Use ¼-inch seams throughout, unless noted otherwise.

To cut the pieces: For the bag, cut three 27½x4¼-inch yellow strips. Cut two 27½x5½-inch yellow strips for the sides. Cut one 27½x18¾-inch yellow piece for the back. Cut one 18¾x5½-inch yellow piece for the bottom. To cover the cardboard bottom, cut two 18¾x5½-inch yellow pieces. Cut 1-inch-wide yellow strips to cover cording.

For the tent top/flap, draw a paper triangle pattern with a 19½-inch base and 10½-inch-long sides. Then draw a 19½x1¾-inch rectangle alongside the base of the triangle. From red fabric, use triangular pattern to cut two tops and two linings. Cut two pieces from fleece. Cut 1-inch-wide red strips to piece and cover cording for piping.

For the scallops, draw a 19¼x3¾-inch rectangle. Mark one long edge into 3¾-inch sections, leaving seam allowances at each short edge. Then mark a parallel line within the rectangle, 1 inch from the long sectioned edge. Draw an even curve, 1 inch deep within each section; cut out. From red, use pattern to cut one scallop and one lining. Cut one piece from fleece.

For the bag front, sew together long edges of yellow and white strips, alternating the colors.

To appliqué the front: Enlarge clown and elephant pattern, page 104. Transfer shapes to tracing paper; label each piece and cut out. Do not add seam allowances to appliqué shapes. Cut elephant body, head, and tail from gray. Cut toes and inner ear from pink. Cut two black eyes. Cut red headpiece and green headpiece border.

Cut clown face and hands from peach and hair from orange. Cut hat from red and hand band and pom-pom from green. Cut one sleeve each from red polka dot and red plaid, the body from blue-on-white pindot, and the leg from blue print. Cut the collar from blue. Cut one red shoe and the pom-pom from green.

Cut matching shapes from fusible webbing.

Arrange the appliqué shapes onto the pieced front, securing with glue stick; fuse shapes to the front. Machine-zigzag-stitch around all shapes with matching thread. Use black thread for the elephant's mouth.

Use two strands of the floss to satin-stitch the clown's nose and smile with red and the eyes with black. Make white eye accents with straight stitches; add black eyelashes. Add a row of red French knots with six plies of floss beneath the green headpiece border. Tack three stars above the clown and one in the lower hand.

To assemble the bag: Make yellow piping. Sew piping to sides and bottom of bag front, raw edges even; clip corners. Sew one side piece to each long edge of the bag front; repeat for the bag back. For the side pleats, match front and back side seams and fold each side piece toward the inside center of the bag; press. At the top, sew the pleats to the bag back.

Sew one bottom piece to the lower edge of the bag. Sew the remaining bottom pieces together, leaving one short edge open. Turn and insert the cardboard. Turn in the raw edges; slip-stitch closed.

Machine-baste fleece to the wrong side of the scallop front. Make red piping. Sew piping to sides and curves of scallop front, raw edges even; clip curves. Sew lining to front, leaving straight edge open; clip curves, trim, and turn.

Machine-baste fleece to wrong side of tent top/flap. With right sides facing, layer straight edges of front, scallop, and front lining, centering the scallop and leaving seam allowances at each side of the tent tops. Sew together along the straight edge. Press the tent tops up, enclosing the seam. Machine-quilt straight lines between each scallop to the tip of the top, pivoting at the seam. Make red piping. Sew piping to top and sides of tent front, raw edges even; clip curves.

Sandwich fleece between the wrong sides of the tent top back and the lining; machine-baste. For the hanger opening, cut away a small section from the tip of the tent top; bind cut edges with bias tape.

Pin the tent top front to the back. Pin the front facing triangle to the back lining atop the hanger opening. Sew along top and sides; clip curves and turn.

Sew the tent top to the bag back. Trim the seam and the top of the bag front. Then bind the seam and the top of the bag front with bias tape.

(Continued)

Sew along the center of a 40-inch length of bias tape. Cut in half, knot the ends, and sew each piece to the bag top, 6 inches from the side.

Cut the green ribbon in half; tie into bows and tack to the top sides of the bag. Insert cardboard into bottom of bag. Cover loop of hanger with bias tape. Insert hanger into top of bag and tie bias into bows around bar of hanger.

❖❖

LOVE RING LINENS
PAGE 93
Finished block is 3 inches square.
Finished size of pillowcase is
19x30 inches.

Materials
Purchased blue-on-white pinstripe pillowcases and top sheet, or sufficient pinstripe fabric to fit the bed you have
½ yard *each* of medium blue print, rose print, white floral, medium blue floral, and dark blue floral fabrics
¼ yard of yellow print fabric
1 yard of white batiste (lining)
Cardboard or plastic for templates

Instructions
Using the patterns, *above right,* make templates for pieces A and B. Set square aside. Patterns are finished size; add ¼-inch seam allowance when cutting the pieces from the fabric.

Draw around the curved pieces onto print and floral fabrics; *adding ¼-inch seam allowances,* cut out pieces. (*Note:* If the fabrics have a directional pattern, be sure to reverse the template for half of the shapes required.)

To prepare pieces for joining, machine-stitch along curved lines, using a long stitch. Clip curves to stitching line.

Referring to pattern, *above right,* assemble each of the blocks, basting along the curved machine-stitched lines. Machine-stitch and remove basting threads as needed. Press seams toward dark fabrics.

Referring to photograph, page 93, join pieced blocks in pairs.

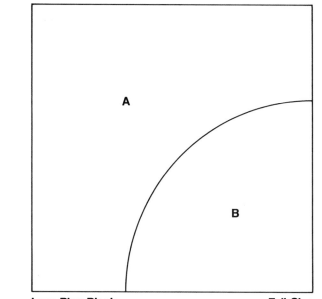

Love Ring Block   **Full-Size**

Then join the pairs, matching colors according to the photograph, into a double row of blocks. For the sheet, make the row longer than the finished width of the sheet; trim away excess during assembly. For each pillowcase, join 14 pairs of blocks.

For the piping, cut 1-inch-wide strips of yellow print fabric; join to same length as sheet and pillowcases. Fold in half lengthwise, raw edges together, and baste. Baste piping to finished patchwork strips on both long edges along seam line; ¼ inch of piping will be visible on the finished projects.

Cut backing fabric 7 inches wide and to fit width of projects. Pin to the patchwork strip on the top edge only, right sides facing; stitch.

For sheet
Trim top hem of sheet. Keeping bottom edge of backing fabric free, sew patchwork strip to sheet. Press seam toward patchwork. Fold under and press raw edge of backing fabric; fold backing to the wrong side of the sheet and slip-stitch along the fold to seam. Hem the side edges of the sheet and patchwork.

For pillowcases
Open side seams of each case about 12 inches, beginning at open end. Trim 5½ inches from case. Join patchwork strip to raw edge as for sheet. Close side seams.

To make linens
Use 60- and 90-inch-wide fabrics to make top sheets. Cut fabric to proper length and complete as directed above.

To make a pillowcase, cut a rectangle from fabric. Join patchwork strip to one edge and finish as for sheet. Join seams.

❖

WINDOW SHADE
PAGE 95
Finished motif is 4¾ x 4¾ inches.

Materials
Roller shade stiffening material *or* firm fusible interfacing
Shade roller and slat
Medium rose print fabric 1 inch wider and 4 inches longer than finished size of shade
Scraps of yellow floral and dark blue floral fabrics
Fusible webbing
Cardboard or plastic for templates
Staple gun

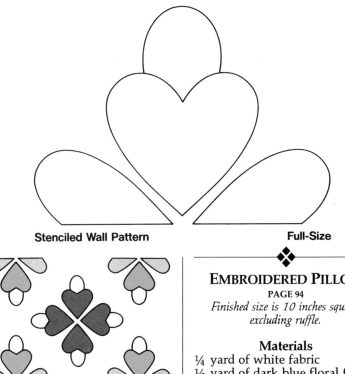

Stenciled Wall Pattern

Full-Size

← 6" →

■ Stencil A   ▦ Stencil C
▦ Stencil B   □ Stencil D

Instructions

Following shade stiffening material directions, mark finished size of shade on fabric.

Referring to pattern, *above,* and to photograph, page 95, plan position of motifs. (Shade shown is 31 inches wide and uses five motifs.) Space motifs side by side (or in position desired), equally spaced. Lightly trace shapes onto rose print fabric.

Make a template of each pattern piece. Cut out hearts from dark blue print fabric and smaller petals from yellow print fabric. Cut out matching shapes from fusible webbing.

Following the fusible webbing manufacturer's directions, fuse the shapes to the shade fabric. Using matching thread, satin-stitch around machine-appliqué shapes.

Following the manufacturer's directions, fuse fabric to stiffening material. Stitch a channel at bottom edge for slat and attach shade to shade roller with staple gun.

❖

EMBROIDERED PILLOW
PAGE 94
Finished size is 10 inches square, excluding ruffle.

Materials
¼ yard of white fabric
⅓ yard of dark blue floral fabric
⅛ yard *each* of medium rose print and yellow floral fabrics
⅓ yard of blue-on-white pinstripe fabric, or linens scraps
1¼ yards of piping cord
Dark blue embroidery floss
Polyester fiberfill, batting
Water-erasable marker

Instructions
To create pattern for embroidery, use four-heart cluster from the pattern for Stenciled Wall Border, *above.* Alter the design by drawing each of the four hearts next to each other, eliminating the space between the motifs.

Embroider design with floss, using stem stitches.

Mark 6-inch square on fabric, centering embroidered design inside it. Cut 1½-inch-wide strips of medium rose and dark blue fabrics. Sew rose strips to opposite sides of square; then, cut and sew rose strips to remaining sides and across ends of first rose strips. Add blue strips in same way.

Baste pillow front to a 10½-inch square of fleece. Outline-quilt embroidery.

Cut 10½-inch square of dark blue floral print fabric for backing; set aside.

Cover cord with yellow print fabric to make piping. Baste piping to seamline.

For ruffle, piece pinstripe fabric to 6x80 inches; join short ends. Fold in half, matching raw edges, and press. Gather to fit pillow and baste to front on seam line. Pin backing fabric and pillow top together, right sides facing. Sew, leaving an opening for turning. Turn, stuff, and slip-stitch closed.

❖

STENCILED WALL BORDER
PAGE 95
Border design repeat is 6 inches wide.

Materials
Basic painting and stenciling supplies
White wall border paper (available from Plaid Enterprises)
Rose, blue, green, and yellow stencil paint
Half-round molding (optional)

Instructions
Referring to photograph, page 95, and pattern, *above,* make a master pattern of the border design. Draw the design two or three more times (or use photocopies); stencil borders are easier to produce with longer stencils. Cut four pieces of acetate to this length.

Cut stencils A, B, C, and D. Label each stencil and add registration markings.

Using a straightedge and making light pencil marks, draw a horizontal line along center of border paper.

Position and tape stencil A to the wall, centering it along pencil line. Stencil with rose paint. Let paint dry and erase pencil line, if desired.

Position and tape stencil B, aligning it with position of stencil A. Stencil with blue paint.

Position and tape stencil C, aligning it with position of stencil B. Stencil with green paint.

(Continued)

Position and tape stencil D, aligning it with positions of stencils A and B. Stencil with yellow paint.

Using wall-covering adhesive, affix border to wall. Paint half-round molding and nail it to wall above and below stenciled border, if desired.

LOVE RING PUZZLES
PAGE 92
Finished size of square puzzle is 13⅝ x 13⅝ inches; rectangular puzzle is 19⅝ x 7⅝ inches.

Materials
Scraps of clear pine 1x2s, ripped to 1-inch widths (frames)
Scraps of ¼-inch hardboard (bottom)
Scraps of 1-inch clear pine (pieces)
Acrylic paints
Polyurethane varnish

Instructions
To make the frames for the puzzles, cut the ripped 1x2s to the lengths listed in the dimensions, *above.* Cut a total of four pieces for each puzzle. Miter each corner at 45 degrees. The ¾-inch-thick surface of the piece is the top edge. Rabbet the bottom inside edge of each piece to receive the hardboard.

Glue and nail the frame pieces together. Cut hardboard to fit inside rabbet; glue and nail in place.

For puzzle pieces, cut 1-inch pine into 3x3-inch blocks. Referring to pattern for Love Ring Linens, page 108, transfer curved line to each block. Cut along curved line with a jigsaw or band saw.

Sand all edges and surfaces. Mix paint to colors desired and dilute with water to make a wash. Paint each puzzle piece; make each quarter-circle the same color within each puzzle; make the corresponding negative shape a contrasting color.

Seal puzzle pieces with two coats of polyurethane varnish, sanding lightly between coats.

❖
AT THE DEPOT QUILT
PAGE 96
Finished square is 3¾ inches.
Finished quilt is 71x92 inches.

Materials
4½ yards of blue print fabric
3 yards of blue stripe fabric
2 yards of red plaid fabric for blocks and binding
6 yards of red stripe fabric for the quilt back
Quilt batting
Red pearl cotton, embroidery floss, or yarn to tie the quilt

Instructions
The instructions for this quilt are written for quick-piecing on the sewing machine. Refer to pages 148–149 for tips on quick-piecing squares and rectangles. Stitch, using ¼-inch seams.

To cut the pieces: The strips and blocks for this quilt can be cut quickly using a rotary cutter, heavy plastic ruler, and a cutting mat. You also can mark the pieces with a ruler and cut them with scissors.

The cutting measurements include ¼-inch seam allowances. The borders are longer than needed; trim them to the exact length when adding them to the quilt top.

From blue stripe fabric, cut:
12 strips, each 1¾x108 inches, (8 strips for the blocks and 4 strips for the borders)

From blue fabric, cut:
24 strips, each 1¾x108 inches, (16 strips for the blocks and 8 strips for the borders)
9 strips, each 4¼x45 inches, for the squares
2 strips, each 6½x45 inches, for the triangles

From red plaid fabric, cut:
9 strips, each 4¼x45 inches, for the squares
1 strip, 6½x45, for the triangles
2 squares, each 3¼x3¼ inches, for the corner triangles
9 strips, each 2½x45 inches, for the binding

To prepare the units: To make the red squares, cut the 4¼x45-inch strips into 83 squares, each 4¼-inch squares.

To make the blue squares, cut the 4¼x45-inch strips into 82 squares, each 4¼-inch squares.

To make the red triangles, cut the 6½x45-inch strip into six 6½-inch squares. Cut the squares in half diagonally, left to right, and right to left, to divide each square into four triangles (total of 24 triangles).

To make the blue triangles, cut the 6½x45-inch blue strips into 7 squares, each 6½ inches square. Following the instructions, above, for the red triangles, divide each square into four triangles (a total of 28 triangles).

To make the corner triangles, cut two 3¾-inch squares from the remaining red fabric. Cut each of the squares in half diagonally to make two triangles (a total of 4 triangles).

To make the striped blocks, sew a long blue strip to both sides of the long blue stripe strips (a total of 8 sets). Press the seams toward the blue strips. Cut the strip sets into 4¼-inch squares (a total of 192 striped squares).

To make the quilt top: Referring to the diagram, *opposite,* join the red, blue, and striped squares into diagonal rows. Begin and end each row with a red or blue triangle, as shown in the diagram. Join the rows to complete the inner quilt top.

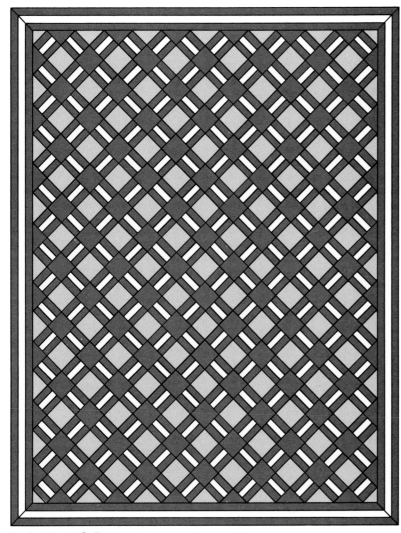

At the Depot Quilt

COLOR KEY   ☐ Blue Stripe   ■ Blue Pindot   ☐ Red Plaid

To make the borders, sew a blue strip to both sides of the four remaining striped strips. Press the seams toward the blue strips.

Sew the borders to the edges of the quilt top, mitering the corners of the borders.

Finishing: To piece the quilt back, divide the red strip backing fabric into two 3-yard lengths. Cut or tear one length in half lengthwise. Sew one half-panel to each side of the full panel, matching selvage edges and using a ½-inch seam. Trim the selvages, leaving about ¼-inch seam allowances. Press the seams to one side.

Layer the quilt back, batting, and quilt top; baste. Quilt as desired, or tie the quilt.

When the quilting or tieing is complete, trim the excess batting and backing fabric even with the quilt top. Join the binding strips into one long piece; fold the binding in half lengthwise with wrong sides together. Pin the raw edge of the binding to the right side of the quilt top; sew. Turn the folded edge of the binding to the wrong side of the quilt and hand-stitch to the quilt back.

STENCILED BLANKET CHEST
PAGE 99

Materials
Unfinished blanket chest
Basic painting and stenciling
  supplies
Stencil paint
Latex paints for base coat and lid
Primer
Polyurethane varnish

Instructions
Sand and prime chest inside and out.

Paint chest with two coats of base color, sanding lightly between coats. Paint lid a contrasting color.

On graph paper, make master patterns, using dimensions of chest surfaces as an outline. Use the blocks and triangle shapes described for the projects featured on pages 96–99 for ideas.

Cut stencils of each shape; label and add registration markings.

Stencil designs.

Seal chest with polyurethane.

STENCILED BULLETIN BOARD
PAGE 96

Materials
Purchased cork bulletin board
Basic painting and stenciling
  supplies
Stencil paint
Latex enamel for frame

Instructions
On graph paper, make master patterns, using dimensions of cork surface as an outline. Use the block and triangle shapes described for the projects featured on pages 96–99 for ideas.

Cut stencils of each shape; label and add registration markings.

Stencil designs.

Paint frame with enamel.

111

❖ CURTAINS

PAGES 98 and 99

Finished height of pieced strip is 5¼ inches.

Materials

Blue ticking stripe fabric
Small amounts of blue pindot, blue ticking stripe, and red plaid fabrics
Cardboard or plastic for templates

Instructions

Note: The instructions are written for quick piecing. The measurements for all pieces *include* ¼-inch seam allowances.

To cut the pieces: The strips, triangles, and blocks for these curtains can be cut quickly using a rotary cutter, heavy plastic ruler, and cutting mat. You also can mark the pieces with a ruler and cut them with scissors.

To cut the triangles, cut 6½-inch squares from blue pindot and red plaid fabrics. Cut the squares in half diagonally, left to right, and right to left, to divide each square into four triangles.

To piece the blocks: To make the striped blocks, cut blue pindot and blue ticking stripe fabrics into 1¾-inch-wide strips. (The stripes should run lengthwise along the strip.) Referring to the instructions for quick-piecing strips,

pages 70–71, stitch together ticking stripe strip between two pindot strips. Press. Cut strips into 4¼-inch squares; this measurement includes seam allowances.

To assemble the pieces: Referring to piecing diagram, *below,* stitch a matching triangle to opposite sides of a pieced block. Then stitch these short rows into a strip as long as necessary for each curtain panel. Straighten the ends of the strip.

To make the curtains: Plan the finished size of each curtain panel; each panel should be approximately the same width as the window. Mark position of pieced strip on panel. If pieced strip is near the bottom of the panel, plan on folding a long hem edge up over the pieced strip to line it. Otherwise, plan for lining the pieced strip.

Cut ticking fabric to size for each panel. Cut it horizontally along top marked edge of pieced strip. Using ¼-inch seams, stitch the pieced strip between pieces of ticking fabric .

Finish side edges of curtain panel. Finish top edge of panel as desired (stitch a rod pocket or hang panel from tabs).

Fold hem of curtain under; press. If hem is placed to line pieced strip, slip-stitch in place. Otherwise, stitch hem and line pieced strip.

❖ PILLOWCASE

PAGES 96 and 97

Finished size is 19¼ x 29½ inches.

Materials

For each pillowcase

1 yard of red pindot fabric
⅛ yard *each* of blue pindot, blue ticking stripe, red ticking stripe, and red plaid fabrics (*Note:* For best results with the quick-piecing method, use full widths of fabric.)

Instructions

Referring to instructions for the At The Depot Quilt on page 110 and the instructions for quick-piecing strips on pages 70–71, cut two 1¾-inch-wide strips from blue pindot. Cut two strips from red plaid. Cut one strip each of blue ticking stripe and red ticking stripe.

Use ¼-inch seams throughout, unless directed otherwise. Stitch the blue ticking stripe between two blue pindot strips; stitch the red ticking stripe between two red plaid strips. Press seams toward darker fabric.

Cut pieced strips into 4¼-inch squares.

Alternating main color of each square, and placing the stripe perpendicular to adjacent squares, stitch 11 squares together to form a row.

Cut red pindot fabric into a 19¾ x 23¾-inch rectangle and a 19¾ x 9½-inch rectangle.

Cut the blue pindot fabric into 1-inch-wide strips. Fold in half lengthwise, wrong sides facing, to make the piping. Matching the raw edges, stitch to pieced strip; trim excess piping.

Stitch pieced strip between red pindot rectangles. Measure 2¾ inches from stitching line on small rectangle; fold fabric to wrong side along this line and press. Fabric folded to inside should extend over piecing to serve as lining. Fold raw edge under and slip-stitch over back of pieced strip.

Fold pillowcase in half and stitch side and end seam.

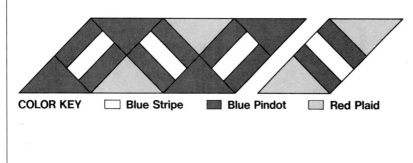

COLOR KEY ☐ Blue Stripe ■ Blue Pindot ☐ Red Plaid

THROW PILLOW
PAGES 96 and 97
Finished size is 16x16 inches, exluding ruffle.

Materials
Scraps of blue ticking stripe and red ticking stripe fabrics
½ yard of red plaid fabric
16½-inch square of backing fabric
Polyester fiberfill

Instructions
To piece top, cut eight 4½-inch squares from both blue and red ticking stripe fabrics.

Join four squares to form a row; join four rows to form pillow top. Referring to photograph, alternate the main color and direction of stripes.

From red plaid fabric, cut a 16½-inch square for pillow back. For flat ruffle, cut four 3½x19½-inch strips.

Align short ends of two strips, right sides facing. Referring to Figure 1, *below,* stitch short ends together in an inverted V. Carefully trim seams and clip corner. Repeat until all four strips have been joined into a square.

Turn ruffle right side out and press, forming mitered corners. Baste raw edges together. Stitch to pillow top, right sides facing. Stitch pillow back to front, right sides together and leaving an opening for turning. Turn, press, stuff, and slip-stitch closed.

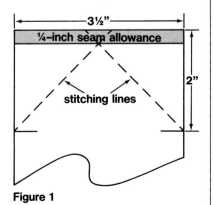

Figure 1

LAUNDRY BAG
PAGE 97
Finished diameter at bottom is 14 inches.

Materials
1½ yards of red plaid fabric
Scraps of blue pindot, blue stripe, blue plaid, red pindot, and red stripe fabrics
2 yards of cable cord
14-inch-diameter circle of poster board

Instructions
Cut scraps into pieces that are 4¼ inches long; cut them in varying widths.

Using ¼-inch seams, stitch the scraps into a 45-inch-long row. Place the fabrics randomly, striving for balanced colors and values.

Cut the red plaid into a 27x45-inch rectangle.

Stitch the pieced strip to the bottom of the rectangle. Fold rectangle in half, aligning edges of pieced strip and matching side edges. Stitch.

Draw a 14-inch-diameter circle on wrong side of red plaid fabric. Adding ¼-inch seam allowances, cut out. Stitch one circle to pieced edge, easing to fit. Clip curves and turn bag right side out.

Fold top raw edge under ¼ inch for seam allowance. Fold under again to make a 2-inch-deep casing. Press and unfold casing.

To position buttonholes for drawstring casing, flatten bag with seam in center. Mark side edges. Make two 1-inch-deep buttonholes at marks, placing bottom edge of buttonholes 1¾ inches down from top fold.

Fold top edge back in place. Stitch along bottom edge of fold and again ½ inch from top edge to create channel.

Cut cord into two lengths. Thread a length through casing, one per side. Pull ends through buttonholes and knot together. Place circle of poster board in bottom of bag; remove to launder.

SEATING CUBES
PAGE 99
Finished size is 16x16x16 inches.

Materials
½-inch plywood
Wood glue; nails
Primer
Basic painting and stenciling supplies
Stencil paint
Latex paint for base coat
Polyurethane varnish

Instructions
Plan construction technique for cubes; either make them using simple butt joints, or miter the edges.

Cut out pieces to make 16-inch cube; glue and nail together.

Fill nail holes. Sand all surfaces; prime.

Paint cubes with base coat.

On graph paper, make master patterns. Use the blocks and triangle shapes described for the projects featured on pages 96–99 for ideas.

Cut stencils of each shape; label, and add the registration markings.

Stencil designs.

Seal cubes with polyurethane.

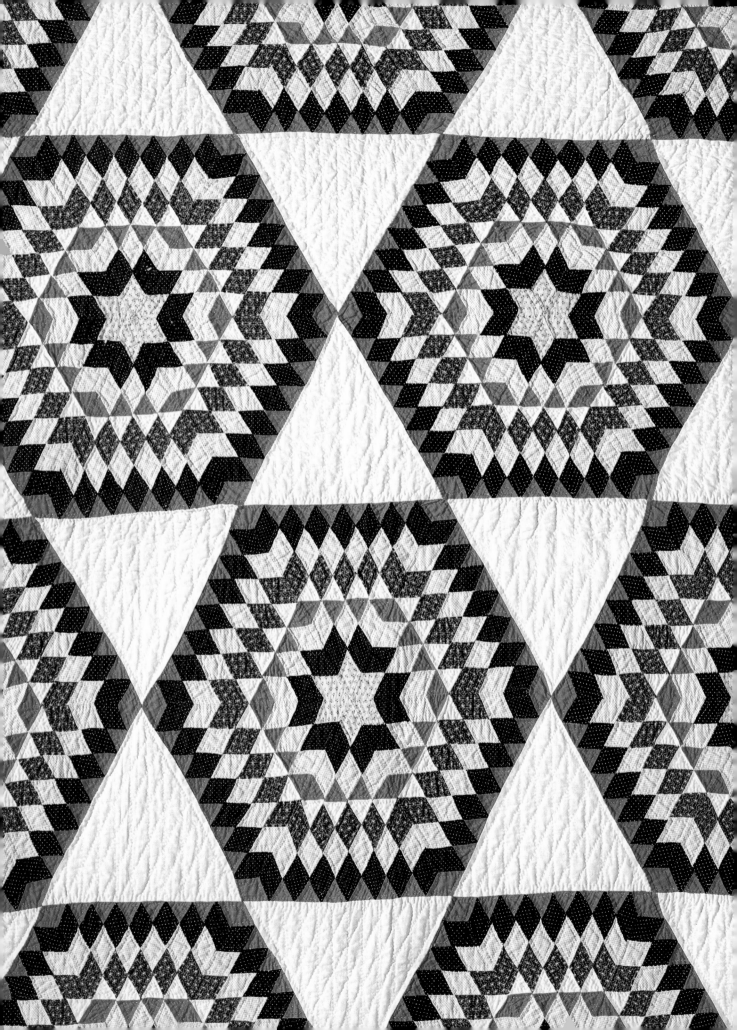

IMAGES FROM A QUILTER'S WORLD

Familiar
objects and surroundings provided
inspiration for America's
pioneer quilters. In fact, many quilt
patterns—including those in this
chapter—were named after
elements of nature and everyday
items used by the early settlers.

The name of this quilt pattern—Delectable Mountains—might sound whimsical to the modern ear. It actually derives from John Bunyan's allegory, *Pilgrim's Progress,* which was published in 1678 and was a favorite text among settlers in the New World.

The relevant passage from *Pilgrim's Progress* describes a beautiful range of mountains, where flocks of sheep graze amid "gardens . . . orchards . . . vineyards and fountains of water."

Today we imagine that such descriptive prose, along with the natural beauty of the New World, inspired many a stitcher. This particular quilt, *left,* is a blue-and-white version of the Delectable Mountains design and was stitched by Rebecca Patchin in the year 1850. The quilt is signed and dated in one corner.

Although the construction of this complex pattern might seem overwhelming, it is composed of just five whole blocks, four half-blocks, and four quarter-blocks. Each of the whole blocks centers around an eight-point star and contains 12 feathered triangles. Because each of these feathered triangles is created with eight squares stitched from a blue and a white right-angle triangle, you can use a quick-piecing technique to speed assembly. See the instructions for quick-piecing on pages 150–151.

Instructions for quilts and accessories in this chapter begin on page 128.

Quilt designs that are as rich in detail as the Delectable Mountains pattern offer plenty of ideas for other craft projects. Here are a crib quilt, footstool, and floorcloth based on the patchwork and quilting motifs from the quilt on the previous pages.

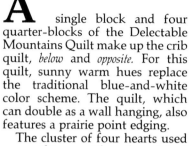single block and four quarter-blocks of the Delectable Mountains Quilt make up the crib quilt, *below* and *opposite.* For this quilt, sunny warm hues replace the traditional blue-and-white color scheme. The quilt, which can double as a wall hanging, also features a prairie point edging.

The cluster of four hearts used as a quilting motif on the original quilt forms the basis for the cross-stitch footstool, *opposite.* With the addition of a border of bright tri-angles and another of tiny hearts, it's a versatile design that also can be used to decorate a pillow or an album cover.

Use the lovely oak leaf appliqué border pattern from the quilt to decorate a floorcloth, *right.* Artist's canvas is a good choice for the background fabric.

❖ ❖ ❖

Today's quilters, like those of yesteryear, continue to design and stitch large and small quilts based on their own visions of nature, as these two contemporary examples demonstrate.

Reminiscent of a migrating flock, the Birds-in-Air wall hanging, *above,* also is an experiment in combining color and pattern. Each of the 32 pieced blocks is made of four squares pieced from two triangles. These squares, alternating with plain blocks, make up the quilt top.

To showcase a favorite quilting motif on a wall quilt such as this, make one of the borders wider than the other three. A pair of birds with a beribboned heart in their beaks appears at the bottom of this quilt.

The large Kalona Star Quilt, *opposite,* is a variation of the many Rolling Star patterns. In this pattern block, however, each of the eight diamonds used in the center star is bisected and pieced from contrasting fabrics. More pieced diamonds and print diamonds are used to make the lively border.

❖ ❖ ❖

Repetition of a single,
striking image, whether
natural or abstract,
often creates a quilt
pattern with great impact.
These two quilts—one
is appliquéd, the
other pieced—aptly prove
the point.

The graceful silhouette of a bird in flight was a popular image among quilters of the late nineteenth century. The appliquéd Red Bird Quilt, *above,* is made with sixteen such birds. A closer look reveals that, while each bird is identically shaped, the birds are not perfectly aligned. This placement gives a sense of animation to the quilt, and is balanced by the lines of shallow zigzag quilting.

The quilt *opposite* is one of many Pine Burr variations. The number, sizes, and shapes of the pieces may vary, but all feature four notched triangles around a center shape. Here, the jagged edges contrast with the graceful feather quilting in the white diamonds.

As with many of the other quilts in this book constructed with right-angle triangles, you can use the quick-piecing method described on pages 150–151 to assemble this quilt top.

❖ ❖ ❖

Quilters have interpreted a star-filled sky as well as any other group of artists has—patterns based on star images abound. Although six-point stars don't show up as often in quilts as eight-point stars, this quilt is a favorite hexagonal pattern.

One nineteenth-century variation of the Tumbling Stars Quilt, *below,* was known as the Seven Sisters. The name derives from the star cluster Pleiades in the constellation Taurus. According to Greek mythology, the Pleiades were the seven daughters of Atlas, whom Zeus transformed first into doves and then into stars, freeing them from the advances of Orion.

Each star is stitched from red and blue diamonds and separated with white diamonds. The star clusters form hexagons.

Use the same diamond piece to make the patchwork accessories, *opposite,* as well as the table runner on page 115. Plan the chair cushions on paper first (there are countless ways to join the diamonds into patterns), and make a single Tumbling Stars block for the patriotic banner. Stuff single stars for the centerpiece.

❖ ❖ ❖

Old-fashioned triangular
irons and an
interpretation of a
limitless, starry prairie sky
surely inspired these two
quilt designs. As with
the Tumbling Stars Quilt
on the preceding pages,
these two quilts are based
on either a hexagon or a
60-degree triangle.

Elements of the Smoothing Iron Quilt, *opposite,* are based on the geometry of an equilateral triangle. Each patchwork unit features a center triangle, three angled side strips, and a diamond in each corner. When the positions of the two colors used for each triangle block are reversed, and the triangles joined in strips with the center triangle color alternating, this intricate-looking design is the result.

Equilateral triangles joined into hexagons compose the Diamond Starburst Quilt, *left.* These intricate hexagons, composed of eight rows of diminutive diamonds and triangles, are balanced by plain triangles and the subdued colors used for the diamonds. To stitch this magnificent quilt, see pages 152–155 for hints on joining 60-degree diamonds.

❖

DELECTABLE MOUNTAINS QUILT
PAGES 116–117
Finished block is 20 inches.
Finished size is 89x89 inches.

Materials
6½ yards of muslin
6½ yards of dark blue print
9 yards of backing fabric
Quilt batting
Water-erasable marker

Instructions
Referring to full-size patterns, *right,* cut pattern templates A, B, BB, D, DD, E, EE, and GG from plastic. In addition, make a template for a 1¹¹/₁₆-inch square (Piece C), a 1-inch square (Piece F), and a 5-inch square (Piece G). These pieces *do not* include seam allowances; add ¼ inch all around before cutting pieces from fabric.

To cut the pieces: The number of pieces to cut for the entire quilt top is listed first, with the number to cut for a single block following in parentheses.
 Label and set aside ¾ yard of blue fabric for binding. Also label and set aside 1 yard of blue fabric for bias vines. Then cut, label, and set aside muslin and blue borders and sashing strips. Dimensions for borders and sashing strips include ¼-inch seam allowances. Except when noted, measurements are for the exact length required.

From muslin, cut:
2 border strips, each 9½ × 87½ inches
2 border strips, each 9½ × 69½ inches

From blue fabric, cut:
2 border strips, each 2⅞ × 67½ inches
2 border strips, each 2⅞ × 62¾ inches
2 sashing strips, each 2½ × 72 inches (includes extra length)
2 sashing strips, each 2½ × 26 inches (includes extra length)

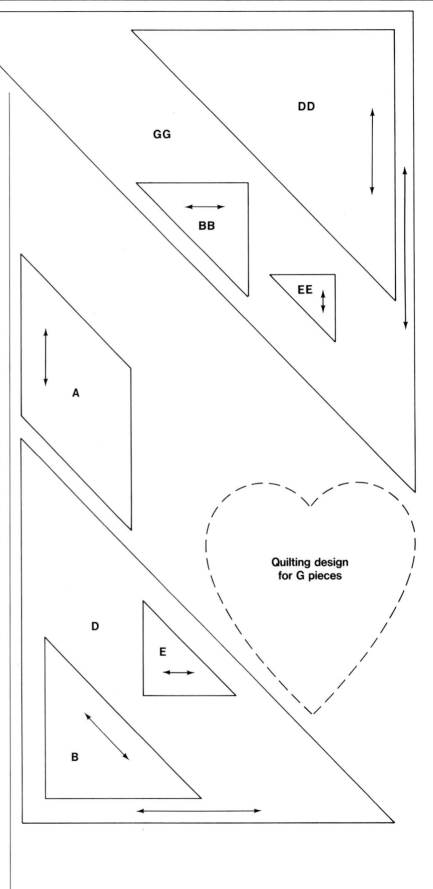

Quilting design
for G pieces

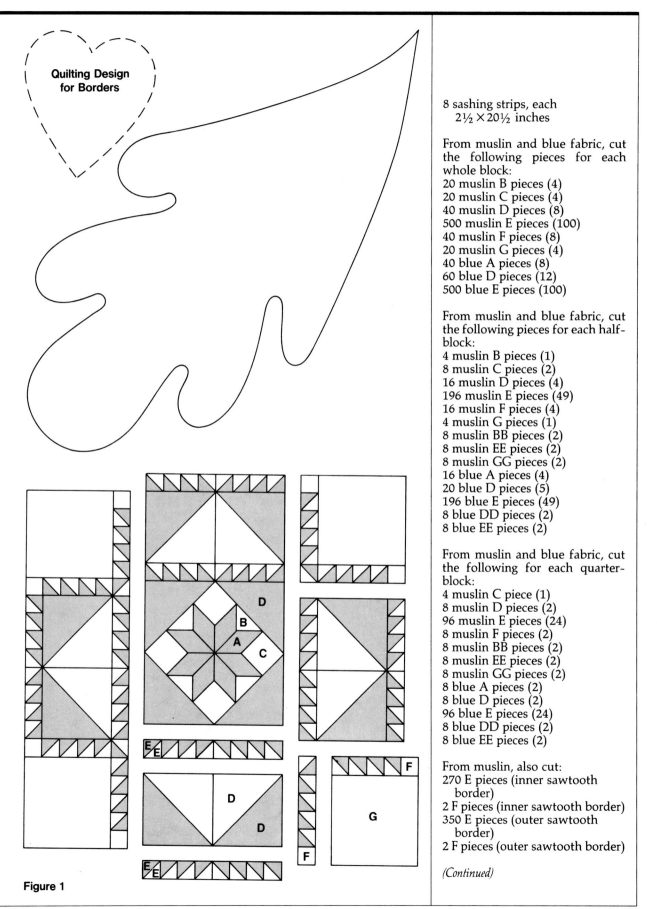

Quilting Design for Borders

8 sashing strips, each 2½ × 20½ inches

From muslin and blue fabric, cut the following pieces for each whole block:
20 muslin B pieces (4)
20 muslin C pieces (4)
40 muslin D pieces (8)
500 muslin E pieces (100)
40 muslin F pieces (8)
20 muslin G pieces (4)
40 blue A pieces (8)
60 blue D pieces (12)
500 blue E pieces (100)

From muslin and blue fabric, cut the following pieces for each half-block:
4 muslin B pieces (1)
8 muslin C pieces (2)
16 muslin D pieces (4)
196 muslin E pieces (49)
16 muslin F pieces (4)
4 muslin G pieces (1)
8 muslin BB pieces (2)
8 muslin EE pieces (2)
8 muslin GG pieces (2)
16 blue A pieces (4)
20 blue D pieces (5)
196 blue E pieces (49)
8 blue DD pieces (2)
8 blue EE pieces (2)

From muslin and blue fabric, cut the following for each quarter-block:
4 muslin C piece (1)
8 muslin D pieces (2)
96 muslin E pieces (24)
8 muslin F pieces (2)
8 muslin BB pieces (2)
8 muslin EE pieces (2)
8 muslin GG pieces (2)
8 blue A pieces (2)
8 blue D pieces (2)
96 blue E pieces (24)
8 blue DD pieces (2)
8 blue EE pieces (2)

From muslin, also cut:
270 E pieces (inner sawtooth border)
2 F pieces (inner sawtooth border)
350 E pieces (outer sawtooth border)
2 F pieces (outer sawtooth border)

(Continued)

Figure 1

129

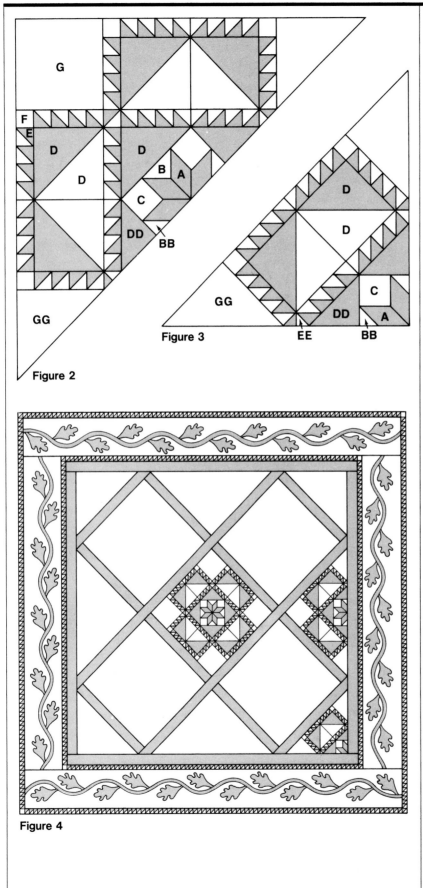

Figure 2

Figure 3

Figure 4

From blue, also cut:
42 leaves (add 1/8-inch seam allowance when cutting these pieces)
270 E pieces (inner sawtooth border)
350 E pieces (outer sawtooth border)

Next, cut the blue fabric set aside for vines into 2-inch-wide bias strips. Fold strips in thirds, so the finished width is approximately 3/4 inch. Piece about 125 running inches of bias for each appliquéd border vine.

To piece whole blocks: For each 20-inch-square block, sew pieces together following Figure 1, page 129. Sew 8 blue A pieces together (star). Add 4 muslin B pieces and 4 muslin C pieces, making a square.

Next, sew 4 blue D pieces to the star block, forming a larger square, which should measure 8½x8½ inches, including seam allowances.

Stitch 8 groups of blue and muslin D pieces into 8 squares. Sew pairs of squares together to form rectangles.

Join muslin and blue E pieces into 100 squares; sew squares into strips, following diagram and adding F pieces as needed. Stitch strips and G pieces as shown.

Make five whole blocks.

To piece the half- and quarter-blocks: Referring to Figure 2 and Figure 3, *left,* and following the stitching sequence for the whole block, *above,* stitch four half-blocks and four quarter-blocks.

To make the quilt top: Lay out whole and partial blocks. Join blocks into rows, using 2½x20½-inch sashing strips.

Join rows, using long sashing strips between them. Use the 26-inch strips at upper left and lower right corners of the quilt. Trim excess sashing even with the quilt top after rows are joined. The inner quilt top should measure 62¾ inches square, including the seam allowances.

To add the borders: Stitch blue borders to all sides of quilt. Trim excess sashing strips.

For inner sawtooth border, stitch blue and muslin E pieces into squares. Stitch squares into strips, following diagram and adding two F pieces at opposite corners. Stitch rows to quilt.

On muslin side borders and top and bottom borders, baste prepared bias vine according to Figure 4. Pin leaves in place. Appliqué vine and leaves, matching thread to appliqués.

For outer sawtooth border, stitch the same as inner sawtooth border, adding F pieces at two opposite corners. Stitch to quilt.

To mark for quilting: Mark quilting motifs as follows: In the G squares, repeat the heart motif, page 128, four times on Piece G. In the smaller (C) squares, mark lines between opposite corners, making an X.

On large and small triangles (pieces D and E), mark quilting lines parallel to the legs and ¾ inch apart; quilting lines will be L-shaped. On sashing strips, mark a zigzag pattern (with lines at 90-degree angles to each other, 45-degree angles to seams), making lines ¾ inch apart. These lines may be established with masking tape or with a straightedge and needle, chalk, or other marker.

Use quilting patterns for large and small hearts and oak leaf to mark border quilting. Note that large heart and leaves fall on the outer edge of the border vine, small heart and leaves fall on the inner edge of the vine.

Finishing: Divide backing fabric into three 3-yard lengths. Tear one length into a 21-inch-wide strip. Sew a full length to each side of the 21-inch strip, using ½-inch seams. Trim selvages, leaving ¼-inch seams. Press seams to one side.

After straightening, seaming, and pressing the backing, lay the backing wrong side up on a flat surface. Smooth batting, cut slightly larger than the finished

top, atop the backing and add the quilt top. Baste layers together. Mount the quilt in a frame, if desired, then quilt, using waxed quilting thread.

Trim batting and backing fabric on outer edges. Bind outer edges with blue fabric (you'll need 375 running inches). Finished binding should be ⅜ inch wide.

DELECTABLE MOUNTAINS CRADLE OR WALL QUILT
PAGES 118–119
Finished size is 37x37 inches.

Materials
2 yards muslin for patchwork and backing
1 yard yellow fabric for patchwork, sashing, and outer border
¼ yard each of 10 solid colors for patchwork and prairie points
Quilt batting larger than 37 inches square

Instructions
From yellow fabric, cut 7 strips, each 2½x44 inches (sashing and borders). These measurements include seam allowances. These strips are longer than necessary; trim excess length before adding strips to the quilt.

From muslin, cut 1⅛ yards for backing; set aside.

Make templates for pieces A, B, C, D, DD, F, G, and GG, page 128. *Adding ¼-inch seam allowances,* cut pieces for patchwork.

From yellow fabric, cut:
8 A diamonds
20 D triangles
8 DD triangles

From muslin, cut:
4 B triangles
4 C squares
16 D triangles
8 DD triangles
4 G squares
8 GG triangles
16 F squares

To cut small triangles: In addition to the pieces noted above, you'll need 204 small colored triangles (Piece E) joined to an equal number of muslin E triangles for the quilt. The E triangles may be cut and sewn individually into triangle-squares. (Cut 21 from each of the 10 colored fabrics.)

Or, assemble triangle-squares using the quick-piecing method explained on pages 150–151. For quick-piecing, cut 10 pieces of muslin, each 6x14 inches. Also cut a 6x14-inch piece from each of the 10 colored fabrics you plan to use in the sawtooth borders. Pair muslin and colored rectangles. Then mark, stitch, and cut 21 E triangle-squares from each 6x14-inch pair.

To piece the quilt: Referring to Figure 1 in the Delectable Mountains Quilt instructions, page 129, and substituting yellow for blue fabric (except E pieces) in the original quilt, construct the 20-inch-square center portion of the small quilt. When assembling sawtooth strips (with E triangles), choose colors randomly, drawing nearly equally from among the 10 colors available.

Use three 2½x44-inch yellow strips to sash the center block. Cut one strip into two 20½-inch lengths; sew them to opposite sides of the block. Cut the two other strips each 24½ inches long; sew to remaining sides of the block.

Then, referring to Figure 3 in the Delectable Mountains Quilt instructions, *opposite,* construct four quarter-block sections, except substitute two muslin DD triangles sewn into a square for the partial star in the four corners.

Sew one quarter-block to each of the four sides of the sashed 20-inch block, centering the large pieced triangle at each side. (After adding the outer border, trim the small excess portion of the sashing strip.)

(Continued)

Use the four remaining 2½x44-inch yellow strips for the outer border. Trim two strips to 31½ inches and two to 35½ inches (dimensions include seam allowances). Sew shorter strips to opposite sides of the quilt; sew longer strips to remaining sides. Trim excess sashing triangle.

Mark four-heart quilting motif in G squares. In muslin D pieces, trace one small heart; in muslin GG pieces, trace two small hearts for quilting. (Plan to outline-quilt these pieces, also.) Mark zigzag pattern for quilting on sashing strips (see large-quilt instructions). Add prairie points before quilting.

To make prairie points: From each of the 10 colored fabrics, cut twelve 2-inch squares. Fold and press each square in half diagonally. Fold each triangle in half again, forming a triangle that measures about 1½ inches on each of the folded sides, and about 2 inches on the side with raw edges.

With the quilt right side up, position and pin about 26 points per side along outer edges of the quilt, matching raw edge of points to edge of quilt top. Select colors randomly, and overlap points as needed to come out even at the corners.

Machine-sew points in place, taking a scant ¼-inch seam.

Finishing: Turn the edges of the quilt so points are away from the center of the quilt; press.

Layer quilt, batting, and backing. Baste and quilt, except for outer border.

To finish prairie point edge, trim batting even with edge of outer border. Trim muslin backing, leaving ¼ inch beyond outer border; turn under raw edge of backing and slipstitch in place. Complete quilting in the outer border.

CROSS-STITCH FOOTSTOOL
PAGE 119

Finished size is 12 inches square.

Materials
14x14-inch piece of off-white hardanger
DMC six-strand embroidery floss; 2 skeins of dark carnation (891), and 1 skein *each* of the following colors: deep lavender (208), dark wedgwood (518), dark cranberry (601), plum (718), medium yellow (743), dark delft (798), medium emerald green (911), and dark aqua (958)
Footstool with a 9½-inch-square opening
Tapestry needle
Embroidery hoop
12x12-inch piece of polyester fleece
Paint *or* stain and varnish

Instructions
Finish footstool frame with paint or stain and varnish. Set aside.

Using sewing thread, mark vertical and horizontal centers of the hardanger; mount fabric in embroidery hoop. Beginning in the center of the fabric and the center of the chart, *opposite,* cross-stitch the design. Use three plies of floss, and work the cross-stitches over two threads of the fabric.

Press finished embroidery on the wrong side. Back hardanger with polyester fleece (centered), then mount on padded cushion insert for footstool. Staple fabric to underside of insert, trimming excess fleece and fabric.

To make a pillow, trim hardanger 1½ inches beyond the outermost row of stitching. Sew piping, ruffles, and backing to pillow front. Turn and stuff.

PAINTED FLOORCLOTH
PAGES 118–119
Finished size is 29x44 inches.

Materials
30x45-inch piece of artist's canvas
White gesso (available from art supply stores)
Paintbrushes
Artist's acrylics in light and medium yellow, medium and dark aqua, and bright pink
Clear acrylic or polyurethane

Instructions
Paint one side of the canvas, using gesso tinted with pink or yellow paint; color should be almost but not quite pure white. Let dry.

Next, using a pencil and straightedge, mark outer border (1½ inches wide) around edge of canvas. Mark middle border (5½ inches wide) and inner border (1 inch wide).

Using patterns A and H and quilting pattern for large heart, draw design in middle border. For stars in corners, sketch a right angle in each inside corner of middle border, ½ inch from and parallel to edge of border. Each leg of the angle should be as long as one side of the A piece. (Pairs of diamonds in eight-point stars form right angles.) With edges of A pieces on sketched lines, trace around diamond twice; finish tracing stars in corners.

Trace heart in center of each side, positioning tip 1¼ inches above edge of border. Sketch ½-inch-wide vines in place; trace leaves (H) along vine (see photograph for placement).

Paint the design as shown in photograph. When dry, trim outer border to 1 inch. Finish floorcloth with at least two coats of clear acrylic or polyurethane.

FOOTSTOOL
Footstool

COLOR KEY

⊠ **Dark Carnation (891)**
☑ **Deep Lavender (208)**
◎ **Dark Wedgwood (518)**
⊞ **Dark Cranberry (601)**
◹ **Plum (718)**

⊡ **Medium Yellow (743)**
◪ **Dark Delft (798)**
⊞ **Medium Emerald Green (911)**
● **Dark Aqua (958)**

❖
❖ ❖

BIRDS-IN-AIR WALL QUILT

PAGE 120

Finished block is approximately 4 inches. Finished quilt is 36x47 inches.

Materials

Various shades of blue solid fabrics, totaling at least 1½ yards

Various shades of yellow solid fabrics, totaling at least 1 yard

½ yard of yellow solid *or* tiny print (borders)

¼ yard of second yellow solid *or* tiny print (plain blocks)

1½ yards of backing fabric

Quilt batting

Instructions

To make this quilt, refer to the instructions for cutting squares and rectangles with a rotary cutter, pages 148–149, and to the instructions for quick-piecing right-angle triangles, pages 150–151.

To cut the pieces: Measurements include ¼-inch seam allowances. The pieces for this quilt can be cut quickly using a rotary cutter, heavy plastic ruler, and a cutting mat. You can also mark the pieces with a ruler and cut them with scissors.

From various blue fabrics, cut: 32 4x7-inch rectangles

From various yellow fabrics, cut: 32 4x7-inch rectangles

From ¼ yard yellow print or solid, cut: 31 squares, each 4½x4½ inches

From ½ yard yellow tiny print, cut: 3 borders, each 3½x45 inches 1 border, 6½x45 inches

To quick-piece the blocks: Place a blue rectangle and a yellow rectangle right sides together; pin together carefully.

See instructions for quick-piecing right-angle triangles, pages

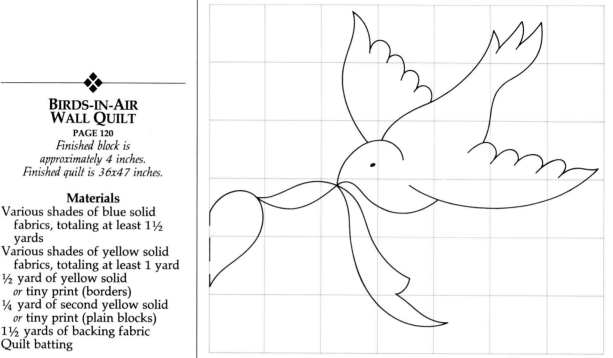

1 Square = 1 Inch

150–151, and mark two 2⅞-inch grid squares on each rectangle. Draw diagonals and stitch, forming four triangle-squares. The triangle-squares should measure 2½ inches, and will finish at 2 inches.

Sew the triangle-squares together to form a four-patch block, with each blue triangle in the upper-right position. Sew the squares together in pairs; sew the pairs together.

Make 32 blocks.

To make the quilt top: Alternating a pieced block with a plain square, and placing a pieced block in each corner, arrange the squares into nine horizontal rows of seven blocks. Stitch the blocks into rows; stitch the rows together.

From blue fabrics, cut 1½-inch-wide strips (inner borders) and 3¾-inch-wide strips (binding). Stitch together, adding small lengths of accent colors randomly. To duplicate look of quilt shown, join predominately light fabrics for inside border; accent with darker blues. Use darker blues for the binding; accent with light blues. Set binding aside.

Stitch a 1½-inch-wide border strip to the sides; trim. Stitch borders to the top and bottom; trim.

For yellow borders, sew a 3½-inch-wide strip to each side; trim

length. Sew the remaining narrow strip to the top and the wider strip to the bottom.

Finishing: Layer backing, batting, and quilt top; baste.

To quilt center, quilt in the ditch around and along triangles in the pieced blocks. Quilt plain blocks with pairs of diagonal lines, spaced ¼ inch apart, that match angles of pieced triangles. Quilt in the ditch along inner border. Beginning at inside edge of narrow borders, quilt lines parallel to side and top edges of inner border at ½, ¾, 2, and 2¼ inches.

To quilt lower yellow border, use pattern, *above.* Reverse design to complete pattern. Center birds-and-heart motif in border; quilt. Fill in lower yellow border with freehand-drawn cloud shapes.

Trim batting and backing 1 inch past yellow borders.

Cut remaining binding into four lengths, each at least ½ inch longer than one edge of the quilt. With right sides facing, and matching raw edges, stitch binding to side of quilt. Fold binding to back side; trim excess length. Fold under raw edge ¼ inch and slipstitch to quilt back. Repeat for opposite border. Repeat for top and bottom binding, turning under raw edges at ends.

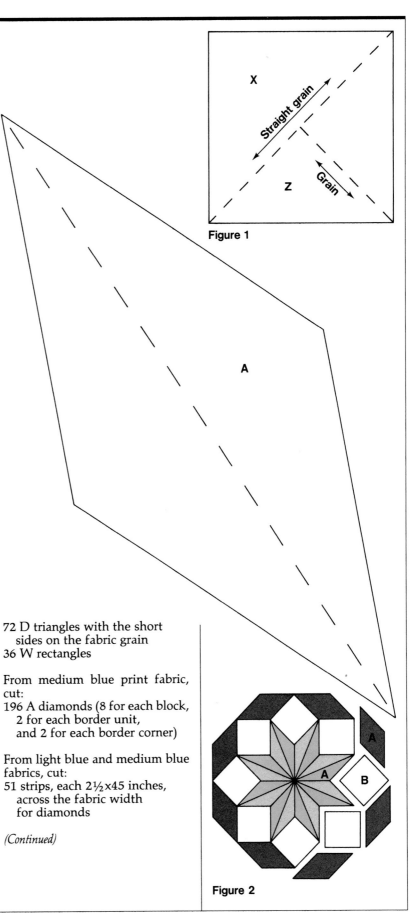

Figure 1

KALONA STAR QUILT

PAGE 121
Finished block is 20 inches.
Finished size is 94x114 inches.

Materials

9 yards of cream fabric
5 yards *each* of light blue and
medium blue print fabric
4 yards of medium blue print
fabric
9 yards of backing fabric
Quilt batting
Cardboard or plastic for templates

Instructions

All patterns are finished size; add
¼-inch seam allowances when
cutting the pieces from the fabric.

Trace and make templates for
pattern Piece A, *right.*

For pieces B, C, and D, draw a
4⅛-inch square on graph paper.
Divide the square as shown in
Figure 1, *above right.* The arrows on
the diagram indicate the fabric
grain indications for the triangle
patterns. Make a template for the
whole square (Piece B), the large
triangle (Piece C), and the small
triangle (Piece D).

Make a 4⅛x7-inch rectangular
template (Piece W).

Draw an 8¼-inch square. Divide the square as shown in Figure
1, *above right.* Make a template for
the entire square, the large triangle (Piece X), and the small triangle (Piece Z).

To cut the pieces: The number of
pieces for the entire quilt is listed
first; the number to cut for a single block follows in parentheses.

From cream fabric, cut:
12 squares
14 X triangles with the long side
of the triangle on fabric grain
4 Z triangles with the short
sides on the fabric grain
164 B squares (8 for each block
and 2 for each border corner)
40 C triangles with the long side
of the triangle on the fabric
grain (1 for each border unit
and 2 for each corner unit)

72 D triangles with the short
sides on the fabric grain
36 W rectangles

From medium blue print fabric,
cut:
196 A diamonds (8 for each block,
2 for each border unit,
and 2 for each border corner)

From light blue and medium blue
fabrics, cut:
51 strips, each 2½x45 inches,
across the fabric width
for diamonds

(Continued)

Figure 2

135

From cream, light blue, medium blue, and medium blue print fabrics, cut:

50 squares from each fabric, each 4½ inches, for prairie point border (measurement includes seam allowances)

To make the pieced diamonds: Sew pairs of medium blue and light blue strips together lengthwise; press seam toward medium blue fabric.

To cut diamonds, position Template A on a strip, lengthwise, with seam running through center of diamond. Mark four diamonds per strip; cut out diamonds, adding seam allowances. Make 204 pieced diamonds (160 for the blocks and 44 for the border).

To make one block: When piecing, sew only on seam lines, not into seam allowances. Avoid stretching bias edges.

Referring to Figure 2, page 135, sew eight pieced diamonds into a star. Position diamonds consistently so they are shaded as in the diagram.

Set a B square into the openings around the outside of the star. Set blue print diamonds into the spaces between squares around the star.

Make 20 star blocks.

To make a single block that will not be joined to other blocks, cut four Z triangles and sew them to blue print A diamonds to square off the block.

To set the quilt top: Lay out the blocks in five rows with four blocks in each row. To make one row, join four blocks by stitching blue print diamonds together. Join rows together by adding large squares between the rows.

Sew a Z triangle into the four corners of the quilt. Set in X triangles into the openings along the outer edges.

To make the borders: Referring to Figure 3, *above right,* sew two pieced diamonds together. Set a C triangle into the opening between the diamonds. Add a D triangle to

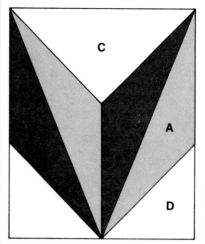

Figure 3

each side of the diamonds to form a rectangle. Make 36 border units from pieced diamonds.

Make 28 border units with pairs of blue print A diamonds similarly.

For the side borders, alternate five pieced-diamond border units with four blue print border units, placing a W rectangle at each end and between each border unit.

Referring to Figure 4, *below,* sew a D triangle to a blue print A diamond as shown in the portion indicated with a heavy line; make two D/A units and two reverse D/A units. Sew a D/A unit to one end and a reverse D/A unit to the opposite end of both side borders. Sew side borders to quilt top.

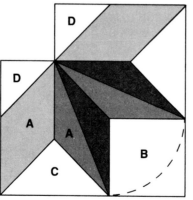

Figure 4

To make the top and bottom borders, alternate four pieced-diamond units with three blue print border units, placing a W rectangle at each end and between each border unit.

Referring to Figure 4, sew border corners from two pieced diamonds, one blue print diamond, two C triangles, one B square, and one D triangle. Make two border corners and two reverse border corners.

Sew a border corner to one end and a reverse border corner to the opposite end of the top and bottom borders. Sew the borders to the quilt. Round off the B corner squares as indicated by the dotted line in Figure 4.

To make the prairie points: Fold a square in half diagonally so it forms a triangle and press. Fold the triangles in half into a smaller triangle; press. Make 200 prairie points, 50 from each fabric.

Sew the prairie points onto the quilt top, alternating fabrics. Place the raw edges of the triangles even with the edge of the quilt and the tips toward the center of the quilt.

Finishing: Divide the backing fabric into three equal lengths. Sew the three panels together, using ½-inch seams. Trim seam allowance to ¼ inch; press. Turn the edges of the quilt top to the wrong side and press so the prairie points are away from the center of the quilt.

Layer and baste together the quilt top, batting, and backing. Transfer the quilt designs to the quilt top. Mark each of the B squares with four small loops. Mark the large squares with four sets of four small loops. Mark two sets of four small loops in each W rectangle.

Referring to the photograph on page 121, mark X triangles around the outside of the quilt with four large loops, extending one loop into the adjacent C triangle.

Leaving the outer 2 inches of the quilt unquilted, quilt around each diamond ¼ inch from the edge. Quilt marked designs.

To finish prairie point edge, trim batting even with the edge of the quilt top. Trim backing, leaving ¼ inch beyond the quilt top. Turn under raw edge of the quilt back and slip-stitch in place.

Complete quilting.

❖ RED BIRD QUILT

PAGE 122

Finished block is 14½ inches.
Finished size is 70x70 inches.

Materials

4½ yards of muslin
2 yards of red fabric
4½ yards of backing fabric
Quilt batting
Black or navy embroidery floss
Water-erasable marker
Cardboard or plastic for templates

Instructions

Enlarge the bird pattern, *below,* and transfer to template material. Cut out. Block and border cutting measurements include ¼-inch seam allowances.

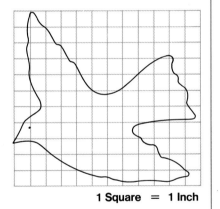

1 Square = 1 Inch

From muslin or white fabric, cut:
2 borders, each 6½x58½ inches
2 borders, each 6½x70½ inches
16 squares, each 15x15 inches
8½ yards of 2½-inch-wide bias binding

From red fabric, cut:
16 bird shapes, adding ¼-inch seam allowances

To make one block: Mark an appliqué positioning guide on the blocks by tracing around the bird template pattern with a water-erasable marker.

Position the bird shape on the background square with the beak slightly below the left middle of the block. Fold under seam allowances around the bird; appliqué. Using either satin stitches or a large French knot, embroider eye. Make 16 blocks.

To make the quilt top: Join the blocks into rows; make four rows with four blocks each. Stitch the rows together.

Stitch the shorter border strips to the top and bottom edges of the top. Stitch the remaining borders to the sides.

Finishing: To piece the quilt back, cut fabric into two 81-inch lengths. Cut or tear one length in half lengthwise. Sew one narrow panel to each side of the wide panel. Match the selvages; use a ½-inch seam. Trim the seams to ¼ inch; press to one side.

Layer the back, batting, and the pieced top. Baste layers together; quilt as desired.

When quilting is complete, trim away excess batting and backing so all edges are even with the quilt top. Fold the binding in half lengthwise, wrong sides together, and press. Sew the binding to the right side of the quilt, raw edges together. Turn the folded edge to the back; hand-stitch in place.

❖ PINE BURR QUILT

PAGE 123

Finished block is 18 inches.
Finished size is 72x80 inches.

Materials

4½ yards of red fabric
(includes fabric for binding)
3¼ yards of navy print
6 yards of muslin
5 yards of backing fabric
Quilt batting
Cardboard or plastic for templates

Instructions

Trace and make templates for the patterns, pages 138 and 139. The patterns are finished size; add ¼-inch seam allowances when cutting the pieces from the fabric.

To cut the pieces: The number of pieces to cut for the entire quilt top is listed first with the number to cut for a single block following in parentheses.

From red fabric, cut:
2 borders, each 2½x74 inches
64 B diamonds (4)
512 C triangles (32)
16 D pieces (1)
9 yards 2½-inch-wide strips for binding

From navy print, cut:
64 A pieces (4)

From muslin, cut:
2 borders, each 2½x74 inches
24 F diamonds
16 E half-diamonds
640 C triangles (40)

To piece one block: Refer to Figure 1, *below.* Stitch a red C triangle to a muslin C triangle along the long edge. Make 32 triangle-squares for each block.

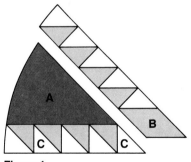

Figure 1

Stitch four squares into a strip; add a muslin C triangle to the end. Make eight strips.

For the points, stitch one red-and-white triangle-square strip to one long edge of the A piece, with seam of single muslin triangle adjacent to point. Stitch a B diamond to a second strip; stitch this strip to the remaining long edge of the A piece and to the end of the muslin triangle. Make four points.

Matching curved edges, sew each A piece to each D piece.

(Continued)

137

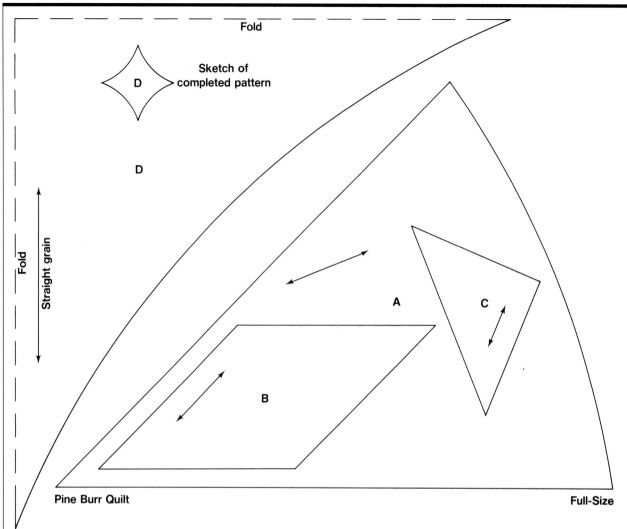

Fold

Sketch of completed pattern

D

D

Fold

Straight grain

A

C

B

Pine Burr Quilt

Full-Size

Make 16 Pine Burr blocks.

If you want to make a single block that will not be combined with other blocks, refer to Figure 2, *below.* Set an E half-diamond into the openings between the points.

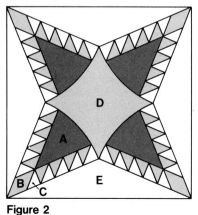

Figure 2

To make the quilt top: Lay out blocks in four rows of four blocks.

To make one row, set in an F diamond between the adjacent blocks. Use a total of three F diamonds for each row. Then set in an E half-diamond on each end.

Repeat for remaining rows.

Join rows in same manner, adding F diamonds between rows.

Set in E half-diamonds into openings between star points at top and bottom of the quilt.

For borders, stitch a red strip to a muslin strip. With the red strip adjacent to the half-diamonds, stitch border to quilt; trim excess.

Finishing: To piece quilt back, cut fabric into two equal lengths. Cut or tear one length in half lengthwise. Sew one narrow panel to sides of the wide panel. Match selvages; use a ½-inch seam. Trim seams to ¼ inch; press to one side.

Referring to the F diamond sketch, *opposite,* complete the quilting design for the F diamonds and E half-diamonds as indicated on the pattern piece. Transfer the quilting design to the F diamonds and E half-diamonds.

Quilt remaining pieces as desired. The D pieces on the quilt shown have parallel diagonal lines, spaced ½ inch apart, forming 60-degree diamonds. Remaining pieces are quilted with parallel diagonal lines, ½ inch apart.

Splice the binding strips together at 45-degree angles. Trim, fold in half lengthwise with wrong sides together, and press.

When quilting is complete, trim away excess batting and backing even with the quilt top. Sew binding to the right side of the quilt, raw edges together. Turn back folded edge; hand-stitch in place.

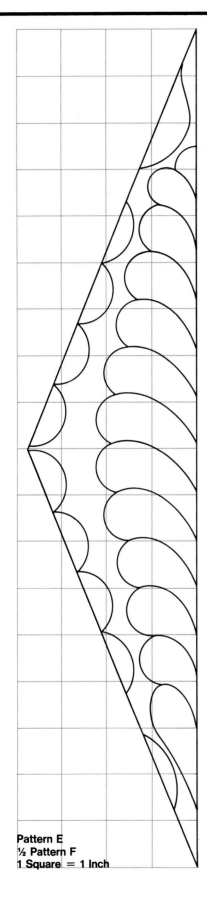

Pattern E
½ Pattern F
1 Square = 1 Inch

TUMBLING STARS QUILT
PAGE 125
Finished size is 65⅝x90½ inches.

Materials
4 yards of white fabric (blocks, sashing, borders)
3¼ yards of blue fabric (stars, inner border, binding)
2⅝ yards of red fabric (stars, middle border)
5½ yards of backing fabric
Quilt batting
Water-erasable marker

Instructions
Trace patterns, page 140, and make templates. Patterns are full-size; add ¼-inch seam allowances before cutting pieces from fabric.

To cut the pieces: The number of pieces to cut for the entire quilt is listed first, with the number to cut for one whole block following in parentheses.

Measurements for borders *include* ¼-inch seam allowances and are 2 to 3 inches longer than required; trim borders to size when adding them to the inner quilt top.

From white fabric, cut:
2 borders, each 2½x69 inches
2 borders, each 2½x90 inches
53 C pieces
6 E pieces
14 D pieces (cut eight with the right angle on the right and six with the right angle on the left)
390 A pieces (18)
126 B pieces (6)

From blue fabric, cut:
2 borders, each 2½ × 59 inches
2 borders, each 2½ × 90 inches
441 A pieces (21)
9½ yards 2½-inch-wide bias-cut strips

From red fabric, cut:
2 borders, each 1¾ × 90 inches
441 A pieces (21)

To piece one block: Each complete block consists of seven stars made of alternating red and blue diamonds.

When piecing this quilt, sew only along seam lines, not into seam allowances. Avoid stretching bias edges. Press seams toward the darker fabric.

For each block, sew six A pieces into a star, alternating red and blue fabrics. Stitch two diamonds together, then add a third; make two sets. Finish by joining the two halves of each star in a center seam. Make seven stars.

Next, set stars together using 12 white A diamonds and referring to Figure 1, page 141. Join pieces carefully so star points are sharp and the block lies flat. Finish the block by setting in six white A diamonds and six B pieces. Make 18 complete blocks.

For half-blocks, piece two stars and three half-stars. See Figure 2, page 141. Join stars and half-stars, using seven white diamonds. Fill in edges with three B pieces and four white diamonds. (Trim diamonds after adding borders.) Make six half-blocks.

Three half-blocks match the Figure 2; for the remaining three, *reverse* the positions of the red and blue diamonds.

To set the quilt top: Referring to Figure 3, page 141, join three complete blocks and one half-block, with C sashing strips between to make each row. Make six rows. Join rows using C pieces between between. To fill out the edges of the inner quilt top, set E pieces into the long sides and D pieces into the top and bottom.

The inner quilt top should measure 55⅝x83 inches, including seam allowances.

(Continued)

139

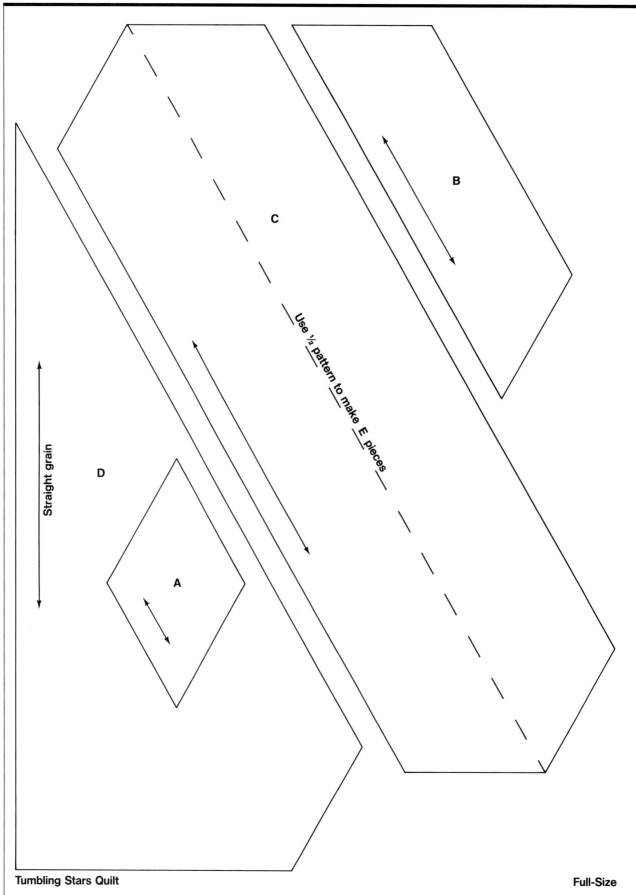

B

C

Use ½ pattern to make E pieces

Straight grain

D

A

Tumbling Stars Quilt

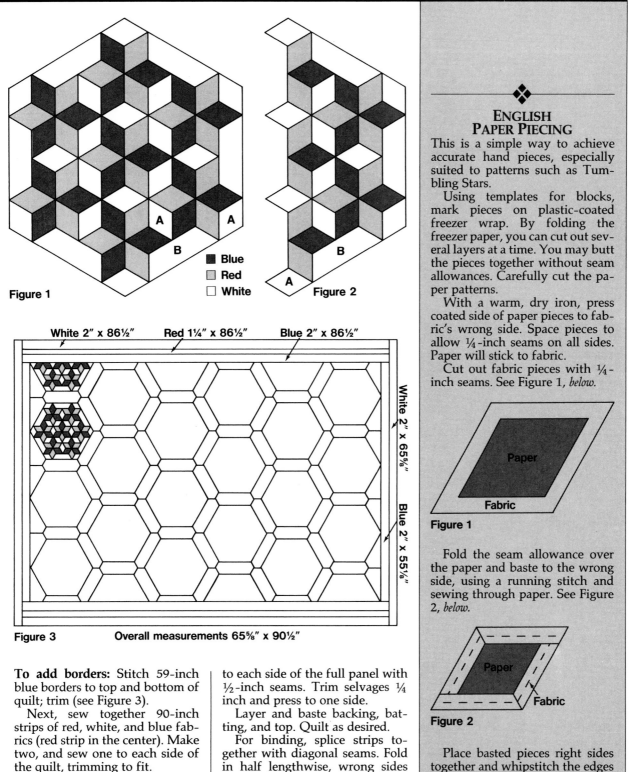

Figure 1

Blue
Red
White

Figure 2

White 2" x 86½"   Red 1¼" x 86½"   Blue 2" x 86½"

White 2" x 65⅝"

Blue 2" x 55⅝"

Figure 3   Overall measurements 65⅝" x 90½"

To add borders: Stitch 59-inch blue borders to top and bottom of quilt; trim (see Figure 3).

Next, sew together 90-inch strips of red, white, and blue fabrics (red strip in the center). Make two, and sew one to each side of the quilt, trimming to fit.

Sew remaining white borders to top and bottom of the quilt.

Finishing: To piece the backing, divide backing fabric into two equal lengths. Cut or tear one length in half lengthwise. Matching selvages, sew a narrow panel

to each side of the full panel with ½-inch seams. Trim selvages ¼ inch and press to one side.

Layer and baste backing, batting, and top. Quilt as desired.

For binding, splice strips together with diagonal seams. Fold in half lengthwise, wrong sides together, and press.

After quilting, trim excess batting and backing even with top. Sew binding to right side of quilt, raw edges together. Turn back folded edge; hand-stitch in place.

❖

ENGLISH PAPER PIECING

This is a simple way to achieve accurate hand pieces, especially suited to patterns such as Tumbling Stars.

Using templates for blocks, mark pieces on plastic-coated freezer wrap. By folding the freezer paper, you can cut out several layers at a time. You may butt the pieces together without seam allowances. Carefully cut the paper patterns.

With a warm, dry iron, press coated side of paper pieces to fabric's wrong side. Space pieces to allow ¼-inch seams on all sides. Paper will stick to fabric.

Cut out fabric pieces with ¼-inch seams. See Figure 1, *below.*

Paper

Fabric

Figure 1

Fold the seam allowance over the paper and baste to the wrong side, using a running stitch and sewing through paper. See Figure 2, *below.*

Paper

Fabric

Figure 2

Place basted pieces right sides together and whipstitch the edges along fold, keeping stitches close together.

When you have joined the pieces on all sides, clip basting thread and remove paper. You can reuse the paper pieces as long as corners remain sharp and pieces will stick to fabric.

141

TUMBLING STARS
CHAIR PADS
PAGES 124–125

Materials
For two chair pads
1 yard of royal blue fabric
¾ yard of red-on-white pindot fabric
Scraps of red fabric
Two 18-inch squares *each* of ¾-inch foam, quilt batting, and muslin
3 yards of cording for piping
Large sheets of paper
Cardboard or plastic for templates

Instructions
Make a template for Piece A of Tumbling Stars Quilt, page 140. Pattern is full size; add ¼-inch seam allowances when cutting pieces from fabric.

For chair pad pattern, draw a hexagon with compass or protractor to fit chair seat. Cut two chair pads each from the pindot, muslin, batting, and blue fabrics. Cut two foam pads the size of the pattern, then trim off ¼ inch around the foam hexagons.

Trace around the diamond template on paper to draw out the designs shown in the photograph on pages 124–125. Determine the colors you wish to make the diamonds within each design. Color placement greatly varies the appearance of the designs.

There are many possible designs to make with diamonds. You may want to experiment to create your own designs by drawing around the diamond template on a sheet of paper.

Mark and cut out the number of diamonds of each color required to make the designs. For the chair pad with the red center star, cut diamonds as follows, adding seam allowances when cutting: 12 *each* from the red and pindot fabrics and six from the blue fabric.

For the chair pad with the blue center star, cut diamonds as follows, adding seam allowances when cutting: 15 from blue fabric, nine from red fabric, and six from pindot fabric.

To piece the blocks: When piecing the diamond designs, sew only on the seam line, leaving the seam allowances unsewn. To piece the red star design, begin by sewing together six red diamonds to form the center star. Sew six pairs of pindot diamonds together, then set them into the center star. Alternately sew red and blue diamonds into the openings between the pindot diamonds.

To piece the blue star design, sew six blue diamonds together to form a star. Set pindot diamonds into outer edges of the star. Sew three half-stars from blue diamonds and three half-stars from red diamonds. Sew the half-stars to the center portion, alternating red and blue half-stars.

Finishing: Baste under the seam allowances on the outer edge of *each* diamond design. Center *each* diamond design on a pindot hexagon; appliqué designs using thread colors to match the diamonds. Remove basting thread when appliqué is complete.

Layer and baste together the muslin backing, batting, and pindot hexagon. Quilt as desired.

To complete one chair pad, cut a 1¼x40-inch blue strip for the ties. Press the long raw edges to the wrong side of the strip center, then fold the strip in half, *lengthwise,* to conceal the raw edges. Stitch along the edge of the strip to secure the folds. Cut the strip into four ties, *each* 10 inches long. Sew pairs of ties to the *right* side of the chair pad at two corners.

For the piping, cut and piece together strips of blue fabric to make a strip 1¼x50 inches. Encase the cording in the fabric strip. Baste the cording to the *right* side of the pindot hexagon on the seam line. Pin the pindot and blue hexagons together, *right* sides facing. Sew around the chair pad, leaving the edge between the ties unsewn. Turn the pad right side out; insert the foam pad and handsew the opening closed.

TUMBLING STARS
TABLE RUNNER
PAGE 115
Finished size is 12x31 inches.

Materials
¾ yard of red-on-white pindot fabric
¼ yard *each* of solid red and blue fabrics
½ yard of white flannel
2½ yards of cable cord for piping

Instructions
Make a template for piece A of the Tumbling Stars Quilt, page 140. Pattern is finished size; add ¼-inch seam allowances when cutting pieces from fabric.

Use the diamond template to mark 20 diamonds *each* from the red and blue fabrics.

From the blue fabric cut and piece together a strip 1x90 inches for the piping.

Cut two 13x32-inch rectangles from the pindot fabric and one rectangle from the flannel. Measurements include ½-inch seam allowances.

To make the runner: Sew the diamonds into two strips, each with 20 diamonds, 10 of each color. Start each strip with a red diamond and end with a blue diamond. Sew only on the sewing line, leaving the seam allowances free. Baste under the seam allowances around the diamond strips.

Pin the diamond strips on the runner, 1 inch in from the runner sides and ends. Appliqué the strips to the runner, matching the thread color to the diamonds.

To make piping, cover the cable cord with the blue fabric strip. Baste the piping to the front of the runner on the seam line.

Layer runner back, flannel and runner top *right* sides together. Sew around the runner, leaving an opening to turn. Trim excess seam allowance, clip corners, and turn right side out. Hand-stitch the opening closed. Outline-quilt around the diamond strips.

STARS AND STRIPES BANNER

PAGE 124

Finished size is 23⅜ x36½ inches.

Materials

1½ yards of red fabric
1¾ yards of white fabric
¼ yard of blue fabric
36-inch length of screen molding

Instructions

Make cardboard or plastic templates for pattern pieces A and B of the Tumbling Stars Quilt, page 140. Patterns are full-size; add ¼-inch seam allowances before cutting the pieces from fabric.

To cut the pieces: Strips include ¼-inch seam allowances.

From red fabric, cut:
9 strips, each 1⅞ x37 inches
21 A diamonds

From white fabric, cut:
25x39-inch banner lining
2x36-inch casing
8 strips, each 1⅞ x37 inches
18 A diamonds
6 B pieces

From blue fabric, cut:
2 binding strips, 1¼ x39 inches
2 binding strips, 1¼ x25 inches
21 A diamonds

To piece the block: Refer to the instructions for the Tumbling Stars Quilt, page 140, to piece one block.

To make the banner: Sew together the red and white fabric strips, *lengthwise*. Press the seam allowances toward the red strips.

Baste under the seam allowances around the Tumbling Star block. Position the block on the striped background with the top of the block even with the raw edge of the top red strip and the white diamond on the block's side ½ inch in from the left side edge of the banner.

Appliqué the star block; remove basting. Trim the red and white striped fabric from behind the block, leaving ¼-inch seam allowances.

Trim off the right side of the banner so the banner measures 23⅞ x37 inches, including seam allowances. Baste the banner to the lining, *wrong* sides facing.

Hand-quilt around the white shapes in the Tumbling Star block. Machine-quilt in the ditch along the seams in the striped portion of the banner. Trim lining even with the banner top.

Baste under ½ inch along one long side and both short sides of the casing strip. Center the casing strip on the lining with the raw edge even with the raw edge of the top red strip. Blindstitch the folded under edge of the casing to the lining.

Sew 1¼ x25-inch blue binding strips, *right* sides facing, to opposite short sides of the banner. Turn under ¼ inch on the raw edges and blindstitch to the lining. Trim excess blue binding. Sew the 1¼ x39-inch binding strips to the long sides of the banner, catching in casing strip at the top edge. Turn under ¼ inch on the raw edges of the binding and blindstitch to the lining. Trim off excess binding, leaving ¼ inch to turn under at the corners. Turn under the seam allowance at the corners and blindstitch in place.

Insert the molding in the casing.

STAR CENTERPIECE

PAGES 124–125

Finished stars are about 5¼ inches from tip to tip.

Materials

Scraps of red, white, and blue fabric
Polyester fiberfill
³⁄₁₆-inch-diameter wooden dowels
½ yard *each* of red, white, and blue ⅛-inch-wide satin ribbon
4-inch length of 2x4
Drill; ¼-inch bit
White spray paint

Instructions

Make cardboard or plastic templates for Piece A of the Tumbling Stars Quilt, page 140. Pattern is full-size; add ¼-inch seam allowances before cutting the pieces from fabric.

Cut out 12 A diamonds *each* from red, white, and blue fabrics.

To make the stars: Sew together the diamonds to piece two stars *each* from the red, white, and blue diamonds. Sew only on seam line, leaving seam allowances unsewn.

Pin together the matching stars, *right* sides facing. Sew around the stars, leaving one star edge unsewn. Clip, turn, and press. Stuff lightly with fiberfill.

Make bows and tack to centers, stitching through all layers.

Finishing: Drill three angled holes in the top of the 2x4. Cut the dowel into three pieces of varying length. Paint block and dowels.

Insert dowel in star and stitch closed. Stand dowels in base.

DIAMOND STARBURST QUILT

PAGES 114–115 and 126–127

Finished block is a 60-degree triangle with 10-inch sides.
Finished size is approximately 75x90 inches.

Materials

4 yards of navy pindot fabric
3½ yards of yellow print
3½ yards of muslin
3¼ yards of red-on-white pindot fabric
1¾ yards of green print fabric
2½ yards of red fabric
5½ yards of backing fabric
Cardboard or plastic for templates
Quilt batting

Instructions

Trace and make templates for the patterns, page 144. Patterns are finished size; add ¼-inch seam allowances when cutting the pieces from the fabric.

(Continued)

143

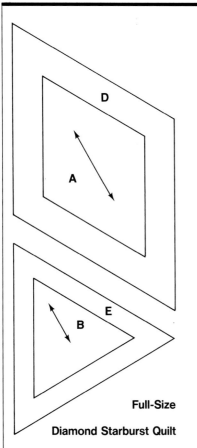

D

A

B

E

Full-Size

Diamond Starburst Quilt

For Piece C, draw an equilateral triangle with sides that measure 9⅞ inches.

To cut the pieces: The number of pieces to cut for the entire quilt top is listed first, with the number to cut for a single block following in parentheses.

From muslin, cut:
448 B triangles (4)
40 C triangles
168 E triangles

From red fabric, cut:
1,344 B triangles (12)

From yellow print fabric, cut:
112 A diamonds (1)

From navy pindot fabric, cut:
896 A diamonds (9)
82 D diamonds (borders)
9½ yards of 2-inch-wide strips for the binding

From the red-on-white pindot fabric, cut:
1,008 A diamonds (9)

COLOR KEY
Y = Yellow print
N = Navy pindot
D = White with red pindot
R = Red
M = Muslin
G = Green

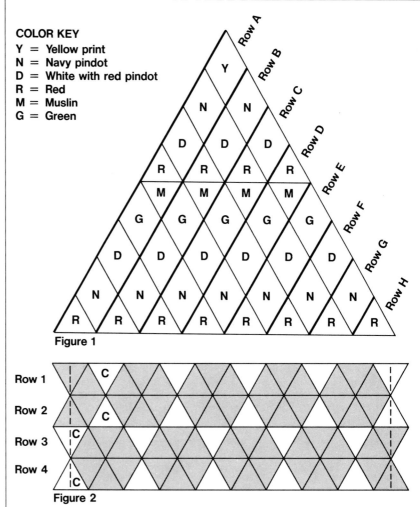

Figure 1

Figure 2

From the green print fabric, cut:
560 A diamonds (5)

To piece one large triangle: Join a red B triangle to a muslin B triangle to form a diamond. Make four diamonds.

Referring to Figure 1, *above,* sew the diamonds into rows. Join the rows to complete a large triangle.

To make the quilt top: Make 112 large triangles.

Referring to Figure 2, *above,* sew the pieced triangles and muslin C triangles into rows. Join the rows to complete the quilt top. To square up the side edges, draw a line along each side edge perpendicular to the bases of the triangles in Row 1 and bisecting each triangle along the edge through its point. *Adding ¼-inch seam allowances,* trim away excess triangles.

To make a border join 84 muslin E triangles and 41 navy D diamonds. Make two borders. Sew

the borders to the sides of the quilt top; trim excess E triangles even with quilt top and bottom.

Finishing: To piece the quilt back, cut fabric into two equal lengths. Cut or tear one length in half lengthwise. Sew one narrow panel to each side of the wide panel. Match the selvages; use a ½-inch seam. Trim the seams to ¼ inch; press to one side.

Layer the back, batting, and pieced top. Baste layers together; quilt.

Splice the binding strips together at 45-degree angles. Trim, fold in half lengthwise with wrong sides together, and press.

When quilting is complete, trim away excess batting and backing so all edges are even with the quilt top. Sew the binding to the right side of the quilt, raw edges together. Turn the folded edge to the back; hand-stitch in place.

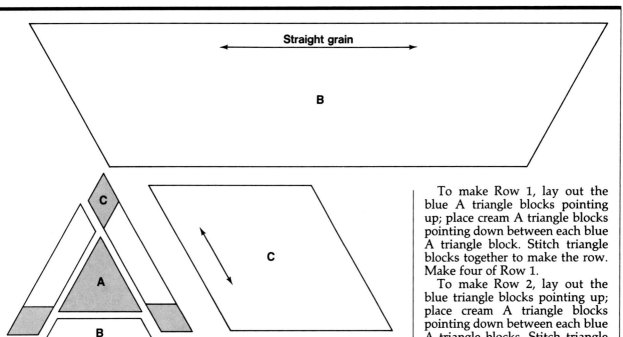

Figure 1

❖

SMOOTHING IRON QUILT
PAGE 126
Finished block is a 60-degree triangle with 9¾-inch sides.
Finished size is 78x88 inches.

Materials
6½ yards of blue print fabric
  (piecing, borders, and binding)
4½ yards of cream print
5½ yards of backing fabric
Quilt batting
Cardboard or plastic for templates

Instructions
Trace and make templates for the patterns, *above.* Patterns are finished size; add ¼-inch seam allowances when cutting the pieces from the fabric.

For Piece A, draw an equilateral triangle with sides that measure 4½ inches.

To cut the pieces: The number of pieces to cut for the entire quilt top is listed first, with the number to cut for a single block following in parentheses.

The cutting measurements for the borders include seam allowances and are longer than what is needed. The borders will be trimmed to exact length when added to the quilt top.

From blue fabric, cut:
4 borders, each 5½x82 inches
10 yards 2½-inch-wide bias
  strips for binding
68 A triangles (1)
204 B pieces (3)
204 C diamonds (3)

From cream fabric, cut:
68 A triangles (1)
204 B pieces (3)
204 C diamonds (3)

To piece the blocks: Half of the triangular blocks for this quilt have blue A and C pieces and cream B pieces; the remaining blocks have cream A and C pieces and blue B pieces. The blocks are pieced identically.

Referring to Figure 1, *above,* stitch a B piece to one side of the A triangle. Sew a C diamond to the end of one B piece; stitch this strip to the adjacent side of the A triangle and to the end of the first B piece. Sew a C diamond to each end of the remaining B piece; sew this strip the last side of the A triangle and to the ends of the B pieces.

Make 68 blocks with blue A triangles and 68 blocks with cream A triangles.

To make the quilt top: For Row 1 of the quilt, use eight blue A triangle blocks and nine cream A triangle blocks. For Row 2, use nine blue A triangle blocks and eight cream A triangle blocks.

To make Row 1, lay out the blue A triangle blocks pointing up; place cream A triangle blocks pointing down between each blue A triangle block. Stitch triangle blocks together to make the row. Make four of Row 1.

To make Row 2, lay out the blue triangle blocks pointing up; place cream A triangle blocks pointing down between each blue A triangle blocks. Stitch triangle blocks together to make the row. Make four of Row 2.

Sew the eight rows together, alternating Rows 1 and Rows 2.

To square up the side edges, draw a line along each side edge perpendicular to the bases of the triangles in Row 1 and bisecting each triangle along the edge through its point. *Adding ¼-inch seam allowances,* trim away excess triangles.

Stitch the border pieces to the long sides; trim length. Stitch the remaining border pieces to the remaining two sides; trim.

Finishing: To piece the quilt back, cut fabric into two equal lengths. Cut or tear one length in half lengthwise. Sew one narrow panel to each side of the wide panel. Match the selvages; use a ½-inch seam. Trim the seams to ¼ inch; press to one side.

Layer the back, batting, and pieced top. Baste layers together; quilt as desired.

When quilting is complete, trim away excess batting and backing even with the quilt top.

For binding, piece bias-cut strips together to make a strip about 10 yards long. Fold binding in half lengthwise, wrong sides together, and press so binding is 1¼ inches wide. Stitch to right side of quilt top with raw edges even with edge of quilt, mitering corners. Turn folded edge to quilt back and hand-stitch in place.

QUICK-PIECING
ON THE MACHINE

Precise piecing
of geometric shapes is critical
when assembling many quilt
blocks. The information in this
chapter offers shortcuts for
piecing squares, rectangles,
right-angle triangles, and
diamonds.

QUICK-PIECING SQUARES AND RECTANGLES

Making a patchwork checkerboard, or any pattern with parallelograms, is easy with this strip technique.

Although the Lincoln Quilt, *above,* appears intricate, the quilt top comprises components that are ideal for quick-piecing.

The first Lincoln Quilt was pieced in 1809 by Abraham Lincoln's mother, Nancy Hanks. The prominent feature of each block is a cross-shape checkerboard surrounded by four eight-point stars.

The quick-piecing method used to create this quilt involves cutting fabric into strips with a rotary cutter, sewing together alternate colors of the strips in sets, and assembling the sets into a checkerboard pattern. Although the squares for this quilt are very small—the finished size of each one is ⅝ inch—the same technique can be used for making any patchwork based on squares and rectangles. Quilt instructions begin on page 158.

The basic construction method for many patchwork designs based on squares and rectangles is to stitch the squares into horizontal rows, and then join the rows together to piece the design. When the squares occur in a regular sequence, they can be quickly pieced into rows on the sewing machine without marking and cutting each individual square.

1 Measure the finished size of the square; add ½ inch to this measurement to allow for ¼-inch seam allowances on all sides.

For the Lincoln Quilt, *opposite,* the center portion of the block is a rectangle made of many small squares. The finished squares are ⅝ inch so the strip width measurement with seam allowances is 1⅛ inches.

Isolate the first row of the design. Count the number of times each fabric is used in the row. For the sample quilt, the first row is made of seven dark pink squares and six white squares.

The second row of the design is made of seven white squares and six dark pink squares. These two rows repeat to make the rectangle.

Use a rotary cutter and ruler to cut 13 strips, each 1⅛ inches wide and approximately 45 inches long, from both the dark pink and white fabrics.

You can mark each strip, then cut the strips with scissors if you do not have a rotary cutter and ruler, but cutting the strips with a rotary cutter and ruler is faster and more accurate.

2 Sew the strips into strip sets using ¼-inch seam allowances. Sew the strips in the same sequence as they occur in the design row.

Make the Strip Set 1 for the first row by alternating seven dark pink strips with six white strips. Press seam allowances all in one direction.

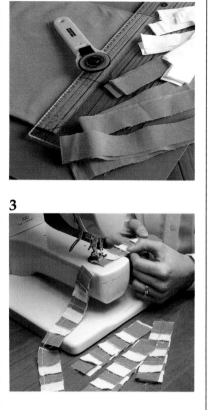

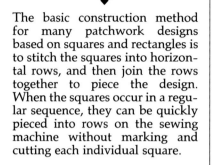

Make the Strip Set 2 for the second row by alternating seven white strips with six dark pink strips. Press the seam allowances in the opposite direction from the way Strip Set 1 was pressed.

Layer the strip sets *right* sides together with the seam allowances going in opposite directions. Using a ruler and rotary cutter, cut the strip sets into segments the same width that the strips were cut (Cut 38 segments, each 1⅛ inches wide for the quilt shown.) Check after cutting every three or four strips to see that the cuts are at right angles to the strips. Trim the edge to square the edge, if necessary, before cutting more strips.

3 Pick a pair of segments (each pair has a Strip Set 1 segment and a Strip Set 2 segment with *right*-sides facing). Stitch the pairs together, matching the squares at each intersection. (You may find it helpful to insert pins so they are perpendicular to the seam lines to align the squares in each segment.) Without clipping the thread, stitch a second pair of segments. Continue to stitch additional pairs. The segments will be chained together with a short length of thread. Chain-piecing the pairs is much faster than stopping and starting after each pair.

4 Join the pairs of segments to other pairs and repeat until the block is the needed size. For the sample quilt, join six pairs of segments then add a single Strip Set 1 segment to complete the center rectangle.

PIECING RIGHT-ANGLE TRIANGLES

Once you've mastered making a triangle-square, you're ready to tackle a Variable Star pattern.

An eye-catching color combination and a dynamic angular pattern make for stunning visual effect in the Amish Variable Star Quilt, *above*.

The quick-piecing instructions for right-angle triangles, *opposite*, provide one way to join pairs of triangles. When two right-angle triangles are joined along their hypotenuses (long sides), the result is a triangle-square. These instructions work well with most Variable Star patterns.

❖

1 The first step is to mark a grid of squares on the *wrong side* of the lighter of the two fabrics to be joined. To determine the size of the squares in the grid, measure the *finished* size of the square made from the two joined triangles. Add ⅞ inch to this measurement to allow for the ¼-inch seam allowances. For example, for the Amish Variable Star Quilt, *opposite,* you need 3-inch finished squares, referred to as triangle-squares; therefore, the grid squares will be 3⅞ inches.

Next, determine the number of grid squares to mark on the fabric. Count the number of triangle-squares of a specific color combination in the quilt design. (There are 24 lavender and teal triangle-squares in the Amish Variable Star Quilt.) Remember, each grid square will make two triangle-squares; therefore, mark only half that number of grid squares. (Mark 12 grid squares.)

It is easiest to work with fabric pieces that are no larger than 18x22 inches. Determine the number of grid squares you can mark on a fabric piece this size or smaller with approximately a ½-inch fabric margin around the grid. Start marking the grid about ½ inch down from the top edge of the fabric and keep the marked grid at least ½ inch in from the fabric edges. (For the lavender and teal squares, you can mark a 3x4-square grid within a 12x16-inch area. To allow for a margin around the grid, cut a 13x17-inch rectangle from the lavender and teal fabrics. Use a wide ruler and pencil or permanent pen to mark a 3x4-square grid of 3⅞-inch squares on the *wrong* side of the lavender fabric rectangle.)

2 Draw a diagonal line through each square with lines going in opposite directions in every other square. Draw only *one* diagonal line through each square.

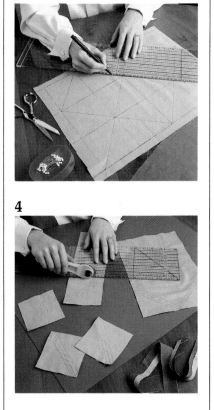

3 Place the marked fabric (lavender) *right* sides together on the second fabric (teal) with the marked fabric on top; press, then pin the layers together. If you pin along horizontal and vertical lines away from intersections of diagonal lines, the pins will not be in your way when you sew.

With your machine set for 12–15 stitches per inch, stitch exactly ¼ inch from both sides of all diagonal lines. It is easiest to stitch the lines on one side of the diagonals and then stitch the lines on the second side. Stitching the diagonals is like going through a maze; if you plan your route carefully, you can stitch continuously along many diagonals without stopping.

On many sewing machines, you can use the edge of the presser foot as an accurate ¼-inch seam guide. You may find it helpful to mark sewing lines ¼ inch to each side of all diagonal lines with a removable marker until you know exactly where to look on your machine's presser foot to guide your stitching exactly ¼ inch from the lines.

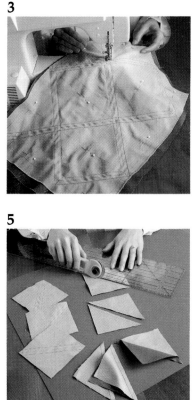

4 Press the stitched piece. Trim the excess fabric around the outside of the grid. Cut on the horizontal and vertical grid lines, cutting the fabric into squares.

5 Cut on the diagonal lines between the rows of stitching, cutting the squares into triangles. (If you added stitching lines in Step 3, cut on the middle diagonal line.)

Open the triangles and press the seam allowances toward the darker fabric. You will have 24 triangle-squares, each 3½ inches square, which will sew down to 3 inches finished size when added to other block units.

PIECING DIAMONDS

Large diamonds stitched from any number of smaller diamonds are perennial favorite quilt patterns. Because this construction is often used for whole quilt tops, efficient piecing is important.

Spectacular whole-top quilt designs like the Broken Star, *opposite,* are prized by quilt collectors. The steps to making this and other large eight-point diamond patterns (such as the Star of Bethelem and the Lone Star) can be simplified.

As with some of our other quick-piecing methods, a fast way to piece diamonds begins with making uniform strips with a rotary cutter, stitching them together in the order they appear on the quilt, recutting them at an angle, and then stitching the angle-cut strips into diamonds.

In addition to the rotary cutter and plastic ruler required for other quick-piecing steps, you'll need a draftsman's 45-degree triangle.

The method, beginning *right,* describes how to quick-piece 45-degree diamonds such as those in the Broken Star Quilt or other eight-point diamond star designs. To modify the method to piece 60-degree diamonds into strips (such as assembling the diamonds for the Hit-and-Miss Quilt shown on page 50) use a 60-degree draftsman's triangle.

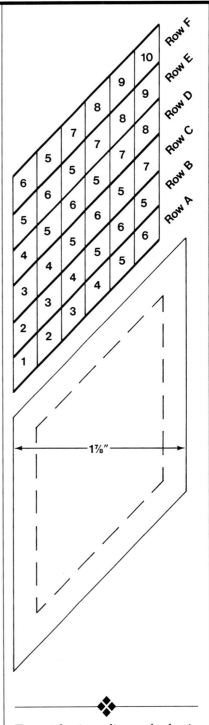

To quick-piece diamonds, begin by sketching one of the large diamonds in the star. Assign a number to each fabric used in the diamond, designating the center diamond as number one. Then assign a color number to each diamond in the sketch.

(Continued)

Label the rows of diamonds with letters, labeling the row with the center diamond Row A. The sample diamond sketch, page 153, is the diamond for the Broken Star Quilt as used in the outer star. The diamonds in the center star are identical but are turned so the blue diamonds are toward the center.

Count the number of times each fabric is used in a large diamond. It is helpful to make a chart similar to the one shown, *below.*

Fabric 1 (green): 1
Fabric 2 (yellow): 2
Fabric 3 (light peach): 3
Fabric 4 (peach): 4
Fabric 5 (hot pink): 10
Fabric 6 (red): 6
Fabric 7 (light pink): 4
Fabric 8 (light lavender): 3
Fabric 9 (lavender): 2
Fabric 10 (blue): 1

If you are working with a *finished-size* diamond pattern, draw a line ¼ inch from the outline to add seam allowances to the pattern. Measure the height of the diamond pattern with seam allowances included. (Measure the distance between two parallel seam allowance lines.) For the sample diamond on page 153, the height is 1⅞ inches.

Cut strips across the width of the fabric (45 inches) that are as wide as the diamond height (1⅞ inches for the sample). Referring to your chart, cut one strip for each time the fabric is used in the big diamond.

For the Broken Star, cut strips as follows: 1 green, 2 yellow, 3 light peach, 4 peach, 10 hot pink, 6 red, 4 light pink, 3 light lavender, 2 lavender, and 1 blue.

1 Referring to the large diamond sketch, sew together the strips for Row A, taking ¼-inch seam allowances. Start by sewing a Fabric 1 (green) strip to a Fabric 2 (yellow) strip, staggering the second

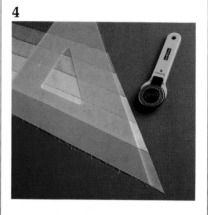

6

strip in about 1½ inches from the first strip. Continue to add strips until all of the strips for Row A are joined; add Fabric 3 (light peach), Fabric 4 (peach), Fabric 5 (hot pink), and Fabric 6 (red). Press seams away from the first strip. Label this strip set Row A.

Repeat to make the strip sets for Rows B, C, D, E, and F.

2 Starting at the top left corner with the Row A strip set right-side up, use a draftsman's 45-degree triangle to mark a 45-degree angle through the Row A strip set; cut along the 45-degree angle mark.

3 Using a wide ruler and rotary cutter, cut 1⅞-inch-wide strips parallel to the 45-degree cut. (Or mark the strips and cut them with scissors.) For the sample project, you can cut 12 strips from each strip set. For other sizes of diamonds, you usually can cut at least eight strips of diamonds (enough diamonds for an eight-pointed star) from a strip set.

4 After cutting every two or three strips, use the draftsman's triangle to make sure you are

maintaining a 45-degree angle; trim excess fabric to correct the angle if necessary. Label the strips of diamonds Row A.

Repeat to cut strips for Rows B, C, D, E, and F.

5 To make a large diamond, begin by pinning a strip of Row A diamonds to a strip of Row B diamonds. Carefully match the diamonds along what will be the sewing line, ¼ inch in from the cut edge. Sew Row A to Row B. Repeat to add Rows C, D, E, and F.

6 When all the rows have been joined, carefully press the seams to one side. Because two sides of the large diamond are on the bias, be careful not to stretch the bias sides when pressing.

❖

PRESSING PIECED PATCHWORK

Any patchwork project requires pressing at several different stages to achieve professional-looking results. Here are the four most important times to press.

Press fabric before marking
Press the fabric with iron set to recommended heat setting; use steam if appropriate. Move the iron *across* the fabric in slow, even strokes, smoothing out wrinkles as you go.

Press after stitching initial seams
For this first stage, and for each subsequent stage of assembly, press all seams to one side or the other; do *not* press them open (as you would in dressmaking).

Piece all similar portions of a pattern block first, then press all seams the same way, before moving on to the next assembly step.

Press seams toward darker fabrics wherever possible, to avoid show-through. If this is not possi-

ble, trim the darker seam allowance slightly so that it does not show beyond the edge of the lighter seam allowance.

Continue pressing after sewing each set of seams and before sewing a second seam *across* the first one.

At each assembly stage, press by lifting the iron and setting it down again in a new spot. Avoid dragging the iron across fabric; you'll risk distorting the edges of the fabric shapes, particularly on bias-cut pieces or curved seams. Clip seams where necessary so that your work lies flat.

Press when blocks are completed
First press the completed blocks gently on the wrong side, making sure that all seams lie as flat as possible and are going in the right directions. Then press the block again on the right side, using the point of the iron to eliminate all folds and wrinkles in the seams. After general pressing, each block should be squared and sized. First, lightly draw a square on the ironing board cover or on a piece of

muslin pinned to the ironing board cover. The square should match the finished block, including seam allowances. Corners should be true right angles.

Next, place the block right side down on the board and pin it along each edge so that the block fits the marked square; make sure that all corners are at right angles.

Cover the block with a damp cloth and press, or press with a steam iron. Use the steam and the weight and motion of the iron to gently shrink or stretch the block to fit the required measurements, if necessary.

Finally, turn the block over and press again on the right side.

Press when quilt top is complete
Iron the finished quilt top on the right side to get it as smooth as possible before basting it together with the batting and backing.

Avoid pressing your quilt or patchwork project after the top has been layered and quilted. Pressing at this stage will flatten the quilting and detract from the overall beauty of your work.

❖ ❖ ❖

Here are three more ways to explore our quick-piecing techniques. The instructions for these quilts are based on the methods explained on the preceding pages.

Because of the number of squares and rectangles used to make a single block, the Young Man's Fancy Quilt, *opposite,* is usually made with only a few blocks. Here, a subtle color combination and delicate quilting offset the impact of the large pieces.

The Barbara Frietchie Rose Quilt, *above left,* is another Variable Star pattern composed of triangle-squares. To introduce a third fabric to this easy block, consider substituting a coordinating print fabric for the pink fabric in the center four triangle-squares.

Each point of the large diamonds on the Prairie Star Quilt, *above right,* is assembled from nine smaller diamonds. Selecting two contrasting fabrics for the two inner rows of each diamond creates a star within a star.

❖

LINCOLN QUILT
PAGE 148
Finished block is 14⅛ inches.
Finished size is 72¾ x 72¾ inches.

Materials
7 yards of white fabric
4 yards of dark pink fabric
1 yards of pink fabric
4½ yards backing fabric
Quilt batting
Plastic or cardboard for templates

Instructions
The instructions for this quilt are written for quick-piecing on the sewing machine. Refer to pages 148–149 for tips on quick-piecing squares. Stitch using ¼-inch seams.

Trace and make templates for the patterns, *above right.* Patterns are finished size; add ¼-inch seam allowances when cutting the pieces from the fabric. Measurements for the sashing strips and strips for quick-piecing squares include seam allowances.

To cut the pieces: The strips for this quilt can be cut quickly using a rotary cutter, heavy plastic ruler, and a cutting mat. You can also mark the pieces with a ruler and cut them with scissors.

From white fabric, cut:
40 sashing strips, each 4¾ x14⅝ inches
63 quick-piecing strips, each 1⅛ x45 inches
356 B triangles with the long side on the fabric grain
292 C squares
64 D squares
128 E triangles with the long side on the fabric grain

From dark pink fabric, cut:
59 quick-piecing strips, each 1⅛ x45 inches
356 diamonds from template A
9 yards of 2½-inch-wide strips for the binding

From pink fabric, cut:
356 A diamonds

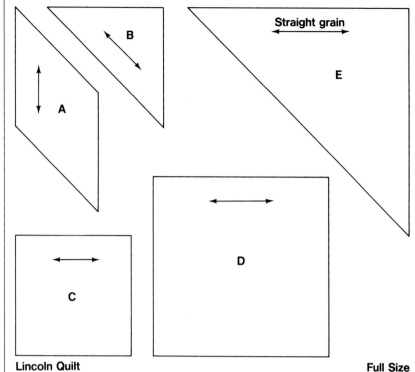

Lincoln Quilt   Full Size

To piece the blocks: Refer to the quick-piecing squares instructions on pages 148–149. Make five each of Strip Set 1 and Strip Set 2 as described in the instructions. Cut a total of 176 pairs of segments. Cut 16 additional segments of Strip Set 2.

Referring to the instructions and Figure 1, *below,* make 16 rectangular center sections for the blocks.

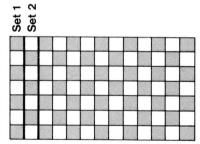

Figure 1

Referring to Figure 2, *below,* use Strip Set 1 segments and Strip Set 2 segments to piece 32 rectangles. Add D squares to the ends of the rectangles.

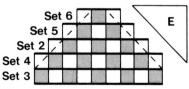

Figure 2

Referring to Figure 3, *below,* make two of Strip Set 3 by sewing together five dark pink strips and four white strips. Cut into a total of 64 segments.

Figure 3

Make two of Strip Set 4 by sewing together five white strips and four dark pink strips. Cut into a total of 64 segments.

Make two of Strip Set 5 by sewing together three white strips and two dark pink strips. Cut into a total of 64 segments.

Make two of Strip Set 6 by sewing together two white strips and one dark pink strip. Cut into a total of 64 segments.

Stitch together the strip segments as shown in Figure 3. Sew an E triangle onto both sides; trim off excess squares along seams. Make a total of 64 Figure 3 units.

Referring to Figure 4, *below,* piece 64 partial star blocks for the block corners.

Figure 5

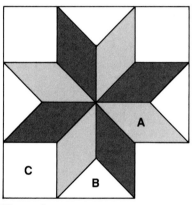

Figure 4

To make one block, refer to Figure 5, *above right.* Sew a Figure 2 unit to opposite sides of a Figure 1 unit. Add Figure 3 units to the sides of the center square. Set in Figure 4 units at the four corners.

To make the quilt top: Make 16 Lincoln Quilt blocks. Referring to Figure 4, *above,* piece 25 star blocks, completing blocks by adding a C square in the open corner.

Sew the blocks into four rows with four blocks in each row, adding sashing strips between the blocks and at the beginning and end of the rows.

Sew five sashing strip rows by sewing together four sashing strips with star blocks between the strips and at the beginning and end of the rows.

(Continued)

Quilting Pattern   Full Size

Sew together the block rows and sashing strip rows.

Finishing: To piece the quilt back, cut fabric into two equal lengths. Cut or tear one length in half lengthwise. Sew one narrow panel to each side of the wide panel. Match the selvages; use a ½-inch seam. Trim the seams to ¼ inch; press to one side.

Trace the quilting design, page 159, and transfer the design to the sashing strips, drawing three leaves on each strip.

Layer the back, batting, and pieced top. Baste layers together; quilt.

Splice the binding strips together at 45-degree angles. Trim, fold in half lengthwise with wrong sides together, and press.

When quilting is complete, trim away excess batting and backing so all edges are even with the quilt top. Sew the binding to the right side of the quilt, raw edges together. Turn the folded edge to the back; hand-stitch in place.

❖❖❖

AMISH VARIABLE STAR QUILT

PAGE 150
Finished block is 12 inches.
Finished quilt is 68x80 inches.

Materials
3 yards of teal fabric
2½ yards of yellow fabric (includes fabric for borders and binding)
¾ yard *each* of royal blue and hot pink fabrics
½ yard *each* of red, green, lavender, and orange fabrics
5 yards of backing fabric; batting

Instructions
The instructions for this quilt are written for quick-piecing on the sewing machine. Refer to pages 150–151 for tips on quick-piecing right-angle triangles for the Ohio Star Quilt. Stitch using ¼-inch seams. All measurements include

seam allowances.

To cut the strips: From the yellow fabric, cut two 4½x76-inch borders and two 4½x72-inch borders; set aside. Borders are longer than is needed; trim them to exact length when sewing them to the quilt top.

From the teal fabric, cut 10 strips, each 3½x45 inches. Cut each strip into twelve 3½-inch squares (120 total). The squares include seam allowances and are for the corners of the star blocks.

To make the star blocks: Piece 30 Variable Star blocks. Each block is made of four teal squares, eight triangle-squares for the star points, and four triangle-squares for the star center. Refer to Figure 1, *below,* to piece the blocks.

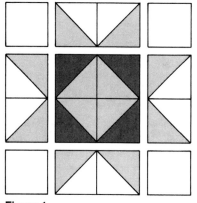

Figure 1

To make four green stars, stitch 32 green and teal triangle-squares. For the star centers, stitch 16 yellow and orange triangle-squares. Piece the stars, using green triangles for the star points and orange triangles in the center.

To make four blue stars, stitch 32 blue and teal triangle-squares. For the centers, stitch 16 red and lavender triangle-squares. Piece the stars, using blue triangles for the star points and lavender triangles in the center.

To make four pink stars, stitch 32 pink and teal triangle-squares. For the centers, stitch 16 green

and blue triangle-squares. Piece the stars, using pink triangles for the star points and blue triangles in the center.

To make four orange stars, stitch 32 orange and teal triangle-squares. For the centers, stitch 16 lavender and pink triangle-squares. Piece the stars, using pink triangles for the star points. Place lavender triangles in the center for two stars and blue triangles in the center for the other two stars.

To make three lavender stars, stitch 24 lavender and teal triangle-squares. For the centers, stitch 12 blue and red triangle-squares. Piece the stars, using lavender triangles for the star points and red triangles in the center.

To make four red stars, stitch 32 red and teal triangle-squares. For the centers, stitch 28 pink and blue triangle-squares; set aside 12 triangle-squares for the yellow stars. Piece the stars, using red triangles for the star points and pink triangles in the center.

To make the seven yellow stars, stitch 56 yellow and teal triangle-squares. For the centers, stitch 16 lavender and green triangle squares. Piece four stars using yellow triangles for the star points and placing green triangles in the center. Piece three yellow stars using the 12 remaining pink and blue triangle-squares for the center. Place the pink triangles in the center.

To make the quilt top: Lay out the blocks in six rows with five blocks in each row, placing a red star at each corner and arranging the stars for a pleasing balance.

Sew the blocks together in rows; join the rows. Add the longer borders to the sides; trim excess. Sew the remaining borders to the top and bottom; trim.

Finishing: To piece the quilt back, cut fabric into two equal lengths. Cut or tear one length in half lengthwise. Sew one narrow panel to each side of the wide panel. Match the selvages; use a ½-inch seam. Trim the seams to ¼ inch;

Layer the back, batting, and pieced top. Baste layers together; outline-quilt ¼ inch from all seams. Quilt borders as desired.

For the binding, cut 9 yards of 2½-inch-wide strips from the remaining yellow fabric. Splice the strips together at 45-degree angles. Trim, fold in half lengthwise with wrong sides together, and press.

When quilting is complete, trim away excess batting and backing so all edges are even with the quilt top. Sew the binding to the right side of the quilt, raw edges together. Turn the folded edge to the back; hand-stitch in place.

❖

BROKEN STAR QUILT
PAGE 152
Finished quilt is 89x89 inches.

Materials
¼ yard each of green and blue fabric
½ yard lavender fabric
⅝ yard each of light peach and light lavender fabric
¾ yard each of peach and light pink fabric
1⅛ yards red fabric
1¾ yards hot pink fabric
1⅝ yards yellow fabric
4 yards white fabric
9 yards of 45-inch-wide backing fabric or 3 yards of 108-inch-wide fabric
Cardboard or plastic for templates
Quilt batting

Instructions
The instructions for this quilt are written for quick-piecing on the sewing machine. Refer to pages 152–155 for instructions on quick-piecing diamonds for the Broken Star Quilt. Stitch using ¼-inch seams. All measurements include seam allowances, unless stated otherwise.

To make templates to cut the white squares and triangles, draw two 12-inch squares on graph paper. Divide one square diagonally into two triangles. Make templates for the square and the triangle. These templates do not

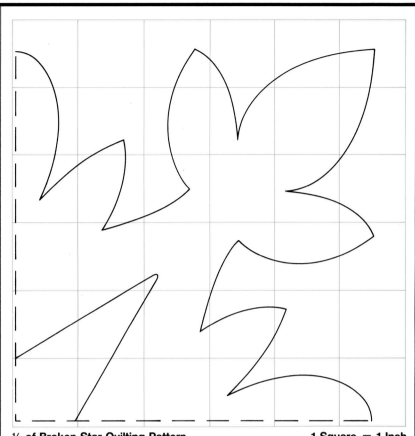

¼ of Broken Star Quilting Pattern   **1 Square = 1 Inch**

include seam allowances; add ¼-inch seam allowances when cutting pieces from fabric.

To cut the pieces: The strips for this quilt can be cut quickly using a rotary cutter, heavy plastic ruler, and a cutting mat. You can also mark the pieces with a ruler and cut them with scissors.

From white fabric, cut:
20 squares
8 triangles with the *long* side on the fabric grain
9 strips, 2½x45 inches, for the binding

From yellow fabric, cut:
8 strips, 4x45 inches, for the borders

To piece the large diamonds: From the colored fabrics, cut strips as described in the diamond quick-piecing instructions on pages 152–155. Cut and piece three sets of strips to make a total of 32 large diamonds, eight diamonds for the center star, and 24 diamonds for the outer star.

To piece the quilt top: Sew eight large diamonds into a star, placing the blue diamonds to the center. Set a square into the openings between the diamond points around the star.

Stitch the remaining diamonds together in groups of three diamonds with the green diamonds together (eight groups total). Set groups of three diamonds into the spaces between the squares, joining groups of diamonds to adjacent diamonds as groups of diamonds are added.

Set three squares into the openings at each of the corners of the outer star. Fill in the openings along the sides with triangles.

Stitch pairs of yellow border strips together into 90-inch-long pieces. Sew a border to the top and bottom of the quilt. Sew borders to the sides; trim excess border fabric.

Finishing: To piece the quilt back, cut fabric into two equal lengths. Cut or tear one length in half lengthwise. Sew one narrow panel

(Continued)

161

to each side of the wide panel. Match the selvages; use a ½-inch seam. Trim the seams to ¼ inch; press to one side.

Enlarge the quilting pattern, page 161, and transfer the design to each of the muslin squares. Divide the pattern in half for the triangles. Outline quilt the small diamonds.

Layer the back, batting, and pieced top. Baste layers together; quilt.

Splice the binding strips together at 45-degree angles. Trim, fold in half lengthwise with wrong sides together, and press.

When quilting is complete, trim away excess batting and backing so all edges are even with the quilt top. Sew the binding to the right side of the quilt, raw edges together. Turn the folded edge to the back; hand-stitch in place.

YOUNG MAN'S FANCY QUILT
PAGE 156
Finished block is 20⅝ inches.
Finished quilt is 77x77 inches.

Materials
4 yards of yellow fabric
3½ yards blue fabric
5 yards of backing fabric
Quilt batting
Cardboard or template plastic

Instructions
The instructions for this quilt are written for quick-piecing on the sewing machine. Refer to pages 148–149 for tips on quick-piecing squares and rectangles and to pages 150–151 for tips on quick-piecing right-angle triangles. Stitch using ¼-inch seams.

Draw a 4⅝-inch square on graph paper; then make a cardboard or plastic template for the square. The square is labeled Template A on Figure 1, *above right,* and the template includes ¼-inch seam allowances.

For the setting squares and triangles, make a 20⅝-inch square template from cardboard or from plastic.

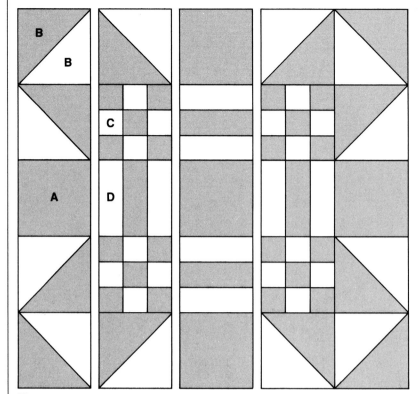

Figure 1

To cut the pieces: The components for the quilt blocks can be cut quickly using a rotary cutter, heavy plastic ruler, and a cutting mat. You can also mark the pieces with a ruler and cut them with scissors.

The cutting measurements include ¼-inch seam allowances unless stated otherwise. The borders are longer than is needed; trim them to the exact length when adding them to the quilt top.

From yellow fabric, cut:
8 strips, each 1⅞x45 inches for the C squares and D rectangles
2 borders, each 6½x67 inches
2 borders, each 6½x77 inches
4 A squares

Adding ¼-inch seam allowances, use the 20⅝-inch square template to mark and cut one setting square. (The cut square will measure 21⅛ inches square.) Set the square aside.

For the setting triangles, draw a diagonal line between opposite corners of the template used for marking the setting squares. Draw a second diagonal line in

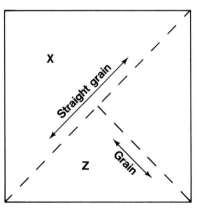

Figure 2

the *opposite* direction, through the lower section of the template (see Figure 2, *right*).

Cut on the drawn lines to form templates X and Z.

Using Template X, mark four setting triangles with the *long* side of the triangle on the straight grain. Adding ¼-inch seam allowances, cut out the triangles.

Next, using Template Z, mark four corner-setting triangles, with the legs of the triangle template on the straight grain. Adding ¼-inch seam allowances, cut out the triangles. Set the X and Z triangles aside.

From blue fabric, cut:
7 strips, each 1⅞x45 inches for
   the C squares and D rectangles
2 borders, each 4x60 inches
2 borders, each 4x67 inches
20 A squares
13 binding strips, each 2½ inches
   wide across remaining fabric
   width (approximately 27 inches
   long)

To quick-piece the block units:
Referring to the instructions on
pages 150–151 to quick-piece
right-angle triangles, make 48 triangle-squares from the remaining
yellow and blue fabric. The finished size of the triangle (labeled
B on Figure 1) is 4⅛ inches so use
a 5-inch grid when making the
triangle-squares.

Refer to the instructions on
pages 148–149 to quick-piece
squares. Using the 1⅞-inch-wide
strips, make 16 nine-patch units
(labeled C on Figure 1).

To make the squares made of
rectangles (labeled D on Figure 1)
make two strips sets in the same
manner as for quick-piecing
squares with a blue strip in the
center and yellow strips to each
side. Cut the strip sets into a total
of 16 segments, each 4⅝ inches
square.

To piece one block: Refer to Figure 1, *opposite.* Assemble the A, B,
C, and D units into rows; then
join the rows to complete the
block.

To make the quilt top: Piece four
Young Man's Fancy blocks. The
quilt top is pieced in diagonal
rows. All blocks are turned on
point. If desired, transfer the
quilting pattern to the yellow setting square and setting triangles
before assembly; see finishing instructions, below.

Join the blocks as follows: Sew
a pieced block to opposite sides of
the yellow setting square for the
center row; sew a Z triangle to
each end. To make the other rows,
add X triangles to opposite sides
of the two remaining blocks.

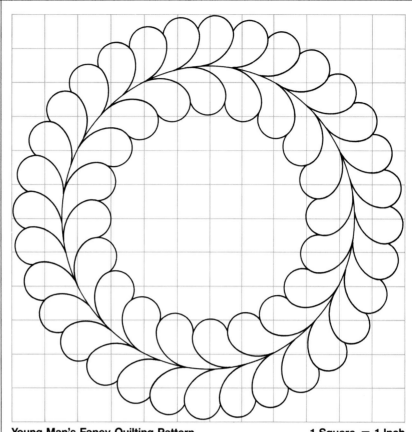

Young Man's Fancy Quilting Pattern   **1 Square = 1 Inch**

Stitch the rows together. Add the
remaining Z triangles to complete
the corners.

Set the 4x60-inch blue borders
to the top and bottom of the quilt
top. Sew the 4x67-inch blue borders to the sides. Trim excess border fabric.

In the same manner, add the
yellow borders to the quilt top.

Finishing: To piece the quilt back,
cut fabric into two equal lengths.
Cut or tear one length in half
lengthwise. Sew one narrow panel
to each side of the wide panel.
Match the selvages; use a ½-inch
seam. Trim the seams to ¼ inch;
press to one side.

Enlarge the quilting pattern for
a feathered circle, *above,* and transfer the design to the large yellow
square. Divide the pattern into

halves and quarters to mark the X
and Z triangles. Trace the feathered heart quilting design, page
164, and transfer a heart into each
corner of the square. Fill open
areas in the triangles with the
heart design or half of the heart
design.

Mark the blue and yellow borders with the border quilting designs, page 164.

Layer the back, batting, and
pieced top. Baste layers together;
quilt.

Splice the binding strips together at 45-degree angles. Trim,
fold in half lengthwise with
wrong sides together, and press.

When quilting is complete, trim
away excess batting and backing
so all edges are even with the quilt
top. Sew the binding to the right
side of the quilt, raw edges together. Turn the folded edge to
the back; hand-stitch in place.

163

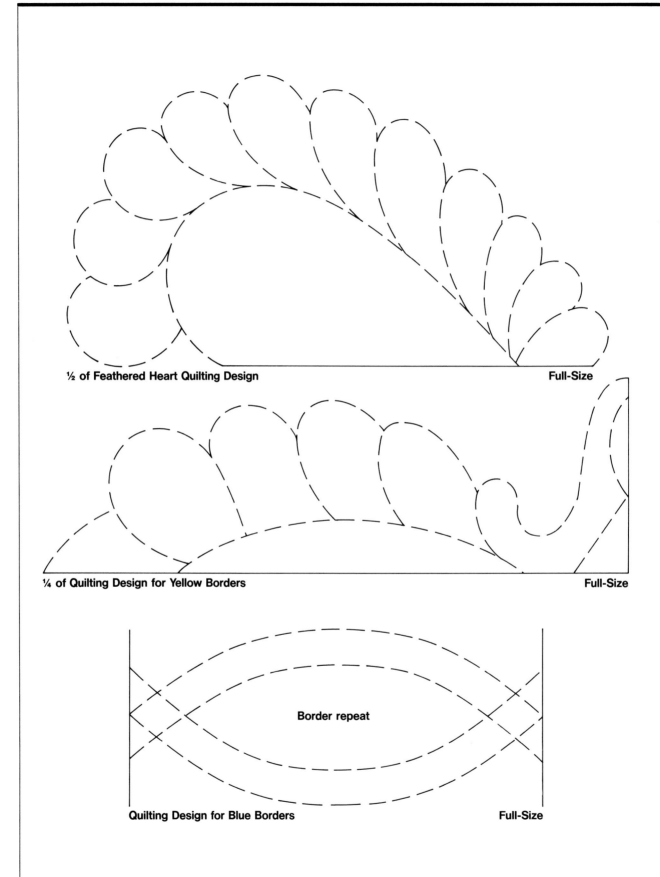

½ of Feathered Heart Quilting Design   Full-Size

¼ of Quilting Design for Yellow Borders   Full-Size

Border repeat

Quilting Design for Blue Borders   Full-Size

Barbara Frietchie Rose Quilt

PAGE 157

Finished block is 10½ inches square. Finished size is approximately 75x90 inches.

Materials

7½ yards of white fabric
2¼ yards of pink fabric
6½ yards of fabric for backing and binding
Quilt batting
Cardboard or plastic for templates

Instructions

The instructions for this quilt are written for quick-piecing on the sewing machine. Refer to pages 150–151 for tips on quick-piecing right-angle triangles. Stitch using ¼-inch seams.

For the setting squares and triangles, make a 10½-inch square template from cardboard or plastic. *Note:* The template is finished size and *does not* include seam allowances.

To cut the pieces: Use the setting square template to cut the setting squares and triangles. The pieces for the star blocks can be cut quickly using a rotary cutter, heavy plastic ruler, and a cutting mat. You can also mark the pieces with a ruler and cut them with scissors.

From white fabric, cut:
Ten 3⅛-inch-wide strips across the width of the fabric
Eight 2½-inch-wide strips across the width of the fabric (binding)

Adding ¼-inch seam allowances, use the 10½-inch square template to mark and cut 20 setting squares. (The cut square will measures 11 inches square.) Set the squares aside.

For the setting triangles, draw a diagonal line between opposite corners of the template used for marking the setting squares.

Draw a second diagonal line in the *opposite* direction, through the lower section of the template (see Figure 1, *below*).

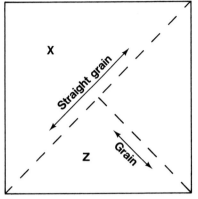

Figure 1

Cut on the drawn lines to form templates X and Z.

Using Template X, mark 18 setting triangles with the *long* side of the triangle on the straight grain. Adding ¼-inch seam allowances, cut out the triangles.

Next, using Template Z, mark four corner-setting triangles, with the legs of the triangle template on the straight grain. Adding seam allowances, cut out the triangles. Set the X and Z triangles aside.

To make the block units: Cut each 3⅛-inch-wide white strip into 12 squares, each 3⅛ inches square (120 total).

Refer to instructions for quick-piecing right-angle triangles as described on pages 150–151.

Cut six 22x19-inch rectangles of both white and pink fabric.

With a pencil, mark a 3½-inch grid on the white fabric. The grid should be five squares by six squares (30 squares total). Draw diagonal lines as directed. Place the white fabric on top of the pink, right sides facing and edges meeting. Complete steps, making 60 triangle-squares from each set of marked rectangles (360 triangle-squares total). The triangle-squares should measure 3⅛ inches at this point.

To piece one block: For each block, use 12 triangle squares and four white 3⅛-inch squares. Referring to Figure 2, *below,* sew the pieces into four rows; join the rows to complete the block.

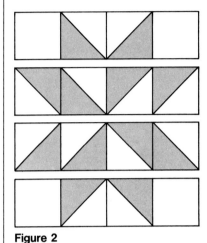

Figure 2

To make the quilt top: Piece 30 star blocks. The quilt top is pieced in diagonal rows with white squares between the pieced blocks; all blocks are turned on point.

Join the blocks as follows: Join five pieced blocks with alternating white squares for one of the center rows; add a Z triangle to one end and an X triangle to the other end. Make another strip exactly like this one. Align the strips so the Z triangles are at opposite ends; stitch together. These two rows form the center of the quilt.

Next, join four pieced blocks with alternating white squares; add one X triangle to each end. Make another strip like this one; add these strips to the center assembly. Continue in this manner, working from center rows outward, and using one less pieced block per row. Add remaining Z triangles to complete corners.

Finishing: To piece the quilt back, cut fabric into two 2¾-yard lengths. Cut or tear one length in

(Continued)

half lengthwise. Sew one narrow panel to each side of the wide panel. Match the selvages; use a ½-inch seam. Trim the seams to ¼ inch; press to one side.

Transfer quilting designs as desired to white blocks.

Layer the backing, batting, and top; baste layers together. Quilt as desired.

Splice the binding strips together at 45-degree angles. Trim, fold in half lengthwise, and press.

When quilting is complete, trim away excess batting and backing so all edges are even with the quilt top. Sew the binding to the right side of the quilt, raw edges together. Turn the folded edge to the back; hand-stitch in place.

❖

PRAIRIE STAR QUILT
PAGES 147 and 157
Finished block is 23 inches.
Finished quilt is 84x84 inches.

Materials
5½ yards of white fabric
2½ yards of gold fabric
1¾ yards of pink fabric
1¼ yards *each* of blue and green fabrics
5 yards of backing fabric
Cardboard or plastic for templates
Quilt batting

Instructions
The instructions for this quilt are written for quick-piecing on the sewing machine. Refer to pages 152–155 for tips on quick-piecing diamonds.

Note: Because the diamonds are larger than those for the Broken Star, cut the strips for the Prairie Star Quilt 2⅛ inches wide.

To make templates to cut the white squares and triangles, draw two 6¾-inch squares on graph paper. Divide one square diagonally into two triangles. Make templates for the square and the triangle. These templates do not include seam allowances; add ¼-inch seam allowances when cutting pieces from fabric.

To cut the pieces: The piecing strips can be cut quickly using a rotary cutter, heavy plastic ruler, and a cutting mat. You can also mark the strips with a ruler and cut them with scissors.

From white fabric, cut:
8 borders, each 3x90 inches
36 squares with the template
36 triangles with the *long* side of the triangle template on the fabric grain
10 strips, each 2½x45 inches for the binding

From gold fabric, cut:
4 borders, each 3x90 inches
9 piecing strips, each 2⅛x90 inches (cut strips in half so they are 45 inches long)

From pink fabric, cut:
27 piecing strips, each 2⅛x45 inches

From blue and green fabrics, cut:
18 piecing strips, each 2⅛x45 inches

To piece the large diamonds: Figure 1, *below,* is a sketch of one large diamond in a Prairie Star block. The pink diamonds are labeled Fabric 1, the blue diamonds Fabric 2, the gold diamonds Fabric 3, and the green diamonds Fabric 4.

Figure 1

Referring to the diamond quick-piecing instructions, pages 152–155 and Figure 1, sew the strip sets for rows A, B, and C. Cut each strip set into eight 2⅛-inch-wide segments. Piece segments into eight large diamonds.

To make one block: Refer to pages 70–73 for tips on assembling diamonds into a star. Sew the eight large diamonds into a star, placing the pink diamonds to the center.

Refer to pages 72–73 for tips on setting the triangles and squares into a star. Set a white triangle into alternate openings between the diamonds. Set a square into the remaining openings.

To make the quilt top: Piece nine Prairie Star blocks. Sew the blocks together into three rows with three blocks in each row. Join the rows.

To make the borders, sew a white border to both long sides of each of the gold borders. Sew the joined borders to the quilt top, centering borders on each side. Miter the corners; trim excess.

Finishing: To piece the quilt back, cut fabric into two equal lengths. Cut or tear one length in half lengthwise. Sew one narrow panel to each side of the wide panel. Match the selvages; use a ½-inch seam. Trim the seams to ¼ inch; press to one side.

Enlarge the quilting pattern, *opposite.* Transfer the large flower pattern to the large white squares created between star blocks; use half the flower on the large rectangles adjacent to borders. Transfer the feathered circle pattern to small squares; use half of the pattern for the triangles.

Layer the back, batting, and pieced top. Baste layers together; quilt.

Splice the binding strips together at 45-degree angles. Trim, fold in half lengthwise with wrong sides together, and press.

When quilting is complete, trim away excess batting and backing so all edges are even with the quilt top. Sew the binding to the right side of the quilt, raw edges together. Turn the folded edge to the back; hand-stitch in place.

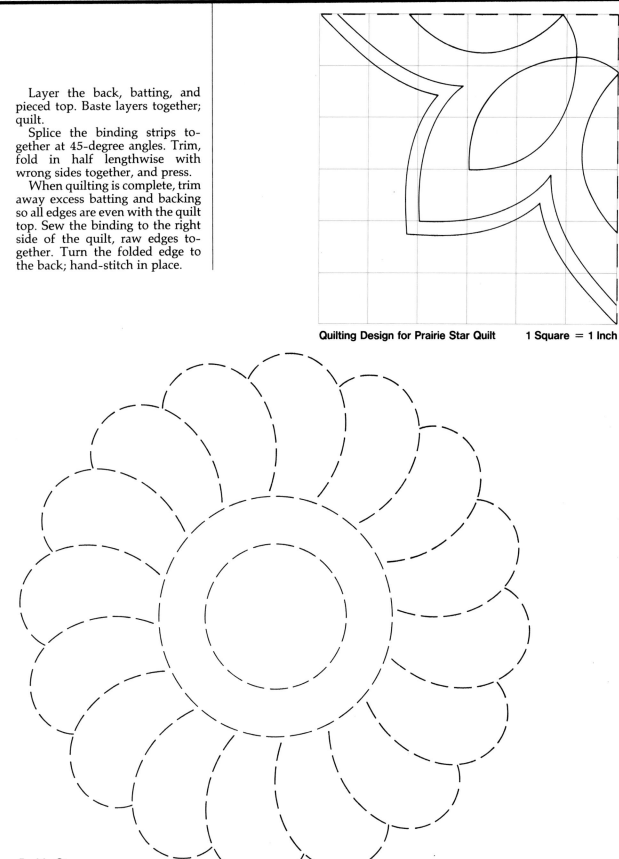

Quilting Design for Prairie Star Quilt   **1 Square = 1 Inch**

**Prairie Star
Quilting Pattern**

Full Size

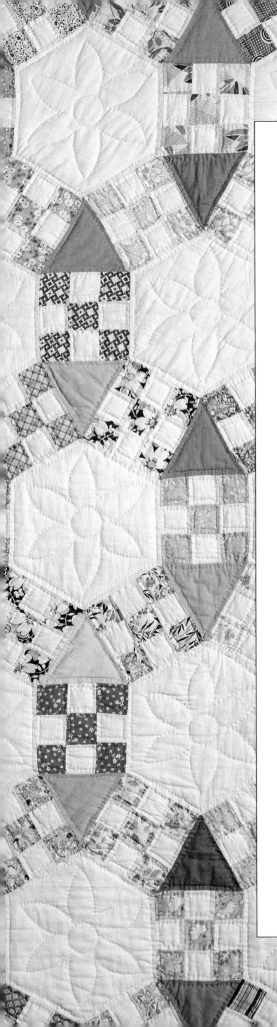

IMAGINATIVE SETS FOR YOUR QUILTS

How you put together all the blocks in a quilt greatly affects the final appearance of the design. In this chapter, you'll explore the different ways of setting a top, and you'll see some beautiful examples of interesting and uncommon sets.

❖ ❖ ❖

**Zigzag sets—beloved by
early quilters—can give
even ordinary patterns an
extraordinary look.**

Of the several ways to create a zigzag (or half-drop) set (including piecing rectangles at right angles between the blocks), joining triangles between the blocks is the easiest. To join the blocks into rows, make right-angle triangles that are half the size of the quilt blocks, turn the blocks on point, and stitch the triangles between the blocks. Fill in the ends of the rows with half-triangles.

The Zigzag Ohio Star Quilt, *opposite,* is an ideal quilt for teaching beginners to create zigzag sets. This popular Variable Star variation is easy to piece and is enhanced by the unusual angles resulting from this set.

The Magic Circle Quilt, *above,* is actually the combination of two quilt set concepts. First, four Bow Tie blocks are pieced into a larger block, so the darker Bow Tie shapes form a ring. Then the blocks are set into zigzag sashings.

Instructions for quilts in this chapter begin on page 180.

171

Not all the design interest in a quilt has to be in the blocks. Try adding pieced work to the ends of the sashing strips to create a small, secondary image on your quilt.

Two popular types of pieced stars fall between the sashing strips of these quilts. One of the star types—for the Carpenter's Wheel Quilt, *below*—is created as a separate block and stitched between the strips, while the stars for the Saint Charles Star Quilt, *opposite,* result from pieced sashing strips and plain blocks.

A lovely pink, rose, and brown color combination is a romantic choice for the Carpenter's Wheel Quilt, *below.* The block for this quilt is made from varying combinations of diamonds and squares. For best results, use ⅛-inch seams for the tiny LeMoyne Star blocks that appear in the sashing.

You'll find many variations of the Saint Charles Star Quilt, *opposite,* but the sashing strips and squares make this one unique. To duplicate this look, make pointed sashing strips and sew a pair of contrasting triangles to each end. Then add sashing squares to match the triangles between the sashing strips.

These two Depression-era quilts demonstrate how unusual quilt sets and the right choice of fabric colors can combine for spectacular results.

Nine-patch blocks joined to equilateral triangles and hexagons form the Jack's Chain Quilt, *below* and on pages 168–169. The hexagons are cut from muslin, and the triangles are cut from bright solids that coordinate with the prints of the nine-patch blocks.

An impressive New York Beauty Quilt, *opposite,* can showcase the many talents of a master quilter. To make the blocks, begin with a muslin square and add pieced arc shapes to each corner. Then piece more points to make the wide, decorative sashing strips, and add sashing squares featuring eight-point stars. Fill the expanse of white in each block with lush feather-quilted arcs and cross-hatched lines.

❖ ❖ ❖

Although both of these quilts feature strong diagonal lines, the methods used to make them vary greatly.

The striking Atlanta Quilt, *opposite,* is made from two alternating pieced blocks. Trim a small triangle off the corners of a large white square and add pieced triangles to each of the remaining long edges of the square. Alternate this block with a 25-patch block that's pieced from squares and triangles.

The interest in the Goose Chase Quilt, *above,* is entirely in the sashing strips, which are pieced in one of the many variations of the Flying Geese pattern. To make a quilt like the one *above,* use sashing strips of five dark triangles between plain blocks and the smaller sashing squares.

You can adapt this idea to incorporate many other pieced patterns to set between plain blocks, such as a pieced checkerboard design or pieced strips. Also consider adding an appliquéd motif to the sashing strips.

Contemporary quilt designers often rely on the combination of simple piecing, unforgettable color combinations, and unusual quilt sets.

The alternating block quilt set, which calls for positioning two kinds of blocks together in checkerboard fashion, always results in a new and intriguing quilt design. These two contemporary designs show different approaches.

Repetition of similar shapes—large squares, small squares, and rectangles—in each of the two blocks makes the Confetti Tablecloth, *below,* a delightful accent. Solid black fabric and a white-on-black pinstripe team with the scrap-bag squares.

To assemble the Contemporary Snowball Wall Hanging, *opposite,* make most of the quilt top from complete blocks of two nine-patch variations. Then add partial blocks along the sides, top, and bottom. Simple quilted squares and diagonal lines complement the lively color scheme.

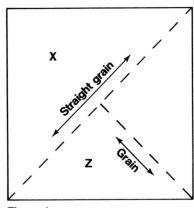

Figure 1

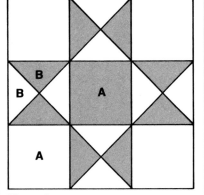

Figure 2

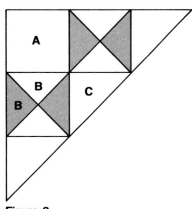

Figure 3

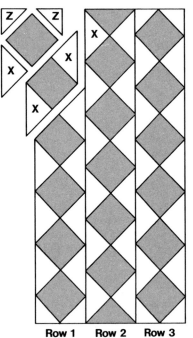

Row 1   Row 2   Row 3

Figure 4

ZIGZAG OHIO STAR QUILT
PAGE 170
Finished block is 9 inches square.
Finished quilt is 62x74 inches.

Materials
2¼ yards of muslin
Assorted blue and gray fabric scraps, totaling about 3 yards
Assorted red and pink solid and print fabric scraps, totaling about 2 yards
1 yard of binding fabric
5 yards of backing fabric
Quilt batting
Cardboard or plastic for templates

Instructions
To make the patterns for the templates, draw two 3-inch squares on graph paper. On one square, draw a diagonal line between opposite corners. Draw a second diagonal line in the *opposite* direction, through the lower section of the square. See Figure 1, *above.*

Make templates of one square (Piece A). Make templates of the small (Piece B) and large (Piece C) right-angle triangles. Mark fabric grain along the long side of the B and C triangles.

For the zigzag setting triangles, draw a 9-inch square on graph paper. Bisect the square as directed in Figure 1. Make templates of the small (Piece Z) and large (Piece X) right-angle triangles. Arrows on triangles indicate grain directions.

Patterns are finished size; add ¼-inch seam allowances when cutting the pieces from fabric.

To cut the pieces: The number of pieces to cut for the entire quilt top is listed first; the number to cut for a single block follows in parentheses.

From blue and gray fabrics, cut:
116 A squares (4)
240 B triangles (8)
8 C triangles

From red and pink fabrics, cut:
28 A squares (1)
240 B triangles (8)
4 C triangles

From muslin, cut:
12 Z triangles
54 X triangles

From binding fabric, cut:
9 yards 2-inch-wide bias strips

To piece one block: Sew a solid B triangle to a print B triangle to make a larger triangle. Sew the pairs together to make a square. Make four squares.

Referring to Figure 2, *above,* place a print A square in center of block. Place a solid A square in each corner and a square pieced from the B triangles between.

Sew the squares into rows; sew the rows together.

Make 28 blocks.

To piece a half-block: Join solid B triangles and print B triangles to make two squares. Referring to Figure 3, *above right,* assemble triangle-squares with one A square and three C triangles.

Make four half-blocks.

To set the quilt top: The blocks are sewn together in five vertical rows. The blocks are set on point and joined with Z and X triangles. See Figure 4, *above right.*

To make the odd rows, join six blocks with 10 X triangles and four Z triangles. Make three odd rows.

To make the even rows, join five blocks with 12 X triangles. Make two even rows.

Sew the rows together, alternating odd and even rows.

Finishing: To piece the quilt back, see finishing instructions for the Magic Circle Quilt, *opposite.*

Mark desired quilting patterns.

Layer the back, batting, and the pieced top. Baste layers together; quilt marked lines. Quilt in the ditch along block seams.

After quilting, trim excess batting and backing. Sew binding to right side of quilt, raw edges together. Turn folded edge to back; hand-stitch in place.

MAGIC CIRCLE QUILT

PAGE 171

Finished block is 8 inches square.
Finished quilt is approximately
71½ x 73½ inches.

Materials

3 yards of pink print fabric
2 yards of assorted navy print
  fabrics
1½ yards of assorted white print
  fabrics (some light blue prints
  are used on the quilt shown)
4½ yards of backing and binding
  fabric
Quilt batting
Cardboard or plastic for templates

Instructions

Trace and make templates for pieces A and B, *right.* Pattern pieces are finished size; add ¼-inch seam allowance before cutting the pieces from the fabric.

Draw an 8-inch square on graph paper. Divide the square as shown in Figure 1, *opposite, above left.* The arrows on the diagram indicate the fabric grain for the triangle patterns. Make templates for the X and Z triangles.

To cut the pieces: The number of pieces to cut for the entire quilt is listed first; the number to cut for one block follows in parentheses. The borders include seam allowances and are longer than is needed; trim to length when adding to the quilt top.

From pink print fabric, cut:
2 borders, each 2½x77 inches
2 borders, each 3½x71 inches
66 X triangles with the long sides
  on the fabric grain
12 Z triangles with the short sides
  on the fabric grain

From white print fabrics, cut:
312 B pieces (8)

From navy print fabrics, cut:
312 B pieces (8)
156 A pieces (4)

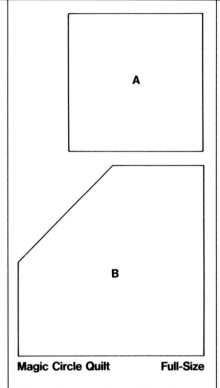

Magic Circle Quilt **Full-Size**

To make one block: Each Magic Circle block is made of four small bow tie units. Referring to Figure 5, *above right,* sew a navy print B piece onto opposite sides of an A square to make a bow tie. Set a white print B piece into each side of the bow tie to form a square.

Make four bow tie units. Sew the units together so the bow ties form a circle as shown in Figure 5. Make 39 Magic Circle blocks.

To set the quilt top: The blocks are sewn together in six vertical rows. The blocks are set on point and joined with X and Z triangles.

To make the half-blocks for the even rows, draw a line on the wrong side of the block diagonally through the block. Adding ¼ inch for seam allowances, cut the block in half. Discard the portion that does not include seam allowances. Cut six half-blocks.

To make the even rows, refer to Figure 4, *opposite.* Join five blocks and two half-blocks with 12 X triangles. Make three even rows.

To make the odd rows, join six blocks with 10 X triangles and four Z triangles. Make three odd rows.

Sew the rows together, alternating odd and even rows.

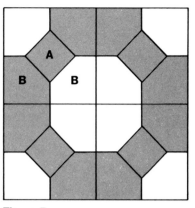

Figure 5

Sew the 3-inch-wide borders to the top and bottom of the quilt; trim. Sew the 2-inch-wide borders to the sides of the quilt; trim.

Finishing: Divide the backing fabric into two equal lengths. Split one panel in half lengthwise. Sew a split panel to each side of the full panel.

Layer and baste together the quilt top, batting, and backing. Quilt as desired.

When quilting is complete, trim the batting one inch larger all around than the quilt top. Trim the quilt back 1½ inches larger all around than the batting.

Turn the quilt back in ½ inch; then, fold the quilt back over to the front. Stitch the quilt back to the quilt top, covering the raw edge of the quilt top.

CARPENTER'S WHEEL QUILT

PAGE 172

Finished block is 13 inches square.
Finished quilt is 70x86 inches.

Materials

3 yards of muslin
1¼ yards of pink fabric
Small amounts of various brown
  prints, totaling about 4½ yards
¾ yards of dark brown fabric
2¾ yards of pink ticking stripe
  fabric
5 yards of backing fabric
Quilt batting
9 yards of pink 2½-inch-wide
  bias binding
Cardboard or plastic for templates

(Continued)

181

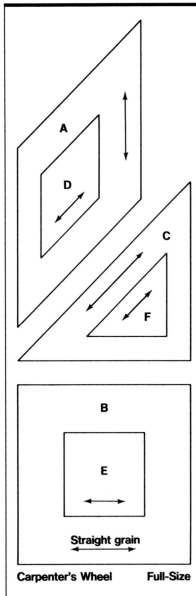

Carpenter's Wheel   Full-Size

Instructions

Trace and make templates for the patterns, *above.* Patterns are finished size. Add ¼-inch seam allowances to pieces A, B, and C when cutting the pieces from the fabric. Add ⅛-inch seam allowances to pieces D, E, and F.

To cut the pieces: The number of pieces to cut for the entire quilt top is listed first; the number to cut for a single block follows in parentheses.

Cut C triangles with the long side on the straight grain. Take care to avoid stretching the A diamonds—two sides are cut on the bias and two are on the straight grain. The neat appearance of the

pink ticking stripe sashing and border pieces relies on cutting the stripes parallel to the strip edges. Measurements for borders and sashing strips include ¼-inch seam allowances.

From pink fabric, cut:
160 A diamonds (8)

From brown prints, cut:
480 A diamonds (24)

From light brown fabric, cut:
80 B squares (4)
104 D diamonds (4)

From dark brown fabric, cut:
104 D diamonds (4)

From muslin, cut:
320 B squares (16)
160 C triangles (8)
104 E squares (4)
104 F triangles (4)

From pink ticking stripe on straight grain, cut:
2 borders, each 5x89 inches
9 sashing strips, each 3½x13½ inches
6 sashing strips, each 3½x10½ inches

From pink ticking stripe across the grain, cut:
4 borders, each 5x32 inches
8 sashing strips, each 3½x13½ inches
8 sashing strips, each 3½x10½ inches

To piece one block: *Note:* When joining and setting in pieces for this block, stitch only from seam allowance to seam allowance, not from edge to edge.

Join two pink print A diamonds. Make four pairs. Sew two pairs together to make a half-star; sew the two halves together to complete the star.

Set in a muslin B square between the points.

To add the brown print A diamonds, sew three A diamonds together. Make eight sets. Set each three-diamond group along the outer edges of the muslin B squares—the inner tip of the cen-

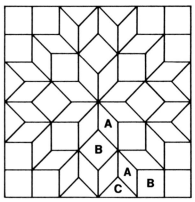

Figure 1

ter brown diamond will touch the pink print diamond of the central star. After all of the groups have been joined to the B squares, join the adjacent edges of the brown print diamonds.

To add the C triangles, set in one C triangle between the points of two brown print A diamonds. Then set in another triangle between the next two points. Skip the spaces between the next two points. Then set in two more C triangles between the following two points. Continue around the block in this fashion until all eight C triangles are set in. The long edges of the C triangles will form the straight sides of the block.

To complete the block, join two muslin B squares and one light brown B square in an L shape, with the light brown square in the corner. Make four sets. Aligning the inner edges of the muslin squares with the brown print diamond points, set a three-square group into each corner of the block.

See Figure 1, *above.*
Make 20 blocks.

To make the sashing squares: Assemble sashing squares as for quilt blocks, stitching only in seam allowances.

Sew a light brown D diamond to a dark brown D diamond. Make four sets with colors in same position. Assemble diamond pairs into a star as for center pink star of block. Set in E and F pieces alternately between points of star to complete sashing square. Make 26 sashing squares. Finished size of sashing square is 3 inches.

To make the quilt top: Sew a sashing square to one end of each 10½-inch-long sashing strip. Sew the blocks, sashing strips, and sashing squares into rows. Sew the rows together. Finished size of quilt top is 61x77 inches.

To add the borders: Center and sew pairs of 5x32-inch border pieces together along short edges to make two 5x63-inch border strips. Stitch a border strip to top and bottom edges of quilt top; trim edges even.

Stitch remaining borders to sides of quilt top and to ends of top and bottom borders; trim edges even.

Finishing: To piece the quilt back, cut fabric into two equal lengths. Cut or tear one length in half lengthwise. Sew one narrow panel to each side of the wide panel. Match the selvages; use a ½-inch seam. Trim the seams to ¼ inch; press to one side.

Layer back, batting, and top; baste together. Outline-quilt around block pieces. Quilt sashing and borders as desired.

After quilting, trim batting and backing even with quilt top. Press binding in half lengthwise, right sides together. Sew binding to right side of quilt, raw edges together. Turn folded edge to back; hand-stitch in place.

❖

SAINT CHARLES STAR QUILT
PAGE 173
Finished block is 13 inches square.
Finished quilt is 86x86 inches.

Materials
3¾ yards *each* of medium blue and beige fabrics
2 yards of white fabric
Approximately 2 yards of assorted blue print fabrics
5 yards of backing fabric
¾ yard of binding fabric
Quilt batting
Cardboard or plastic for templates

(Continued)

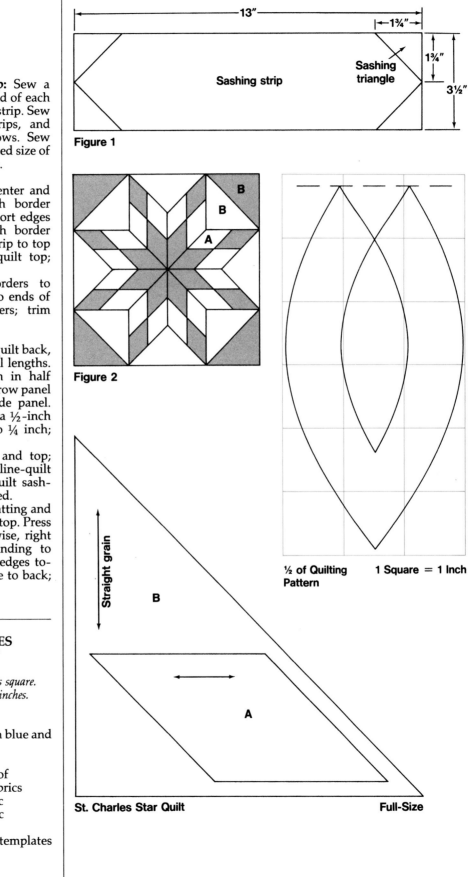

Figure 1

Figure 2

½ of Quilting Pattern   1 Square = 1 Inch

Straight grain

B

A

St. Charles Star Quilt   Full-Size

Instructions

Trace and make templates for pattern pieces A and B, page 183.

To make the pattern for the sashing strips and the sashing triangles, draw a 3½x13-inch rectangle on graph paper. Referring to Figure 1, page 183, mark 1¾-inch triangles at the ends of the strip. The long, pointed piece is the sashing strip; one right-angle triangle (with 1¾-inch short legs) is a sashing triangle.

Draw a 3½-inch square on graph paper to make the pattern for the sashing squares.

Make templates for sashing strips, triangles, and squares.

All pattern pieces are finished size; add ¼-inch seam allowances before cutting the pieces from fabric.

To cut the pieces: The number of pieces to cut for the entire quilt is listed first; the number to cut for one block follows in parentheses.

From blue fabric, cut:
60 sashing strips
100 triangles from Template B, with the long sides of the triangle on the fabric grain (4)

From beige fabric, cut:
200 triangles from Template B, with the long sides of the triangle on the fabric grain (8)
240 sashing triangles, with the short sides of the triangle on the fabric grain
36 sashing squares

From white fabric, cut:
400 A diamonds (16)

From blue prints, cut:
400 A diamonds (16)

From binding fabric, cut:
10 yards 2½-inch-wide bias

To piece one block: Referring to Figure 2, page 183, piece two of the white diamonds and two of the blue print diamonds into a larger diamond. Make eight of the large diamonds.

Sew pairs of large diamonds together; join pairs to form star halves. Join star halves.

Set a beige B triangle into the openings between diamond points. Sew a blue B triangle to alternate beige B triangle, matching long sides to form a square.

Make 25 blocks.

To piece the sashing rectangles: Referring to Figure 1, sew pairs of sashing triangles onto each pointed end of a sashing strip to form a rectangle.

Make a total of 60 pieced sashing rectangles.

To make the quilt top: To make one row of blocks, sew together five blocks, with sashing rectangles between the blocks and at the ends of the row. Make five rows with five blocks in each row.

To make one row of sashing rectangles and squares, sew together five sashing rectangles with a sashing square between each rectangle and at the ends of the row. Make six rows.

Beginning and ending with a sashing rectangle/square row, alternate rows of blocks with rows of sashing squares. Sew the rows together.

Finishing: To piece the quilt back, cut fabric into two equal lengths. Cut or tear one length in half lengthwise. Sew one narrow panel to each side of the wide panel. Match the selvages; use a ½-inch seam. Trim the seams to ¼ inch; press to one side.

Enlarge the cable quilting pattern, page 183, and transfer to sashing rectangles.

Layer the back, batting, and the pieced top. Baste layers together. Quilt cables; quilt remaining areas as desired.

When quilting is complete, trim excess batting and backing even with quilt top.

Cut 2½-inch-wide strips of bias for binding. Piece binding strips at 45-degree angles; fold in half lengthwise, wrong sides together, and press. Sew binding to right side of quilt, raw edges together. Turn folded edge to back; hand-stitch in place.

❖

JACK'S CHAIN QUILT
PAGES 168–169 and 174
Finished nine-patch block is 4 inches square.
Finished quilt is 81x91 inches.

Materials

6 yards of muslin
Assorted fabric scraps for nine-patch blocks, totaling about 3¾ yards
Assorted solid fabrics for setting triangles, totaling about 1½ yards
3 yards of 90-inch-wide muslin quilt backing fabric, *or* yardage to piece quilt back
15 yards of 1¼-inch-wide bias-cut binding
Quilt batting
Cardboard or plastic for templates

Instructions

Trace and make templates for pieces B and C, *opposite.* For pattern for Piece A, trace and repeat six B triangles to form a hexagon; see Figure 1, *opposite.* Then bisect A hexagon and make a template for a half-hexagon. Patterns are full-size; add ¼-inch seam allowances when cutting pieces from fabric.

To cut the pieces: The number of pieces to cut for the entire quilt is listed first; the number to cut for one block follows in parentheses.

From muslin, cut:
59 A hexagons
8 half-hexagons
832 C squares (4)

From solid fabrics, cut:
150 B triangles

From print scraps, cut:
1,040 C squares (5)

To piece nine-patch block: Gather five matching print C squares and four muslin C squares. Make a 3x3-square block, alternating fabrics in checkerboard fashion. Stitch squares into rows; stitch rows together.

Make 208 nine-patch blocks.

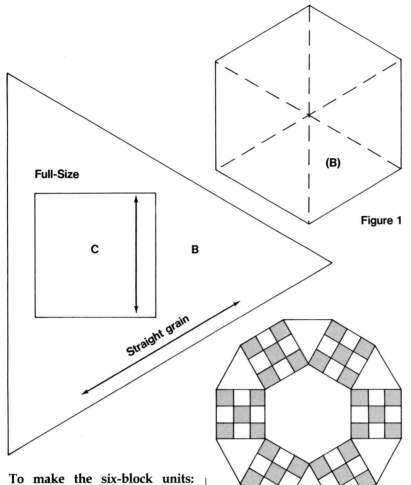

Full-Size

C   B

Straight grain

Figure 1

(B)

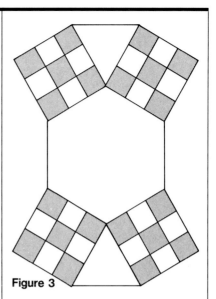

Figure 2

Figure 3

To make the six-block units:
Gather six nine-patch blocks, one A hexagon, and six B triangles. *Note:* Hereafter, when joining elements, stitch only along the seam allowance, not from edge to edge.

Referring to Figure 2, *above,* join a side of each block to a side of the hexagon. Set in the B triangles between each nine-patch block.

Make 20 six-block units.

To make the four-block units:
Gather four nine-patch blocks, one A hexagon, and two B triangles. Referring to Figure 3, *above*

right, join a block to two sides of a B triangle; make two of these sets. Stitch these groups to opposite sides of the hexagon.

Make 15 four-block units.

To make the quilt top: Refer to Figure 4, *below.* To make the odd rows, alternate four six-block units with three four-block units.

Stitch together. Make five odd rows.

To make the even rows, alternate seven nine-patch blocks with six A hexagons. Stitch together. Placing the wide edge of the half-hexagon at the outside edge, stitch a half-hexagon to the nine-patch block at each end of the row. Make four even rows.

Stitch the rows together.

Finishing: Mark top for quilting, using patterns desired.

Piece quilt back, if necessary, and layer backing, batting, and quilt top. Baste layers together.

Quilt the nine-patch blocks in the ditch. Quilt the designs.

When quilting is complete, trim away excess batting and backing so that all edges are even with the quilt top. Sew the binding to the right side of the quilt, raw edges together. Turn under unsewn edge of binding ¼ inch. Turn the folded edge to the back; hand-stitch in place.

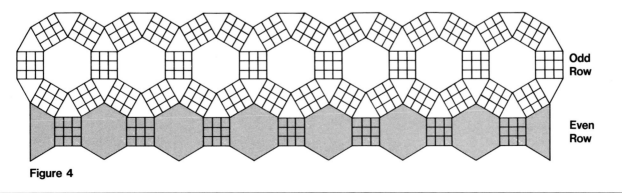

Odd Row

Even Row

Figure 4

❖

NEW YORK BEAUTY QUILT
PAGE 175

Finished block is 16¼ inches square.
Finished quilt is 70¾ x 92½ inches.
Sashing is 5½ inches wide.

Materials

7¼ yards of white fabric
3½ yards of green fabric
3 yards of lavender fabric
6 yards of backing fabric
Quilt batting
Cardboard or plastic for templates

Instructions

To make pattern for Piece A, draw a 16¼-inch square on graph paper. Setting a compass radius at 5 inches, place point in corner of square; swing arc to sides. Repeat at each corner. Cut away quarter-circles in each corner for pattern.

To make a pattern for Piece E, draw a 2¼ x16¼-inch rectangle on graph paper.

Make template of the A and E pieces.

Trace and make templates for pattern pieces, *right.* Patterns are full-size; add ¼-inch seam allowances when cutting the pieces from fabric. (*Note:* Because there are so many small pieces, and accurate cutting is essential, we recommend using plastic template material.)

Take care to transfer the dots on curved pattern pieces.

To cut the pieces: The number of pieces to cut for the entire quilt is listed first; the number to cut for one block follows in parentheses.

From white fabric, cut:
12 A pieces (1)
80 H triangles (4)
80 I squares (4)
806 F sashing triangles (26)
288 D curved triangles (6)
48 DD pieces (4)
48 DD pieces, reversed (4)

From green fabric, cut:
744 F triangles (24)
62 FF triangles (2)
62 FF triangles, reversed (2)

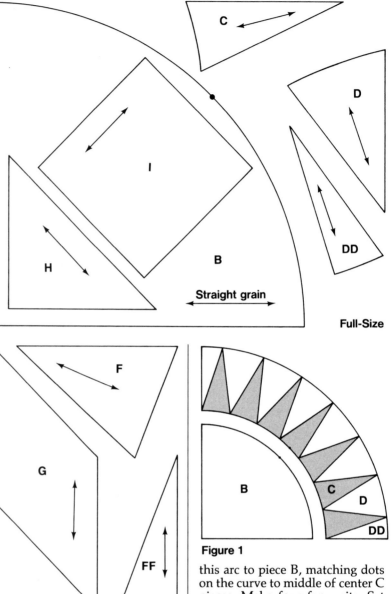

Straight grain

Full-Size

New York Beauty Quilt

336 C pieces (28)
10½ yards of 2½-inch-wide bias binding

From lavender fabric, cut:
31 E strips (1)
48 B quarter-circles (4)
160 G diamonds (8)

To piece one block: Referring to Figure 1, *above right,* piece seven green C triangles and 6 white D triangles together to form an arc. Sew a DD and a reversed DD piece to each end of the arcs. Ease

Figure 1

this arc to piece B, matching dots on the curve to middle of center C pieces. Make four fan units. Set the fans into piece A, matching dots to point of center C pieces and easing fullness at the curve.

Make 12 blocks.

To piece the sashing strips: Referring to Figure 2, *opposite,* alternate 13 white F triangles and 12 green F triangles; stitch together along long sides to form a strip. Stitch an FF and a reversed FF piece to each end of the strip. Make two strips.

Stitch a strip to each long side of the E rectangle, with green triangles adjacent to the lavender rectangle.

Make 31 sashing strips.

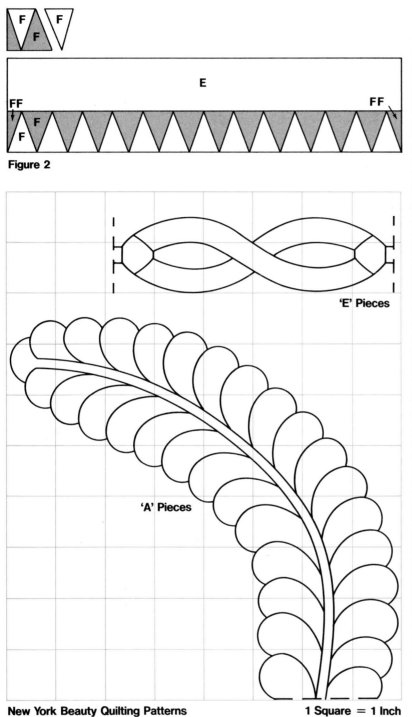

Figure 2

'E' Pieces

'A' Pieces

New York Beauty Quilting Patterns

1 Square = 1 Inch

Finishing: Enlarge the quilting patterns, *left,* and transfer to the A and E pieces.

Fill in center of A pieces and B pieces with a grid of ¾-inch squares.

Layer the backing, batting, and top; baste together. Quilt marked designs and outline-quilt ¼ inch from seams.

To piece the backing, divide the fabric into two equal lengths. Cut or tear one length in half lengthwise. Sew one narrow panel to each side of the wide panel. Match the selvages; use a ½-inch seam. Trim the seams to ¼ inch; press to one side.

Trim away excess batting and backing so that all edges are even with the quilt top. Piece binding strips together at 45 degrees. Fold in half lengthwise, wrong sides facing, and press. Sew the binding to the right side of the quilt, raw edges together. Turn the folded edge to the back; hand-stitch in place.

❖

GOOSE CHASE QUILT
PAGE 177
Finished quilt is approximately 69x74 inches.

Materials
3 yards of white and black print fabric
3 yards of muslin
½ yard of rust plaid fabric
Approximately 2 yards of assorted rust, tan, green, and brown print fabrics
4½ yards of backing fabric
Cardboard or plastic for templates
Quilt batting

Instructions
This Goose Chase Quilt is not sewn in pieced blocks like most quilts. The blocks actually are large, unpieced squares set on point. The illusion of pieced blocks is created by the pieced sashing strips that run diagonally across the quilt top between the squares.

(Continued)

To piece the star blocks: Join eight G diamonds to form a star. Set in H triangles and I squares to make a square.

Make 20 corner blocks.

To make the quilt top: Arrange the quilt blocks in four rows of three blocks. Place a sashing strip between each block and along outer edges. Place a star block at the ends of each sashing strip.

Sew the units into rows; sew the rows together.

187

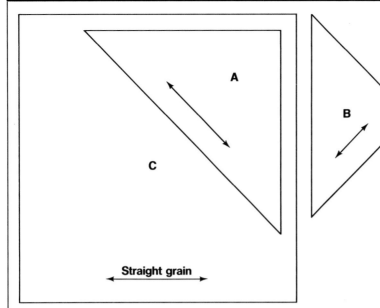

Goose Chase Quilt

Full-Size

To make patterns for the large squares and triangles, draw a 7½-inch square on graph paper. Make a template for the square. Draw a diagonal line to divide the square into two triangles. Make a template for the triangle.

Trace and make templates for the patterns *above*. Patterns are finished size; add ¼-inch seam allowances when cutting the pieces from the fabric. Border measurements include seam allowances and are longer than is needed.

To cut the pieces: The number of pieces to cut for the entire quilt is listed first; the number to cut for one rectangular unit follows in parentheses.

From the white and black print fabric, cut:
2 borders, each 5½x62 inches
2 borders, each 5½x77 inches
31 large squares
18 large triangles (cut with long side on the fabric grain)

From muslin, cut:
800 triangles from Template B (10)
20 squares from Template C
8½ yards of 2½-inch-wide strips for binding

From the rust plaid fabric, cut:
26 squares from Template C
4 triangles from Template A (cut with the *short* sides on the fabric grain)

Figure 1

From assorted print fabrics, cut:
400 triangles from Template A (5)

To piece one sashing strip: Sew a B triangle to the short sides of an A triangle to form a rectangle (referred to as a goose). Make five geese.

Referring to the rectangular sashing strip enclosed by a heavy line in Figure 1, *above*, sew together five geese, with the geese all heading the same direction.

Piece 80 sashing strips.

To make the quilt top: Referring to Figure 1, *above*, lay out the sashing strips to form "blocks." Lay out five rows of "blocks" with four "blocks" in each row.

Place a muslin C square in the center of each "block." Place a rust plaid C square between the

sashing strips so the muslin and rust plaid squares alternate between the strips. Place the remaining rust plaid C squares at the ends of the strips around the outer edge of the quilt top. These outer C squares will be trimmed to triangles when the borders are added. Place a rust plaid A triangle at the four corners of the quilt top.

Fill in the openings around the perimeter with white and black print triangles. Fill in the square openings between strips with white and black print squares.

Join the pieces in diagonal rows. Beginning in the lower left corner, sew the rust plaid A triangle to the end of the sashing strip. Sew a white and black print triangle to each side of the sashing strip to make the first row.

To make the second row, sew together a rust plaid C square, a sashing strip, a muslin C square, a sashing strip, and a rust plaid C square. Continue until all pieces are joined in diagonal rows; join the rows.

To square up side edges, draw a line on wrong side of fabric diagonally through the outer rust C squares. *Adding ¼-inch seam allowances,* trim excess squares.

Stitch shorter borders to the quilt top and bottom edges; trim excess. Stitch the remaining border pieces to the sides; trim.

Finishing: To piece quilt back, cut fabric into two equal lengths. Cut or tear one length in half lengthwise. Sew one narrow panel to each side of wide panel. Match selvages; use a ½-inch seam. Trim seams to ¼ inch; press to one side.

Layer the back, batting, and the pieced top. Baste layers together; quilt as desired.

When quilting is complete, trim away excess batting and backing even with quilt top.

For binding, piece strips together. Fold binding in half lengthwise, wrong sides together. Stitch to right side of quilt top with raw edges even with edge of quilt. Turn folded edge to quilt back and hand-stitch in place.

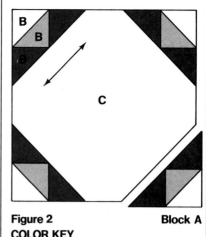

Figure 2   **Block A**

COLOR KEY
☐ **Muslin**
■ **Red**
▨ **Teal**

ATLANTA QUILT
PAGE 176
Finished block is 8¾ inches square.
Finished quilt is 69¼ x 86¾ inches.

Materials
5 yards of muslin
2⅝ yards of red fabric
2⅓ yards of teal fabric
5¼ yards of fabric (backing and
    self-binding)
Quilt batting
Plastic or cardboard for templates

Instructions
To make the patterns for the A
and B pieces, draw two 1¾-inch
squares on graph paper. Bisect
one of the squares diagonally. The
square is Piece A; one of the triangles is Piece B.

Make templates for all pieces.
Mark short sides of B triangle for
fabric grain. Patterns A and B are
finished size; add ¼-inch seam
allowances when cutting the
pieces from fabric.

To make the pattern for Piece
C, draw an 8-inch square on
graph paper. Trace the trimming
triangle, *below.*

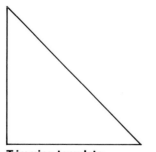

Trimming template
(Seams included)

To cut the pieces: The number of
pieces to cut for the entire quilt is
listed first; the number to cut for
one block follows in parentheses.
Border measurements include
seam allowances and are longer
than needed; trim to length when
adding to the quilt top.

From muslin, cut:
2 borders, each 2½x82 inches
2 borders, each 2½x71 inches
32 C squares (1 for Block A)
376 B triangles (4 for Block A
    and 8 for Block B)
124 A squares (4 for Block B)

From teal fabric, cut:
2 borders, each 2½x82 inches
2 borders, each 2½x71 inches
376 B triangles (4 for Block A
    and 8 for Block B)

From red fabric, cut:
403 A squares (13 for Block B)
256 B triangles (8 for Block A)

To make the C octagons: Referring to Figure 1, *below,* use the triangular trimming template to cut
a triangle off the corners of the C
squares to make the C octagons.
Do not add seam allowances
when using the trimming template; the template pattern allows
for seam allowance.
    Make 32 C pieces.

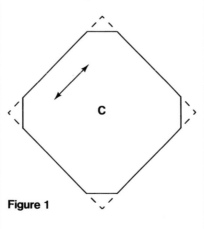

Figure 1

To piece the A blocks: Sew four
teal B triangles to four muslin B
triangles along the long sides to
make four squares. Referring to
Figure 2, *above right,* sew two red A
triangles to each side of the teal
and muslin squares to form a triangle; make four pieced triangles.
Sew a pieced triangle to each long
(on the straight of grain) side of a
C octagon.
    Make 32 A blocks.

To piece the B blocks: Sew eight
teal B triangles to eight muslin B
triangles along the long sides to
make eight squares. Referring to
Figure 3, *below,* sew red and muslin
A squares and squares made from
teal and muslin triangles into five
horizontal rows. Join the rows to
complete the block.
    Make 31 B blocks.

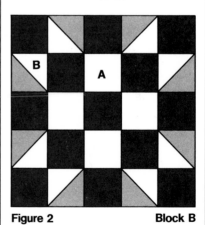

Figure 2   **Block B**

To set the quilt top: Alternating
A blocks and B blocks, sew the
blocks together in nine horizontal
rows with seven blocks in each
row.

Sew matching-length teal and
white borders together lengthwise
into pairs. Sew the longer border
pairs to the quilt sides; trim. Sew
the shorter pairs to the top and
bottom of the quilt; trim.

(Continued)

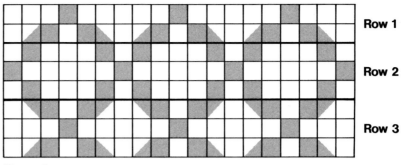

Figure 1

Finishing: To piece the quilt back, cut fabric into two equal lengths. Cut or tear one length in half lengthwise. Sew one narrow panel to each side of the wide panel. Match the selvages; use a ½-inch seam. Trim the seams to ¼ inch; press to one side.

Layer the back, batting, and the pieced top. Baste layers together; quilt as desired.

When quilting is complete, trim batting even with quilt top. To finish the edges with a self-binding, trim the quilt back ½ inch larger than the quilt top on all sides. Turn in ¼ inch on the quilt back. Turn folded edges of the quilt back over to the quilt top, covering the raw edge. Blindstitch the folded edge in place.

❖

CONTEMPORARY SNOWBALL WALL QUILT
PAGE 179
Finished block is 6 inches square.
Finished quilt is 51½x63½ inches.

Materials
Various shades of blue, blue-green, and green fabrics, totaling about 2 yards
Various shades of white and off-white fabrics, totaling about 1½ yards
54x20-inch piece of white *or* off-white fabric (borders)
4 yards backing fabric
Quilt batting
Cardboard or plastic for templates

Instructions
To make the patterns, draw a 2-inch square. Cut out a template. Divide the square in half with a diagonal line. Cut out a template of one right-angle triangle. These patterns are finished size; add ¼-inch seam allowances when cutting the pieces from fabric.

To plan the quilt top: To devise the color scheme for the inner quilt top, refer to Figure 1, *above* (which represents the first three rows of the quilt); draw the complete inner quilt top on graph pa-per. Alternating rows 2 and 3, draw Row 2 for a total of four times and Row 3 for a total of three times, ending with the reverse of Row 1 to complete the bottom.

Referring to photograph, page 179, tape or pin a snippet of blue, blue-green, or green fabric to each shaded piece. Use this scheme for piecing the quilt top.

To cut the pieces: The number of pieces to cut for the entire quilt top is listed first with the number to cut for a single block following in parentheses.

Border measurements include seam allowances and are longer than is needed; trim away excess after stitching to the quilt top.

From border fabric, cut:
4 borders, each 4¾x52 inches

From white and off-white fabrics, cut:
252 squares (4 for Block A and 5 for Block B)
96 triangles (4 for Block B)

From various blue, blue-green, and green fabrics, cut:
127 squares (5 for Block A)
96 triangles (4 for Block B)
1½-inch-wide strips (inner border)
3½-inch-wide strips (binding)

To piece the blocks: Using ¼-inch seams, stitch a colored triangle to a light triangle along long sides. Repeat to make 96 triangle-squares. Press seams toward darker fabric.

Referring to piecing diagrams for Block A and Block B, select combinations of colors according to master pattern. For each whole block, sew three squares (or triangle-squares) together to form a

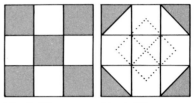

Block 'A'   Block 'B'

row; sew three rows together. Make 17 A blocks and 18 B blocks. Repeat to make 14 partial A blocks, 10 partial B blocks, and 4 corner blocks.

To make the quilt top: Referring to your master pattern, stitch the quilt top into rows; stitch the rows together.

For inner border, stitch 1½-inch-wide strips together. Vary the length of each strip and add short lengths of contrasting colors as accents. Make each strip slightly longer than the adjacent side, and trim after stitching. Sew inner borders to sides of quilt; trim. Sew inner borders to top and bottom of quilt and to ends of side inner borders; trim.

Sew white borders to sides of quilt; trim. Sew remaining white borders to top and bottom and to ends of side borders; trim.

Finishing: Mark the quilting design as indicated with blue lines on the piecing diagram.

Piece the quilt back. Layer backing, batting, and quilt top; baste.

Quilt Block A in two diagonal lines from corners to corners and in the ditch along each block. Quilt Block B as marked and in the ditch along triangle-square seams.

Quilt border as desired.

Trim batting and backing 1 inch past white borders.

For binding, piece four lengths of 3½-inch-wide fabrics, each piece slightly longer than a side of the quilt. With right sides facing, and matching raw edges, stitch binding to right side of quilt. Fold binding to back side; trim excess length. Fold under raw edge ¼ inch and slip-stitch in place. Repeat for opposite border. Repeat for top and bottom binding, turning under raw edges at ends.

❖

CONFETTI TABLECLOTH
PAGES 169 and 178
Finished block is 5 inches square.
Finished tablecloth is 58½ x 58½ inches.

Materials
Fabric scraps in various shades of reds, oranges, yellows, greens, blues, and violets
⅔ yard black fabric
1½ yards white-on-black pinstripe fabric
½ yard red fabric
⅓ yard blue fabric
3½ yards backing fabric
3½ yards flannel
Cardboard or plastic for templates

Instructions
Draw pattern pieces on graph paper first, then cut out templates. Draw a 2-inch square (Piece A), a 1-inch square (Piece B), a 3-inch square (Piece C), a 2x1-inch rectangle (Piece D), and a 3x1-inch rectangle (Piece E). Patterns are finished size; add ¼-inch seam allowances before cutting the pieces from fabric.

To cut the pieces: The number of pieces to cut for the entire tablecloth is listed first; the number to cut for one block follows in parentheses. Measurements for borders and binding include ¼-inch seam allowances.

From greens, blues, and purples, cut:
244 A squares (4 for A block)

From reds, oranges, and yellows, cut:
301 B squares (1 for A block and 4 for B block)

From black fabric, cut:
60 C squares (1 for B block)

From pinstripe fabric, cut:
244 D rectangles (4 for A block)
240 E rectangles (4 for B block)
(*Note:* Cut pinstripe pieces with the stripes parallel to the short sides of the rectangles.)

From blue fabric, cut:
6 strips, each 1¼ x45 inches across the fabric width (border)

From red fabric, cut:
6 strips, each 2½ x45 inches across the fabric width (binding)

To piece the blocks: For each A block, gather one B square, four A squares, and four D rectangles. For each B block, gather one C square, four B squares, and four E rectangles.

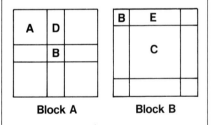

Block A   **Block B**

Referring to Figure 1, *above,* and using ¼-inch seams, assemble blocks. To assemble either block, stitch the pieces into rows and then stitch the rows together.

Make 61 A Blocks and 60 B blocks.

Note: To duplicate the look of the tablecloth shown, make A blocks using four squares in colors from the same family. For example, divide the A pieces into

groups of blue, blue-green, green, turquoise, blue-violet, and violet; assemble the block using four squares from any one group. For B blocks, use bright yellow squares sparingly; distribute these evenly across tablecloth during assembly.

To piece the top: Lay the blocks out on the floor in 11 rows of 11 blocks, alternating A blocks and B blocks and placing an A block in each corner. Reposition the squares, if necessary, until you have a pleasing arrangement.

Sew the squares into rows; sew the rows together.

To add the border: Cut two of the blue strips in half. Stitch the short ends of a long and a short blue strip together to form borders; make four. Stitch a border to opposite sides of the tablecloth top; trim ends. Stitch remaining strips to remaining sides of tablecloth top and to ends of first borders; trim.

Finishing: To piece the backing, divide fabric into two equal lengths. Cut or tear one length in half lengthwise. Sew one narrow panel to each side of the wide panel. Match the selvages; use a ½-inch seam. Trim the seams to ¼ inch; press to one side.

Repeat with the flannel.

Layer backing, flannel, and tablecloth top; baste layers together. Tack layers together at corners of each block.

Trim flannel and backing 1 inch beyond tablecloth top.

Cut and piece red binding strips together as for borders. With wrong sides together, press in half lengthwise. With right sides together, and matching raw edges, stitch one binding strip to edge of border; trim excess. Fold binding to wrong side and hand-stitch in place. Repeat for opposite side. Repeat for remaining two sides, stitching ends of binding to raw edges of borders.

ROMANTIC DESIGNS
FOR PERSONAL STYLE

Creating a
patchwork design that both reflects
the quilting tradition and exhibits
a touch of individuality is one
challenge that intrigues today's
quilters. The projects in this
chapter are based on time-honored
designs that invite adaptation.

**The lovely patterns—both
appliquéd and quilted—of this
Rose Quilt are great sources for
new designs. Turn the page to see
our adaptations of the Rose
appliqué design and the feathered
circle and floral quilting patterns.**

Although the block of the Rose Quilt, *opposite,* is flat appliqué, some of its design elements give it dimension and vitality. The large four-petaled rose in the center of the block is accented with a circle and two rings of bias tape. And each block is set on point so that the roses are in a more natural position.

This quilt, as with many antique quilts of similar age, is ideal for today's twin-size beds. However, if you'd like to adjust the size of this quilt—or any small quilt in this book—you'll need to take a few basic steps.

First, determine the quilt's ideal finished size. Measure your bed or the bedcovers you already have, or look at the sizes of coverlets and bedspreads as listed in a catalog or at a store. Then, divide the width and length measurements of the quilt by the dimensions of the quilt block. Allowing for borders or other elements, plan the new quilt top according to the number of blocks that will fit. In the case of quilt blocks set on point, as with this quilt, draw a quilt block on paper and measure from one corner to another corner for the width and length of the block.

Instructions begin on page 206.

❖ ❖ ❖

The charming appliqué designs and classic quilting patterns from the Rose Quilt shown on the preceding pages appear on these delicate accessories.

Perfect for protecting a treasured dress, the floral appliquéd garment bags, *opposite,* are also showcases for an appliquér's talents. These bags are ingeniously constructed and can be made in full or half lengths. Special touches include eyelet lace trim and fabric ties.

A single flower bud, executed in cross-stitch, decorates the pincushion, *above right.* It's a fun scrap project you can complete in one evening.

The jewelry case, *above right,* is a practical accessory for a lady who travels. The elegant feathered circle quilting motif from the plain blocks of the Rose Quilt is a classic pattern you'll want to use for many quilting projects.

Another equally versatile quilting pattern is used for the chair seat, *below right.* This motif—without the quilted grid in each petal—is used to outline the appliqué motifs on the Rose Quilt.

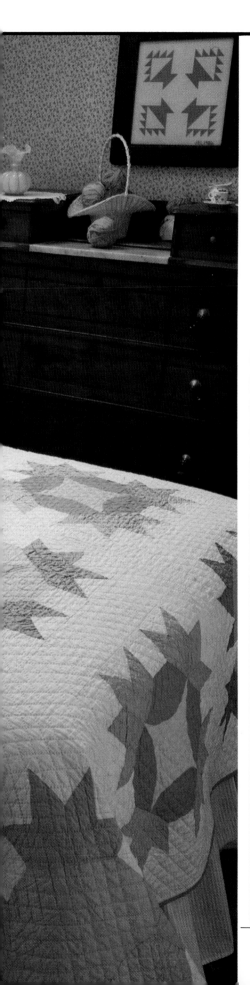

❖ ❖ ❖

Selecting and using just the right colors for quilting can turn an ordinary design into an inspired piece of patchwork. Here are two spectacular examples of how fabric choice can make the difference.

Marked by the contrast of crisp points and gentle curves, the Hands All Around Quilt, *opposite,* is a striking design that benefits from thoughtful interpretation. Here, the quilter chose bright, clear colors, perhaps inspired by a bouquet of summer flowers. And because there are no print fabrics used, and the quilting is just an allover grid pattern, the lack of detail only emphasizes the pieced shapes.

Note the similar color combination used for the Stanley's Squares Wall Quilt, *above.* A group of 25 nine-patch blocks, which are set on point, make up the quilt top. Because each patch is small, and the center patch of each block is a distinctive fabric, the quilt top contains many surprising accents.

The popularity of crazy patchwork—the ultimate scrap craft—never seems to fade.

Crazy patchwork, with its apparently haphazard arrangement of motley bits of fabric, is one quilting style that is universal. Whether stitched in humble calicoes or pricey taffetas and velvets, the result is always successful.

The simple clutch bag, *above,* is constructed in one piece atop a rectangle of polyester fleece. First make a rectangle of 1-inch-wide stripes for the front and back. Then add the curved flap in crazy patchwork.

The technique for making the crazy-patch hearts on the pillow, *above,* is based on assembling random-patch pieces as described on pages 72–73.

The graceful arched mirror, *opposite,* is another way to use this fascinating technique. Cut a piece of plywood to this or any other shape, and cover it with crazy patchwork. Use clips to hold the mirror in place.

❖ ❖ ❖

The Princess Feather design is a dynamic appliqué pattern that always seems in motion.

In addition to being one of America's oldest appliqué patterns, the Princess Feather design is one that has undergone countless adaptations. All, however, feature scalloped, notched, or curved petallike feathers.

The Princess Feather Quilt, *above,* uses 16 motifs for the quilt top. These motifs were stitched onto two strips, but you also can make it block by block.

Patterns with shapes as distinctive as the Princess Feather lend themselves to stenciling. To make a valance like the one *opposite,* first build a shallow plywood cornice to fit the window. Make paper cutouts of the shapes in the directions for the quilt and arrange the motifs to fit the valance front.

Cut a separate stencil for each paint color that will be used in the design. Stencil the shapes onto the background fabric (we used lightweight canvas). Pad the cornice with batting and staple the stenciled fabric to the cornice.

❖ ❖ ❖

Grape motifs, with twining vines, lush fruit, and corkscrew tendrils, were motifs favored by the Victorians.

The areas of rich appliqué are balanced by plain white fabric on the Grapevine Quilt, *opposite.*

Stitch nine large appliquéd blocks, and separate them with generous sashing strips, to make this quilt top. Four small sashing blocks—each with four grapes and four leaves—are used to join the ends of the sashing strips.

For the border, use bias strips stitched in curving lines accented with grape clusters and leaves.

To make the accompanying pillows, *below,* start with a fabric background that is the same size as a quilt block or a sashing square, but change the squares' seam allowances to ½ inch. Then, following appliqué directions for the Grapevine Quilt, sew the grapes and leaves to the background. Edge the squares with piping, if desired, and add a ruffle before assembly.

❖ ❖

ROSE QUILT
PAGES 194–195
Finished block is 11½ inches.
Finished size is 57¾ x 75 inches.

Materials
5½ yards of white fabric (borders, blocks, setting squares, and triangles)
1½ yards of green fabric
1¼ yards of pink print fabric
¾ yard of rose fabric
⅛ yard of yellow fabric
3½ yards of backing fabric
Quilt batting
Water-erasable marking pen

Instructions
Trace and make templates for the patterns, *right*. Patterns are finished size; add ¼-inch seam allowances when cutting the pieces from the fabric.

For the setting squares and the triangles, make an 11½-inch square template from cardboard or plastic.

On tracing paper, draw an 11½-inch square. Referring to Figure 1, *below right*, use the templates to draw entire rose pattern inside square. Use this pattern as a positioning guide for appliqué.

To cut the pieces: The number of pieces to cut for the entire quilt is listed first, with the number to cut for one block following in parentheses. Border measurements include ¼-inch seam allowances.

From white fabric, cut:
Two 5x78-inch borders
Two 5½x51-inch borders

From green fabric, cut:
36 B pieces (3)
144 E pieces (12)
80 inches of ¾-inch-wide bias-cut strips (6 inches)

From rose fabric, cut:
36 A pieces (3)
12 C pieces (1)

From pink print fabric, cut:
Approximately 7 yards of ⅝-inch-wide bias-cut strips (approximately 15½ inches)
Approximately 8 yards of 1¼-inch-wide bias-cut strips

From yellow fabric, cut:
12 D pieces (1)

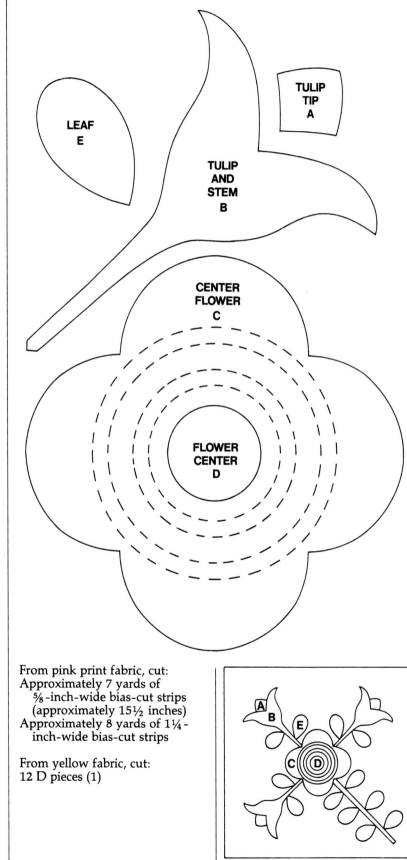

LEAF
E

TULIP
TIP
A

TULIP
AND
STEM
B

CENTER
FLOWER
C

FLOWER
CENTER
D

Figure 1

From remaining white fabric, *and adding ¼-inch seam allowances,* use the 11½-inch square template to mark and cut 18 squares from white fabric; 12 blocks are for appliqué and 6 blocks are plain setting squares. Set the squares aside.

For the setting triangles, draw a diagonal line between opposite corners of the template used for marking the setting squares. Draw a second diagonal line in the *opposite* direction, through the lower section of the template (see Figure 2, *below*).

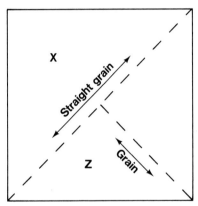

Figure 2

Cut on the drawn lines to form Templates X and Z.

Using Template X, mark 10 setting triangles on the white fabric with the *long* side of the triangle on the straight grain. Adding ¼-inch seam allowances, cut out the triangles. Using Template Z, mark four corner-setting triangles on the white fabric, with the *legs* of the triangle on the straight grain. Adding seam allowances, cut out the triangles.

Set the X and Z triangles aside.

For the appliqué shapes, trace the template on the *right side* of the fabrics. Cut out, adding a scant ¼-inch seam.

To appliqué one block: Fold 12 squares in half diagonally; crease lightly and unfold. Then fold in half in the other direction; crease lightly and unfold.

(Continued)

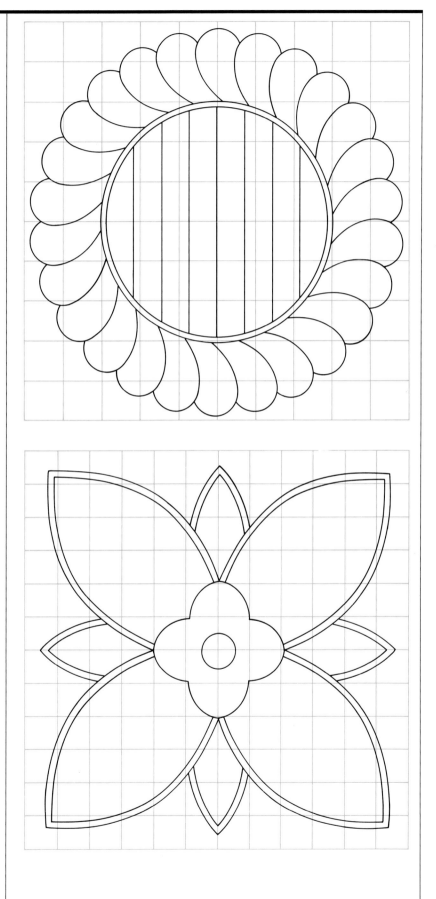

At a window or atop a light box, trace block flower outline *lightly* on muslin squares with a water-erasable marker. Use the fold lines to align the stems of the tulips within the squares.

Trace the rose trim outlines onto each center rose (C piece).

For each block, pin the tulip tips, tulips with stems, leaves, and the center rose in place.

To make the flower stem, fold the green bias in thirds lengthwise and press. Cut into 6-inch lengths for each stem. Pin a stem to each block.

Appliqué the shapes in place. (*Note:* To hand-appliqué, fold under and baste raw edge of each shape to outline. Position on background and stitch in place using tiny, invisible stitches.)

Center the flower centers and appliqué. To trim each center rose, fold the pink print in thirds lengthwise; press and baste to hold the ends in place. For each rose, cut off a 6-inch strip of pink print bias for the inner trim circle; cut a 9½-inch strip for each outer trim circle.

Baste the trim strips to each rose within the guidelines. Trim off excess length and turn under the ends of the trim. Appliqué the inner edge of each trim first and then the outer edge of each circle.

To make the quilt top: When appliqué is complete, arrange blocks and setting squares to form four horizontal rows, each with three blocks. All blocks are set on point; position each block with stem at bottom. If desired, transfer the quilting pattern to the plain blocks before assembly; see finishing instructions below.

Add one Z triangle to each corner; add X triangles to sides.

Using ¼-inch seams, join blocks and triangles into diagonal rows. Stitch rows together.

Stitch the shorter borders to the top and bottom edges of the quilt top. Trim excess border. Stitch the remaining borders to the sides of the quilt top. Trim excess border.

Finishing: To piece the quilt back, cut fabric into two equal lengths. Cut or tear one length in half lengthwise. Sew one narrow panel to each side of the wide panel. Match the selvages; use a ½-inch seam. Trim the seams to ¼ inch; press to one side.

Enlarge the feathered circle quilting design, page 207, and transfer the design to each of the plain squares. Divide the pattern into halves and quarters to mark the X and Z triangles.

Enlarge the four-petaled quilting design, page 207, and transfer it to the appliquéd blocks.

Layer the back, batting, and the pieced top. Baste layers together; quilt.

Splice the binding strips together at 45-degree angles.

When quilting is complete, trim away excess batting and backing so all edges are even with the quilt top. Sew the binding to the right side of the quilt, raw edges together. Turn under the edge ¼ inch and hand-stitch fold to the quilt back.

FULL-LENGTH GARMENT BAG
PAGE 196
Finished size is 30 inches long.

Materials
1 yard *each* of peach fabric (front panel), light green fabric (front panel), rose (piping), green large print (garment bag), and white flannel (panel interfacing)
1¼ yards batiste or broadcloth (lining)
½ yard rose print (piping and tulip tips)
⅓ yard of green small print (tulips, leaves, stem)
2 yards piping cord
2½ yards ⅞-inch-wide gathered eyelet
Water-erasable marking pen
Bias tape (optional)

Instructions
(*Note:* Use ¼-inch seams throughout, unless noted otherwise.)

To make master pattern for garment bag, draw a 21-inch-wide, 30-inch-high rectangle on tracing paper. Draw a line at center from top to bottom. To make cutout at top, draw a 4-inch-diameter half-circle at top of center line. To make slope for shoulders, mark each side of the rectangle 4 inches down from the top of each 30-inch side; connect the points on the side to the edge of the half-circle. Round the corners at the shoulder. See Figure 1, *below.*

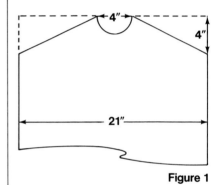

Figure 1

Adding ¼-inch seam allowances, cut this shape from green large print and lining fabrics for back of garment bag.

For front pieces, mark peach fabric for the 3¾-inch-wide, 30-inch-high center panel. Mark a line along peach panel for vertical center.

Mark light green fabric for one 2x30-inch strip and one 6¼x30-inch strip for front panel. Add ¼-inch seam allowances to green strips and cut out.

To appliqué front panel: To make appliqué pattern, refer to pattern pieces and Figure 1, page 206, for Rose Quilt. Cut only templates of pieces A (tulip tip) and B (tulip stem); cut template for piece E (leaf), extending stem 2 inches.

Plan position of appliqués on peach panel. Use a total of five tulip motifs, each spaced 5⅝ inches apart. Add four leaves beneath each tulip shape.

Working over a light box or against a window, trace appliqué design on peach panel, centering stem along center line, and aligning bottom of stem with bottom of panel. Referring to instructions for Rose Quilt, page 206, appliqué shapes to background. Use green small print for stem, leaves, and tulips (B and E pieces). Use rose fabric for tulip tips (A pieces).

When appliqué is complete, baste flannel to wrong side of peach fabric.

Cover cording with rose fabric to make piping. Stitch piping to long edges of peach panel. Stitch long green strips to peach panel, placing the narrow strip on the left-hand side of peach panel (as it faces you) and the wider strip on the remaining side.

Assembly: Mark front panel fabric to finished 12-inch width; with right-hand piped seam at center, mark neckline half-circle. Cut two lengths of eyelet to edge long edges of front panel and one length to edge neckline. Stitch eyelet to sides and cutout neckline edge of front panel.

Stitch a 5-inch-wide strip of green large print fabric to right-hand (as it faces you) edge of front panel.

Aligning neckline cutout to master pattern, cut out front appliquéd assembly to match back shape. Cut a lining piece to this shape.

For remaining front side piece, mark a strip of green large print fabric sufficiently wide to extend from side seam to left-hand edge of neckline cutout (approximately 8 inches). Add seam allowances and shape top edge to match shoulder slope as for other front piece. Cut lining piece similarly.

For ties, cut four 1⅛x8½-inch strips from peach fabric. Turn under ¼ inch on each short end; press. Press long edges toward center, then fold in half length-

wise and press. Topstitch along folded edges.

Position ties at left-hand edge of neckline cutout and at left-hand edge of front panel; baste.

Finishing: Stitch side and shoulder seams of garment bag. Repeat for lining pieces. Place lining and garment bag right sides together. Stitch along all edges, leaving bottom edges open and catching ends of ties in stitching line.

Turn. Tack lining in place at shoulders. Bind bottom edge with green bias binding or make binding from green fabric.

HALF-LENGTH GARMENT BAG
PAGE 196
Finished height is 18 inches.

Materials
⅝ yard *each* of pale yellow fabric (panel), large yellow print fabric (garment bag and flower appliqué), and white flannel (panel interfacing)
1¼ yards batiste or broadcloth (lining)
½ yard rose fabric (piping, flower tips, and circles)
⅓ yard of green small print (tulips, leaves, stem)
Scrap of bright yellow fabric (flower center)
1⅞ yard piping cord
Water-erasable marking pen
Bias tape (optional)

Instructions
(*Note:* Use ¼-inch seams throughout, unless noted otherwise.)

To make master pattern for garment bag, draw a 21-inch-wide, 18-inch-high rectangle on tracing paper. Draw a line at center from top to bottom. To make cutout at top, draw a 4-inch-diameter half-circle at top of center line. To make slope for shoulders, mark each side of the rectangle 4 inches down from the top of each 18-inch side; connect the points on the side to the edge of the half circle. Round the corners at the shoulder. See Figure 1, *opposite.*

Adding ¼-inch seam allowances, cut this shape from yellow print and lining fabrics for back of garment bag.

For front pieces, mark yellow fabric for the 12-inch-wide, 18-inch-high center panel.

To appliqué front panel: To make appliqué pattern, refer to pattern pieces and Figure 1, page 206, for Rose Quilt. Make a master pattern of this design on tracing paper. Extend stem to 7½ inches long and trace a total of eight leaves along stem, four on each side.

Mark a line along vertical center of yellow fabric. Working over a light box or against a window, trace appliqué design on yellow panel, centering stem along center line, and aligning bottom of stem with bottom of panel. Referring to instructions for Rose Quilt, *opposite*, appliqué shapes to background. Use green small print for stem, leaves, and tulips. Use yellow print for center rose, bright yellow for rose center, and bias strips cut from rose fabric for circular rose trims. Appliqué all shapes in place; press. Baste flannel to wrong side of yellow fabric.

Assembly: Mark yellow fabric to finished 12-inch width; mark neckline half-circle. Cover cord with rose fabric for piping. Stitch piping to sides and cutout neckline edge of yellow panel.

Stitch a 5-inch-wide strip of yellow print fabric to right-hand (as it faces you) edge of yellow panel.

Aligning neckline cutout to master pattern, cut out front appliquéd assembly to match back shape. Cut a lining piece to this shape.

(Continued)

For remaining front side piece, mark a strip of yellow print fabric sufficiently wide to extend from side seam to left-hand edge of neckline cutout (approximately 8 inches). Add seam allowances and shape top edge to match shoulder slope as for other front piece. Cut lining piece similarly.

For ties, cut four 1⅛x8½-inch strips from green fabric. Turn under ¼ inch on each short end; press. Press long edges toward center, then fold in half lengthwise and press. Topstitch along folded edges.

Position ties at left-hand edge of neckline cutout and at left-hand edge of yellow panel; baste.

Finishing: Stitch side and shoulder seams of garment bag. Repeat for lining pieces. Place lining and garment bag right sides together. Stitch along all edges, leaving bottom edges open and catching ends of ties in stitching line.

Turn. Tack lining in place at shoulders. Bind bottom edge with green bias binding or make binding from green fabric.

❖

JEWELRY CASE
PAGE 197
Finished size is 12x24 inches, unfolded.

Materials
½ yard *each* of main fabric, fleece, and lining fabric
½ yard contrasting print fabric (bias-cut binding)
Water-erasable marking pen
Hook-and-loop fastening dot

Instructions
Cut 13x25-inch rectangle from main fabric, lining, and fleece. Mark finished size of case onto main fabric. Draw a line through the center of the rectangle, making two 12½x13-inch rectangles.

Enlarge feathered circle quilting pattern for plain block of Rose Quilt, page 207. Transfer pattern to one of the rectangles on main fabric, with lines in center of circle parallel to the long edges of the large rectangle.

Layer main fabric, fleece, and lining; baste layers together.

Quilt design with contrasting thread.

For pocket, cut a 12x16-inch rectangle; fold in half to form an 8-inch-deep pocket. Matching raw edges, baste to lining fabric along sides and bottom; position pocket on opposite end of rectangle, away from quilted design. Sewing through all layers, make two 4-inch-wide dividers in pocket.

For binding, cut 1¼-inch-wide bias strips from print; join ends with diagonal seams. Stitch binding to raw edges of case, right sides together. Fold under remaining raw edges twice; slip-stitch in place.

Fold case in half to close. Sew fastening dot to center of lower inside edge.

❖

ROSE PINCUSHION
PAGE 197
Motif is 42x56 stitches.
Finished size is 4x5½ inches.

Materials
Scrap of light green 14-count Aida cloth
DMC embroidery floss: Small amounts of dark seafoam green (561), dark dusty rose (961), and deep dusty rose (3350)
Scraps of fleece and backing fabric
⅝ yard piping cord, covered with bias-cut fabric
Small amount of fiberfill
Water-erasable marking pen

Instructions
Referring to chart, *below,* work design on Aida cloth. Use three plies of floss and work the cross-stitches over one thread. When stitchery is completed, steam-press on the wrong side.

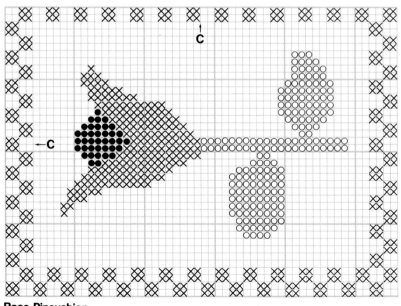

Rose Pincushion

COLOR KEY
▨ **Dark Seafoam Green (561)**
⊠ **Dark Dusty Rose (961)**
● **Deep Dusty Rose (3350)**

To assemble, mark fabric 1 inch past cross-stitches. Cut out stitchery, fleece, and backing. Mark ½-inch seams on Aida cloth.

Baste fleece to stitchery. Baste piping to seam line.

Place backing and stitchery right sides facing. Stitch along seam line, leaving an opening for turning. Turn. Stuff with fiberfill. Slipstitch closed.

CHAIR CUSHION

PAGE 197
Finished size of quilted motif is 10½ inches square.

Materials

½ yard *each* of main fabric, fleece, muslin, and cushion backing fabric
¼ yard contrasting print fabric (ruffle and ties)
1-inch-thick foam

Instructions

On tracing paper, draw outline of chair seat for master pattern. Transfer outline to main fabric. Adding ½-inch seam allowance, cut cushion backing from this shape; set aside.

Enlarge four-petaled quilting pattern for appliquéd blocks of Rose Quilt, page 207, and transfer to center of cushion outline with water-erasable marking pen. Add a grid of ½-inch squares to large petal shapes.

Layer main fabric, fleece, and muslin; baste layers together.

Quilt design with contrasting thread. Stitch around cushion outline and trim excess fabric close to stitching.

Cut four 3x30-inch ties from print fabric; finish long edges and one end. Matching raw edges, baste a pair of ties to rear corners of cushion.

Make sufficient 1½-inch-wide ruffle for front edge and sides of cushion. Ruffle should be about 1½ to 2 times as long as measurement of front and sides of cushion. Gather ruffle. Matching raw edges, baste to cushion top, tapering edges of ruffle at ties.

With right sides facing, stitch cushion back to top, leaving back edge of cushion open. Turn. Cut foam to cushion shape and slip inside cushion. Close opening.

HANDS ALL AROUND QUILT

PAGES 198–199
Finished block is 14 inches.
Finished size is 72x89 inches.

Materials

4¾ yards of white fabric (blocks, borders, and sashing)
1½ yards of dark pink fabric (blocks and binding)
¾ yard *each* of light pink, orange, yellow, grey, tan, lavender, and blue fabric (blocks)
5½ yards backing fabric
Quilt batting
Water-erasable marking pen

Instructions

Trace and make templates for the patterns, page 212. Transfer the center markings on the D and E patterns to the templates. Patterns are finished size; add ¼-inch seam allowances when cutting the pieces from the fabric.

Cut border and sashing pieces from fabric first.

To cut the pieces: The number of pieces to cut for the entire quilt is listed first, with the number of pieces to cut for one block following in parentheses.

Border and sashing strip measurements include ¼-inch seam allowances. Lengths listed for borders and long sashing strips are longer than needed; trim excess fabric from borders after assembly. The short sashing strips are correct length. When marking and cutting D and E pieces, transfer the center marks to the fabric pieces.

From white fabric, cut:
Two 4×93-inch white borders
Two 4×76-inch white borders
Three 3½×86-inch white sashing strips
Sixteen 3½×14½-inch white sashing strips
160 B pieces (8); notice the grain line on piece B; cut the triangles with the *long* side on the fabric grain
160 C pieces (8)

From dark pink fabric, cut:
40 D pieces (4)
10 yards 2-inch-wide bias-cut strips

From light pink fabric, cut:
40 D pieces (4)

From orange fabric, cut:
10 E pieces (1)

From yellow fabric, cut:
10 E pieces (1)

From green, gray, tan, lavender, and blue fabrics, cut:
64 A pieces from each color (16)

To piece one block: Stitch the pieces together following the piecing diagram. Press seams toward darker fabric as you go.

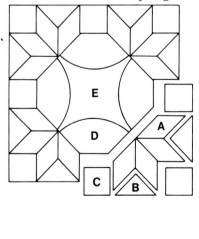

(Continued)

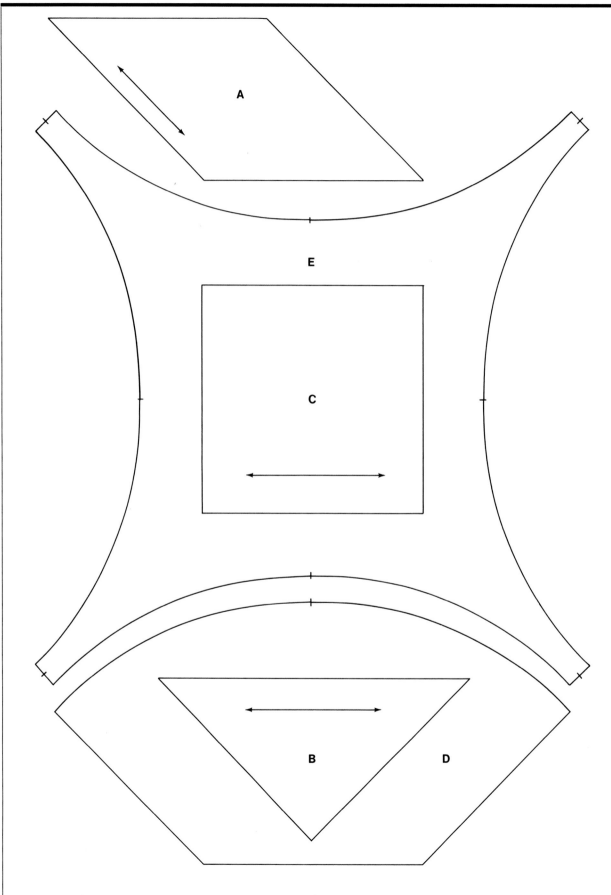

You may stitch by hand or machine; however, the block lends itself to hand-stitching because so many pieces require setting in. If you use a machine, stitch only from seam line to seam line, not edge to edge.

For all blocks, use this piecing order. Sew four D pieces to E piece, matching center marks. Stitch four A diamonds into half-stars. Stitch the half-stars into the corners along the edges where D pieces meet. Set in B pieces, then C pieces. See piecing diagram, page 211.

Instructions follow to duplicate the color combination of this quilt. Ten blocks have yellow centers (E pieces) and deep pink D pieces (Type 1 blocks), and 10 blocks have orange centers (E pieces) and light pink D pieces (Type 2 blocks).

To Type 1 centers, stitch diamonds in green, gray, tan, lavender, and blue. Each diamond color is used twice on Type 1 blocks.

To Type 2 centers, stitch diamonds the same way, so each diamond color appears on two blocks.

To make the quilt top: Lay out 20 completed blocks in four rows of five blocks each. Alternate Type 1 and Type 2 blocks, striving for a pleasing balance of colors.

Stitch five blocks together in a row, using 3½x14½-inch sashing strips in between. Make four rows. Stitch long sashing strips between each row, aligning each row of blocks. Trim sashing strips.

The quilt top should measure 65½x82½ inches, including seam allowances. Stitch the borders to the quilt top, mitering the corners; trim the excess. Finished top is 72½x89½ inches, including seam allowances.

Finishing: To piece the quilt back, cut fabric into two equal lengths. Cut or tear one length in half lengthwise. Sew one narrow panel to each side of the wide panel. Match the selvages; use a ½-inch seam. Trim the seams to ¼ inch; press to one side.

Quilt as desired. The quilt shown has quilting stitches in an allover diagonal pattern of ¾-inch squares.

Trim batting and backing fabric on outer edges.

Piece binding together making diagonal seams. Fold in half lengthwise with wrong sides together to make a 1-inch-wide strip.

Sew raw edges of strip to top of quilt with ¼-inch seams. Turn folded edge to back and hand-stitch in place.

STANLEY'S SQUARES WALL QUILT
COVER and PAGE 199
Finished block is 3 inches.
Finished quilt is 30¾x30¾ inches.

Materials
½ yard of muslin
Small amounts of various solid and tiny print fabrics
¼ yard of light brown fabric
⅝ yard of peach fabric
1 yard of backing fabric
Quilt batting
Cardboard or plastic for templates

Instructions
To make template for nine-patch blocks, draw a 1-inch square on graph paper.

For the setting squares and triangles, make a 3-inch square template from cardboard or plastic.

The patterns are finished size and *do not* include seam allowances. Add ¼-inch seam allowances to all pieces before cutting them from fabric.

To cut the pieces: Adding ¼-inch seam allowances, use the 3-inch square template to mark and cut 16 setting squares from muslin. (The cut squares will measure 3½ inches square.) Set the squares aside.

For the setting triangles, draw a diagonal line between opposite corners of the template used for marking the setting squares. Draw a second diagonal line in the *opposite* direction, through the

lower section of the square (see Figure 1, *below*).

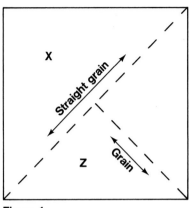

Figure 1

Cut on the drawn lines to form templates X and Z.

Using template X, mark 16 setting triangles on muslin with the *long* side of triangle on the straight grain. Adding ¼-inch seam allowances, cut out triangles.

Next, using template Z, mark four corner-setting triangles on the muslin, with the legs of the triangle on the straight grain. Adding seam allowances, cut out the triangles. Set the X and Z triangles aside.

Border cutting measurements include seam allowances and are exact length needed.

From fabric scraps, cut:
225 small squares

From light brown fabric, cut:
Two 1½x21¼-inch inner borders
Two 1½x23¼-inch inner borders

From peach fabric, cut:
Two 4¼x23¼-inch outer borders
Two 4¼x30¾-inch outer borders

To make the blocks: If desired, draw entire quilt top on graph paper before beginning. Then, use colored pencils (or tape snippets of fabric to each square on paper), to determine combination and position of fabrics. Or simply cut a supply of fabric squares and combine them freely as you work.

(Continued)

213

Lay out nine squares for one block. Choose one square for the center piece in the block. Place four squares cut from a second fabric adjacent to the center piece. Fill in the corners of the block with four squares cut from a third fabric.

Using ¼-inch seams, stitch the squares into rows; stitch the rows into a block. Make 25 blocks.

To make the quilt top: The quilt top is pieced in diagonal rows with muslin squares between the pieced blocks; all blocks are turned on point.

Lay out all of the blocks first, making five rows of five blocks with alternating muslin squares. Adjust position of pieced blocks, if necessary, to balance color. Add large setting triangles along the sides and small setting triangles in the corners.

Using ¼-inch seams, stitch the blocks and the triangles together in diagonal rows. Stitch the rows together.

Stitch the short inner border strips to the sides of the quilt top; stitch the long inner border strips to the top and bottom of the quilt top and to the ends of the shorter strips.

Repeat with the outer border strips.

Finishing: Layer backing, batting, and quilt top; baste layers together.

Outline-quilt inside each muslin square and triangle ¼ inch from seam. Outline-quilt outer border ½ inch from raw edge and ¼ inch from edge of inner border. Quilt remainder of outer border as desired.

Trim batting and backing 1¾ inches larger than the quilt top on all sides.

To make pieced border, join several 4-inch-wide pieces of various colored fabric scraps to a length of at least 36 inches. Make four pieces.

Fold borders in half lengthwise with wrong sides together; press. With right sides facing, and matching raw edges, stitch one border strip to side of quilt. Fold

border to back side; trim excess length. Fold under raw edge ¼ inch and slip-stitch in place. Repeat for opposite border, then for remaining edges.

To make a casing for hanging, cut a 9x29-inch strip from backing fabric. Finish short edges and fold strip in half lengthwise with wrong sides together. Stitch long edges together, taking ¼-inch seams, to form a tube. Flatten tube and slip-stitch to top edge of backing.

CRAZY-PATCH CLUTCH BAG
PAGE 200
Finished size is 12x6½ inches.

Materials
⅛ yard *each* of about 16 different fabrics, including satins, taffetas, brocades, challis, and printed silks
½ yard *each* of muslin, fleece, and lining fabric
1½ yards narrow satin piping *or* string and fabric to make piping
1 large snap
Tailor's chalk
Decorative button or small brooch (optional)

Instructions
To make pattern for bag, draw a 12x17¾-inch rectangle on paper. Measure up 6½ inches from the bottom line; draw a horizontal line for bag front. Measure up 7 more inches; draw a horizontal line for bag back. Draw a curved line on remaining 4¼-inch-deep area for flap. See Figure 1, *above right.* Pattern does not include seam allowances.

Mark bag outline on muslin.

Cut 12 different strips from fabrics, each 1½x12 inches. Four of the strips used for the bag shown are pieced from two different fabrics; choose fabrics in the same color family.

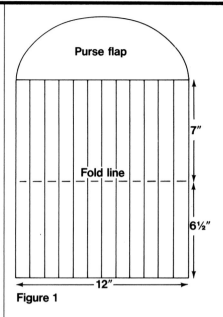

Purse flap

Fold line

7"

6½"

12"

Figure 1

To piece the bag front and back, position the first strip on the muslin. Place the strip right side up, and align the raw edge ¼ inch past outline. Stitch along the bag outline.

Place the second strip atop the first strip, right sides facing and matching raw edges. Using ¼-inch seams, stitch through second and first strips and muslin. Fold second strip over so the right side is up; press open.

Continue in this manner until all 12 strips are stitched to the muslin.

For the flap, random-piece several fabric scraps together to a 12-inch width. With right sides facing, sew this assembly to the muslin above the strips. Press scrap assembly open.

When all patches are stitched to the muslin, trace bag outline onto pieced work. Layer pieced work atop fleece; machine-stitch around outline. Trim seam allowance to ¼ inch.

Mark bottom fold of bag. Sew piping along outline of straight 12-inch edge. Press seam to wrong side. Sew piping to outline, beginning at bottom fold, continuing around curve of flap, and ending at opposite end of fold line.

Cut lining fabric to same shape as bag. Press under ¼ inch along the straight 12-inch edge. With right sides facing, sew lining to bag on curve of flap on piping line. Clip seam allowance.

Fold bag in half along fold line. With right sides facing, sew front to back. Sew lining in same manner. Turn flap right side out; press. Turn bag right side out; press side seams. Tuck lining into bag and slip-stitch straight edge.

Cover large snap with lining fabric and sew in place beneath lower center of flap. Add a decorative button or pin to flap, if desired.

❖

CRAZY-PATCH MIRROR FRAME
PAGE 201
Finished size is 14½x21½ inches.

Materials
⅛ yard *each* of about 20 different fabrics, including satins, taffetas, brocades, challis, and printed silks
1¼ yard (45 inches wide) fleece
20x28-inch piece of muslin
3½ yards narrow satin piping *or* string and fabric to make piping
Tailor's chalk
Size 8 pearl cotton
Fabric glue
½-inch plywood, flat black paint
7x14-inch piece of single-thickness mirror
Mirror clips, sawtooth hanger

Instructions
To create the pattern for mirror frame, draw a 14-inch square on graph paper. Find center point of top of square. Using a compass with radius set at 7 inches, swing an arc atop square to create arch shape.

For cutout, draw a 6x10-inch rectangle inside the arch shape. Position the rectangle's 6-inch bottom edge 4 inches up from bottom and 4 inches in from each side. Find the center point of the top edge of the rectangle. With the compass radius set at 3 inches, swing an arc atop square to create arch shape.

(Continued)

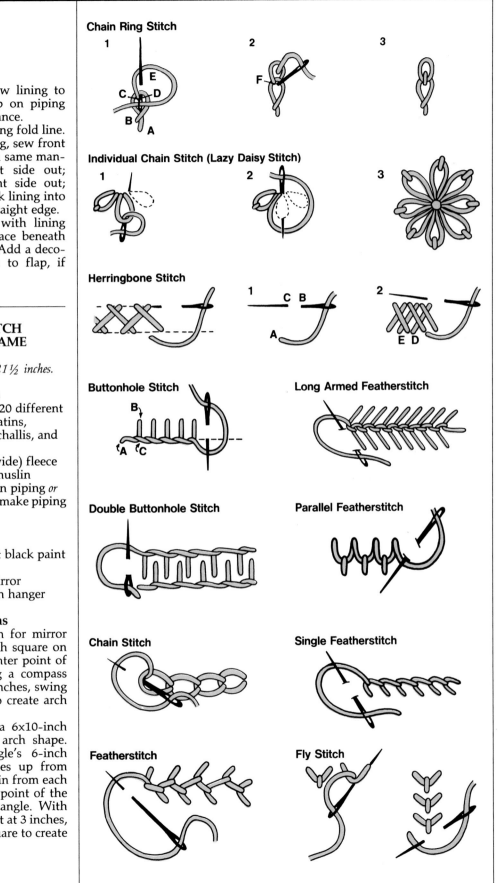

Transfer frame shape to muslin. Mark ¼-inch seam allowances along inside and outside edges of outline.

Crazy patchwork: Refer to the instructions for piecing random patches, pages 72–73.

Cut two or three irregularly shaped fabric scraps. Stitch together with right sides facing; press open. (Make sure pieced strip is wide enough to extend across frame shape.)

Place the first pieced strip right side up atop muslin, within outline. Stitch in place.

Make a similar, second strip of scraps. Place second strip atop first strip with right sides together; stitch.

Trim excess fabric where pieces overlap and press open.

Continue in this manner until all of the mirror frame surface is covered.

Assembly: With tailor's chalk, trace frame outline on right side of patchwork. Machine-stitch along this line. Referring to hand-embroidery stitches, page 215, and using pearl cotton, add accent stitches along prominent seam lines.

Line shape with fleece and stitch. Make piping if necessary, and stitch to inside and outside edges of patchwork, clipping piping as necessary. Trim away all seam allowance from fleece. Grade seam allowance of piping and frame, leaving ⅜ inch on piping and ¼ inch on frame edge.

Cut frame shape from plywood. Sand edges and surfaces. Paint edges and back of mirror frame flat black.

Cut frame shape from two layers of fleece. Cut out fleece ⅜ inch smaller on inside and outside edges. Glue fleece to plywood.

Press under piping seam allowance of patchwork and glue seam allowance *only* to plywood.

Secure mirror behind opening with mirror clips. Add sawtooth hanger to top back edge.

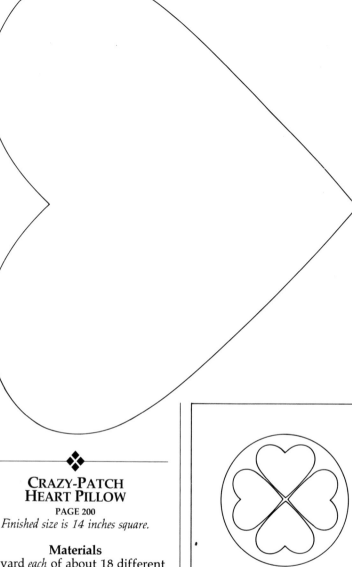

❖

CRAZY-PATCH
HEART PILLOW
PAGE 200
Finished size is 14 inches square.

Materials
⅛ yard *each* of about 18 different fabrics, including satins, taffetas, brocades, challis, and printed silks
1 yard of fabric (backing and shirred piping)
½ yard *each* of fleece, muslin, and cotton velveteen
Size 8 pearl cotton
Transparent nylon thread
2 yards of thick cable cord
14-inch pillow form
Tailor's chalk
Plastic-coated freezer paper

Instructions
Refer to pattern, *above,* for heart shape.

Cut out four heart shapes from freezer paper. Referring to instructions, pages 72–73, for piecing random patches, piece two or three fabrics atop freezer paper. Leave paper pattern affixed to patchwork.

Layer patchwork and a muslin scrap, right sides facing. Stitch around heart shape. Trim seam to ¼ inch and clip as necessary. Remove freezer paper.

Make a small slit in muslin; turn heart to right side and press. Cut velveteen to 14 inches square. Center hearts within square, positioning them side by side and about ¼ inch apart. See Figure 1, *above.* Slip-stitch in place. Referring to hand-embroidery stitches, page 215, and using pearl cotton, add accent stitches along prominent seam lines of heart shapes.

For pillow border, draw a 14-inch square on muslin. Draw a 10-inch diameter circle in center of square. Portion of square between circle and edges of square will be pieced. Referring to instructions for Crazy-Patch Mirror Frame, *opposite*, cover muslin border with fabrics.

With tailor's chalk, trace border shape on right side of piecing. Machine-stitch on inside and outside edges. Trim inside circle seam allowance to $3/8$ inch; clip seam allowance every $1/8$ inch around circle. Turn raw edge under on machine-stitching line; baste. Center pieced border atop velveteen square; pin and baste together around circle. Topstitch border to velveteen with transparent nylon thread close to folded edge. Trim velveteen seam allowance to $3/8$ inch. Using pearl cotton, embroider featherstitches around the circle.

Line pillow top with fleece. Trim outside square of pieced border to $1/2$ inch. Cut backing fabric the same size as top.

Shirred piping: Cut and piece 3-inch-wide strips of fabric into a piece $1\frac{1}{2}$ yards long. Divide the length of the strip into fourths; mark fourths with pins. Baste the raw edge under $1/2$ inch at ends. Fold the strip in half lengthwise, wrong sides together, over cable cord. Sew two rows of gathering threads on each fourth, $1/2$ and $1/4$ inch from raw edge.

Pull cable cord and gathering threads so the piping within each fourth measures 14 inches.

Sew the piping to the outside edge of pillow. Tape cable cord edges together. Slip-stitch shirred ends together.

Sew backing fabric to top with right sides together on piping line; leave opening for turning. Trim corners and turn. Insert pillow and slip-stitch closed.

❖

GRAPEVINE QUILT
PAGE 204
Finished block is 16 inches.
Finished quilt is 86x86 inches.

Materials
12 yards of white fabric (top and quilt back)
$2\frac{1}{4}$ yards of purple fabric
$3\frac{1}{4}$ yards of green fabric
Quilt batting
Cardboard or plastic for templates
Water-erasable pen
Tracing paper
Black permanent marker

Instructions
Trace and make templates for the leaf and stem patterns, *above.* You can use a quarter as the template for the grapes. Patterns are finished size; add $1/4$-inch seam allowances when cutting the pieces from the fabric.

Use patterns to create a $1/4$-block drawing. Trace onto tracing paper four times, rotating the quarters around the block center to create a drawing of the full block. Darken the lines with a black permanent marker.

To cut the pieces: The number of pieces to cut for the entire quilt is listed first, with the number to cut for large block following in parentheses. The cutting measurements include $1/4$-inch seam allowances.

(Continued)

217

From white fabric, cut:
Two 90-inch-long lengths (for the quilt back)
4 borders, each 9½x68½ inches
4 border corners, each 9½ inches square
12 sashing strips, each 9x16½ inches
4 sashing squares, each 9x9 inches
9 blocks, each 16½ inches square

From the green fabric, cut:
136 leaves (8)
36 stems (4)
1-inch-wide bias strips for the vine (join the bias strips into 8 pieces, each approximately 66 inches long)

From the purple fabric, cut:
2 borders, each 2x65½ inches
2 borders, each 2x68½ inches
Ten 2-inch-wide strips across the width of the fabric (binding)
836 grapes (60)

To make the blocks: With water-erasable pen trace the block design onto the fabric blocks. For each block, prepare eight leaves, four stems, and 60 grapes for appliqué by basting under the seam allowances. Position the pieces over the corresponding outlines on the block and appliqué, using thread to match the shapes being appliquéd. Make nine blocks.

To make the sashing blocks: To create positioning guides for appliqué, fold the blocks in half and press lightly; fold them in half the other direction and press. For each square, prepare four leaves and four grapes for appliqué. Appliqué four grapes in the center of the block; appliqué a leaf in each corner of the block. Make four sashing blocks.

To make the borders: To make a placement guide for the vine, cut a 4½x13½-inch paper rectangle. Fold the paper in half lengthwise and crosswise. Cut the folded paper so it is a tapered oval shape when opened out. On each border, mark five vine patterns 1 inch from the inner edge of the border.

Fold the vine bias in thirds lengthwise, so it is about ⅜ inch wide; press. Baste the vine along the placement lines, trimming excess vine.

For each border, prepare 60 grapes and 10 leaves for appliqué. Appliqué clusters of 10 grapes below the vine at the ends of the borders at each point where the vines cross. Appliqué a leaf along the lower edge of the vine to each side of the grape clusters. Make four borders.

To make the border corners, fold corner blocks in half diagonally and press. For each corner, prepare two leaves and 10 grapes for appliqué. At the inner corner of the square, appliqué a leaf to each side of the crease. Appliqué a grape cluster below the leaves. Make four corners.

To make the quilt top: Make three rows by stitching together three blocks with sashing strips between the blocks. Make two sashing rows by stitching together three sashing strips with sashing squares between the strips. Join the rows, alternating block rows and sashing rows.

Sew the shorter purple border to the quilt top and bottom. Sew a border corner square to the ends of the remaining two borders; stitch to the quilt sides.

Finishing: To piece the quilt back, cut or tear one quilt back length in half lengthwise. Sew one narrow panel to each side of the wide panel. Match the selvages; use a ½-inch seam. Trim the seams to ¼ inch; press to one side.

Layer the back, batting, and the pieced top. Baste layers together; quilt as desired. The leaf and grape patterns can be arranged into quilting designs for the sashing strips.

Splice the binding strips together at 45-degree angles. Trim, then fold in half lengthwise with wrong sides together to 1 inch wide; press.

When quilting is complete, trim excess batting and backing even with the quilt top. Sew the bind-

ing to the right side of the quilt, raw edges together. Turn the folded edge to the back; hand-stitch in place.

PRINCESS FEATHER QUILT
PAGE 203
Finished block is 13 inches.
Finished panel is 26x52 inches.
Finished quilt is 70x70 inches.

Materials
4½ yards muslin *or* white fabric
3½ yards red fabric
2 yards green fabric
¼ yard orange fabric
4½ yards backing fabric
13½-inch square of paper
Quilt batting
Water-erasable marker
Cardboard or plastic for templates

Instructions
Trace and make templates for patterns, *opposite* and page 220. The patterns are finished size; add a ¼-inch seam allowance when cutting pieces from fabric.

To cut the pieces: *Note:* The inner top of the antique quilt shown on page 203 was put together in two panels. The following instructions include using two panels *or* making 16 blocks for the inner quilt top.

The number of pieces to cut for the entire quilt is listed first, with the number to cut for one block following in parentheses.

Measurements for borders and panels (or blocks) include seam allowances. Borders are longer than needed; trim to length when added to the quilt.

From muslin, cut:
2 borders, each 7½x72 inches
2 borders, each 7½x58 inches
2 panels, each 26½x52½ inches, *or* 16 squares, each 13½ inches square

(Continued)

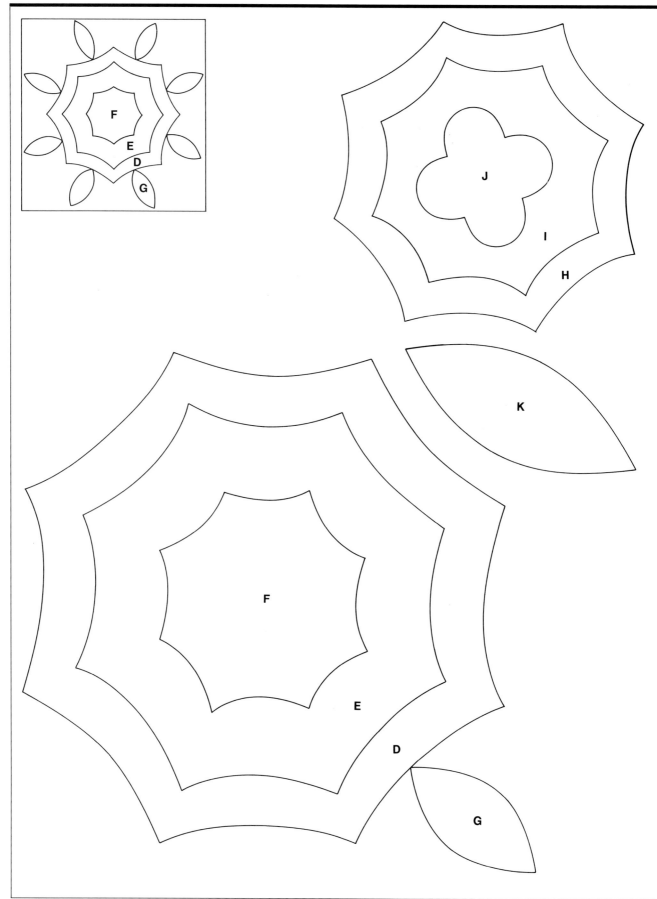

From red fabric, cut:
4 borders, each 2½×58 inches
64 B pieces (4)
10 D flowers (borders)
10 F flower centers (borders)
9 H flowers (borders)
12 G buds (borders)

From green fabric, cut:
64 A leaves (4)
16 C flowers (1)
10 E flowers (borders)
80 G leaves (borders)
9 J flower centers (borders)
34 K leaves (borders)
Approximately 7½ yards of
    ¾-inch-wide bias, folded in
    thirds to ¼ inch wide
Approximately 8½ yards of
    1½-inch-wide bias (binding)

From orange fabric, cut:
9 I flower centers (borders)

To make block patterns: Fold four creases in the 13½-inch square (horizontally, vertically, and diagonally in both directions). Referring to block drawing, page 219, use templates of pieces A, B, and C to draw the block design on the square.

To make one block: Use one of the 16 muslin squares. Using a water-erasable pen, trace the paper pattern onto a fabric block.

Baste under the seam allowances of the appliqué pieces. Position and appliqué four A leaves and four B pieces, using thread to match both fabrics. Position and appliqué a C flower in the center of the block.

To make one panel: Use one of the two muslin panels. Fold panel in half lengthwise; press and unfold. Fold the panel in half widthwise; press (do not unfold). Fold the panel in half widthwise again; press and unfold. These folds should divide the panel into eight equal sections, each approximately 13 inches square.

Referring to the instructions to make one block, *above,* appliqué a block in each section of the panel.

To make the quilt top: Make 16 blocks *or* two panels. Sew the 16 blocks into four rows of four blocks *or* sew the two panels together.

Center and sew a red border to each side of the quilt, mitering the corners.

Center and sew a 58-inch-long muslin border to opposite sides of the quilt; trim excess. Center and sew the 72-inch-long border to remaining two sides and to the ends of the shorter borders; trim.

To appliqué the borders: On one border, use template D to mark position guides for five flowers. Baste vine bias in gentle curves between the flower outlines. Prepare pieces to appliqué five flowers made with D, E, and F pieces. Prepare eight G leaves for each flower; see block drawing, *opposite.* Pin flowers in place; appliqué flowers and vine to border. Repeat to make a second border on the opposite side of the quilt.

To make the borders for the remaining sides, use template H to mark the position of five flowers, template G to mark the position for three pairs of buds, and template K to mark the position for 16 leaves on one border.

Prepare pieces to appliqué five flowers made from H, I, and J pieces. Prepare 16 K leaves and six red G buds. Baste vine bias in curves between the flower and positions. Pin flower, bud, and leaf pieces in place; appliqué flowers, leaves, buds, and vine.

Repeat to mark and appliqué vine bias, four H, I, and J flowers, three pairs of buds, and 18 K leaves on the opposite border.

Finishing: To piece the quilt back, cut fabric into two equal lengths. Cut or tear one length in half lengthwise. Sew one narrow panel to each side of the wide panel. Match the selvages; use a ½-inch seam. Trim the seams to ¼ inch; press to one side.

Layer the back, batting, and the pieced top. Baste layers together; quilt as desired.

When quilting is complete, trim away excess batting and backing so all edges are even with the quilt top. Sew bias binding into one long piece. Sew the binding to the right side of the quilt, raw edges together. Turn the folded edge to the back; hand-stitch in place.

NEEDLE-ROLLING APPLIQUÉ

Some appliqué shapes, such as the Princess Feather Quilt's feather pieces, have very tight curves. Traditional ¼-inch seam allowances are impossible to manage in such cases; there just isn't enough fabric between the curves to allow for them. By using the following technique to stitch such designs, you'll get excellent results—and be able to appliqué all manner of intricate designs in the future.

Begin by tracing around the appliqué shape (the feather) onto the *right* side of the fabric. The drawn line will be the *sewing* line. Cut out the shape, adding only ⅛ *inch* all around for seams.

Next, using the pattern's template and a water-erasable pen, mark placement lines for the motif on the background fabric.

Pin the appliqués to the background, carefully matching the drawn line on each appliqué piece (the sewing line) to the placement lines on the background fabric.

Using your fingertips and the tip of the needle, pinch and roll under a small section of the seam allowance on the appliqué shape, adjusting the position of the folded edge so it just covers the placement line on the background (border) fabric. Pin the appliqué in place as needed.

Next, sew each appliqué in place. As you stitch, continue using the tip of the needle to tuck under the seam allowance along the drawn line and match it to the placement line. Use sharp, small scissors (manicure scissors work well) to clip the tight curves as needed.

MASTERING THE ART AND CRAFT OF QUILTING

Graceful
quilting designs, coupled with
meticulous craftsmanship, are two
hallmarks of the American
patchwork style. In this chapter,
learn how to prepare quilt tops for
quilting and how to hand-quilt
pieced and plain fabrics like
a professional.

Patchwork projects chosen to represent the methods demonstrated in the teaching chapters of this book are all based on star motifs, including the Feather-Quilted Amish Star Quilt, *above.*

This design, which is also suitable for wall hangings, features a central star surrounded by a feathered circle and set into a larger eight-point star. Stitch four additional stars to fill in the corners of the center panel. Beyond the

contrasting inner borders, quilt a continuous feather vine and a grid of diagonal lines.

Through the beginning of this teaching chapter, we use this quilt to demonstrate how to mark fabric with quilting designs, how to baste together quilt layers, and how to hand-quilt. Additional information follows, detailing how to mount a quilt in a frame.

Instructions for projects in this chapter begin on page 232.

MARKING QUILTING DESIGNS

The first step in quilting any project is transferring the quilting motifs to the fabric. Careful placement of correctly scaled motifs is critical.

1 Choose a removable marker to mark the quilting design on your quilt top. **Test any marker to make sure it will show up on your fabric and will be easy to remove after you have finished quilting.** Some good markers for light-colored fabrics (shown from left to right in the photo, *above*) are: a lead pencil (with number 3 or harder lead), a water-erasable marking pen, a colored tailor's chalk pencil, and a chalk dispenser. Some suggested markers for dark fabrics (shown from left to right on the burgundy fabric) are: a soapstone marker, yellow and silver artist's colored pencils, a chalk dispenser, and a sliver of a bar of hand soap.

2 Enlarge the quilting design to full size or trace the individual portions of the design to get a full pattern. For the Feather-Quilted Amish Star design, draw the complete pattern for the center star and draw one border with both corners.

Press the quilt top. To determine the quilt center and establish marking guidelines, fold the top in half; press lightly. Fold in half in the other direction; press.

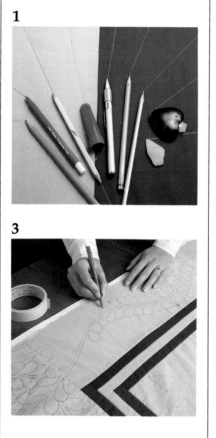

On tracing paper, draw an area with dashed lines (such as a triangle or square) that is the same size as the area to be marked on the quilt top. These lines will be edge guides to help position the quilt top on the pattern.

Trace the quilting design onto the tracing paper within the marked area. Retrace all lines with a black permanent marker; allow to dry. (Use a permanent marker so the ink will not rub off onto the quilt top.)

Use masking tape to secure the traced design. Matching the seams on the quilt top to the edge guides on the pattern, tape the quilt top over the pattern, using the seams and center creases to help position the quilt top.

3 Starting at the center and working out toward the edges, use a removable marker to trace the quilting designs onto the quilt top. Mark the more complex designs first. Use a ruler as a guide when tracing straight lines.

For the Feather-Quilted Amish Star pattern, mark the star design in the center of the quilt top first. Then mark the four borders.

4 After the complex quilting motifs have been marked, fill in the background grid to complete the border.

For the Feather-Quilted Amish Star pattern, background design on borders is 1-inch cross-hatching (use a diagonal grid of 1-inch squares). Use a ruler to mark the grid of squares. It is easiest to begin marking at the center of a border and mark all the parallel lines in one direction along a border side first, then mark the lines in the opposite direction.

1

2

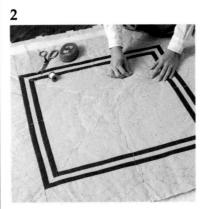

3

BASTING THE QUILT TOP, BATTING, AND BACKING

Assembling the layers of a quilt properly ensures a smooth, wrinkle-free fabric background for your quilting stitches.

1 When the marking is complete, you are ready to baste your quilt.

First, take the quilt batting out of its package and leave it unfolded for a few days to remove some of the wrinkles. You also can relax the batt by tumbling it in a clothes dryer for a few minutes on the air-dry setting.

Piece the quilt backing so it is at least 2 inches larger on all sides than the quilt top. Press the quilt back. To create positioning guides, fold the back in half and lightly press. Fold the back in half in the other direction and press.

Using masking tape, secure the quilt back *wrong* side up to a hard surface, such as a wood or vinyl floor. (Don't plan to baste on a fine wood dining table; you may scratch the surface.) Often a school or church recreation hall is a convenient place to baste a quilt; you'll find plenty of floor space or large banquet-size tables.

Even if you are basting a large quilt, you can work on a table if this is more comfortable and convenient for you. Center the quilt back on the table, letting the excess back hang down. The weight of the excess fabric hanging down will help keep the quilt back smooth while you are basting, or you can use large paper clips and clip the back to the tabletop. After you have basted one area, slide another section onto the table and continue basting.

Cut the batting to at least 1 inch larger all around than the quilt top. Center the batting on the quilt back; smooth any wrinkles.

Tape or pin the batting to the quilt back, gently pulling the batting to straighten it if necessary.

Fold the quilt top in half, right sides together. Line up the fold in the quilt top with the center creases on the back. The *wrong* side of the quilt top should be toward batting. Unfold quilt top, keeping the top centered on the batting.

2 Beginning at the center and working toward the edges, baste the three layers together. If your quilt has sashing strips, baste along the strips first, then fill in the additional basting between the strips.

Use white thread to baste. Colored thread may leave colored lint in your quilt. If a colored thread breaks inside the quilt when you are removing the basting after quilting, the thread may be visible through the quilt top. These threads are almost impossible to remove after the quilting has been completed.

Continue to add basting until the quilt is basted about every 4 inches. The basting stitches can be very large and you can skip 3 to 4 inches between stitches.

3 To keep the batting from fraying if you plan to quilt in a hoop, fold the quilt back over the batting and quilt top; baste.

QUILTING

There are many methods for sewing quilting stitches. With experience and practice, each quilter develops an individual technique. Here are instructions for one common method.

1 To begin, hold the needle between your thumb and first finger. Place your other hand under the quilt, with the tip of the index finger in the spot where the needle will come through the quilt back. With the needle angled slightly away from you, push the needle through the layers until you feel the tip of the needle with the finger beneath the quilt.

2 As soon as you feel the needle tip, slide the finger underneath the quilt toward you, pushing up against the side of the needle to help return the needle to the top. At the same time, with your top hand, roll the needle away from you. Gently push the needle forward and upward, through the quilt's layers, until the amount of needle showing is the length you want the next stitch to be.

3 To form successive stitches on your needle, reposition your top hand to rest the eye of the needle on the end of your thimble, placing your thumb slightly ahead of where you are stitching. Rock the needle up so it is almost perpendicular to the quilt top. Push down on the thimble until you feel the needle tip with your finger underneath the quilt.

1

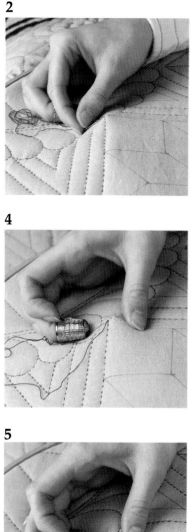

2

3

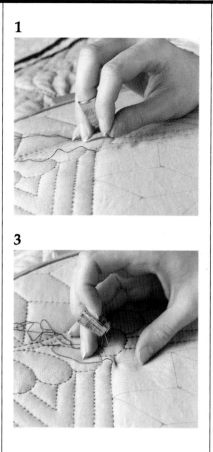

4

4 While helping redirect the needle to the quilt top with your finger underneath the quilt, roll the needle down and then forward with your thimble. Push down on the quilt top with your thumb, just ahead of where you are stitching, to help return the needle to the top.

5 Repeat the motions of steps 3 and 4 to fill your needle with several stitches. Push the needle forward with your thimble. Then, grasp the needle with your thumb and forefinger and pull it through the layers of the quilt. Tug on the thread until the stitches are snug but not puckered.

5

1

2

3

MOUNTING A QUILT IN A FRAME

Mounting an assembled quilt in a frame, regardless of the frame's style, calls for the same basic steps. It's best, however, to carefully read the manufacturer's directions that accompany your quilt frame.

1 Referring to pages 225 and 226, mark the quilting design on the quilt top and baste the quilt top, batting, and quilt back.

Check to make sure your quilting frame is large enough for your quilt. The frame rails should be as long as the quilt is wide, plus long enough to fasten in the frame.

Tack or staple 6-inch-wide muslin strips along the rails.

Place the rails on the floor parallel to each other. Pin or baste the width of the backing to the muslin strips on each rail.

Carefully roll the quilt evenly around one rail to the middle of the quilt, rolling the quilt so the quilt back is facing out. Roll the other end of the quilt around the rail in the opposite direction, with the quilt top out. Rolling the sides in opposite directions will help keep an even tension on the quilt when it is in the frame. It is easier to roll a large quilt evenly if at least two people help.

2 Fasten one of the rails in the frame. Unroll the other rail and fasten it in the other side of the frame, exposing the center section of the quilt top. The quilt should be stretched firmly between the rails.

3 Cut 2-inch-wide strips of muslin or scrap fabric. Pin a fabric strip to the excess quilt back along the side of the quilt near one of the rails. Wrap the strip around the side brace of the frame and then pin it again to the quilt back, stretching the quilt as you wrap. Continue to wrap and pin until the side is stretched. Repeat for the other side.

Begin quilting in the center and work toward the edges. When the center section is quilted, unpin the muslin strips that stretch the sides. Unroll another section of the quilt and continue until you reach the end. Then, reroll the quilt to the center and work toward the other end.

Hand-Quilting Tips

To many observers, the method used to make quilting stitches is not as important as the result. Here are some guidelines by which to judge your quilting, as well as some general information on quilting equipment and accessories.

❖

Hand-quilting is stitching a series of small, even running stitches through all three layers of the project. Quilting holds the layers of the quilt together and keeps the batting from shifting and lumping. Stitches should be small, straight, and evenly spaced. Quilting seven or more stitches per inch (counting on the top) is considered fine quilting. The stitches on the back of the project ideally should be the same size as those on the front.

Needles: Betweens needles are ideal for quilting. Betweens needles are short needles of fairly uniform diameter. Most quilters prefer needles in the size range of 7 to 12; the higher the number, the shorter the needle.

It usually is easier to make small, even stitches with short needles because short needles are easier to control than longer needles. If you are accustomed to a longer needle for general sewing and embroidery, work your way down to a small needle. Set your goal to use a needle that is as small as you can comfortably thread and that will not break too easily when used on your project.

Thread: Waxed or specially treated quilting threads are stronger, smoother, and less likely to tangle than conventional sewing thread. Use cotton or cotton-covered polyester thread for quilts that contain cotton fabrics because polyester thread may cut the cotton fabric.

Regular sewing thread may be used for small projects; treat the thread with beeswax to strengthen it and make it more tangle-free.

Choose thread that complements both the quilt top and quilt back. Use matching or contrasting thread, but keep in mind that stitching irregularities are more obvious with contrasting thread.

Keep your quilting thread relatively short—18 to 24 inches long is a workable length. Long threads are more likely to snarl, break, and wear thin from being pulled through the fabric.

Thimbles: You will be more comfortable when quilting if you wear a thimble on the middle finger of your sewing hand. The thimble protects your finger and helps push the needle through all three layers.

Metal thimbles come in varying sizes. Choose a thimble that fits snugly and has small, deep dimples to hold your needle. The dimples should not be smooth and dished like those on a golf ball. Special quilting thimbles have a raised rim at the top to help prevent the needle from slipping.

Several types of leather thimbles also are available. Some quilters find these easier to adapt to than metal thimbles.

Quilting hoops: Since today's homes seldom have space to accommodate a full-size quilting frame, many quilters use a round or oval quilting hoop.

Wooden quilting hoops are similar to large embroidery hoops, but they have thicker, deeper hoops and a larger screw adjustment. Hoops are available in a variety of sizes and with or without a stand. A 14-inch-diameter hoop is a good all-purpose size.

Quilting with a hoop: The process of forming the quilting stitches is similar with either a hoop or a frame. For instructions on how to form the quilting stitches, refer to page 227.

When quilting with a hoop, begin quilting at the center of the quilt and work out in concentric circles.

To fit the quilt in a hoop, position the inner hoop under the area to be quilted. Loosen the screw adjustment on the outer hoop so it will slip easily over the quilt. Fit the outer hoop over the quilt and inner hoop. Pull on the quilt top and back to smooth out any wrinkles; then, tighten the screw adjustment to hold the quilt snugly in the hoop.

If the quilt is stretched drum-tight, it's difficult to make stitches. But it also should not be so loose that puckers and wrinkles are stitched into the quilt.

Beginning and ending stitches: To begin, thread a needle with 18 to 24 inches of quilting thread: knot one end. Run the needle into the batting about half a needle-length away from the point where quilting is to begin. Bring the needle up at the starting point. Pull on the thread to pop the knot into the batting. If the knot is stubborn and does not want to pop through the quilt top, try pushing down on the knot with your thumbnail while you pull on the thread.

End the thread by tying a knot about ¼ inch from the quilt top. Run the needle through the batting; then, pop the knot into the batting. No knots should show on either surface of a project.

Move from one area of quilting to another by running the needle through the batting or by knotting off and restarting, depending on the distance to the next part of the design.

❖ ❖ ❖

Quilted designs are the focal points of these three projects. You'll find many uses for these classic quilting motifs.

Sashiko is the name given to the style of quilting used for the yoke of the jacket, *left,* and on page 223. This style originated in Japan in the early 18th century, and is characterized by a repeat pattern of interlocking geometric shapes. Our quilted yoke is based on a hexagonal motif.

The flattering quilted collar, *above,* features graceful tulip motifs. This detachable accessory also can be worn with the opening at the back.

The spectacular whole-cloth quilt, *opposite,* is a fine example of a bridal quilt. In the mid-1800s, about when this quilt was created, fine white fabric was expensive. Projects calling for large amounts of such fabric were reserved for special times, such as weddings.

This design, also pictured on pages 222-223, features feathered circle motifs in varying sizes, and a central circle of interlocking rings.

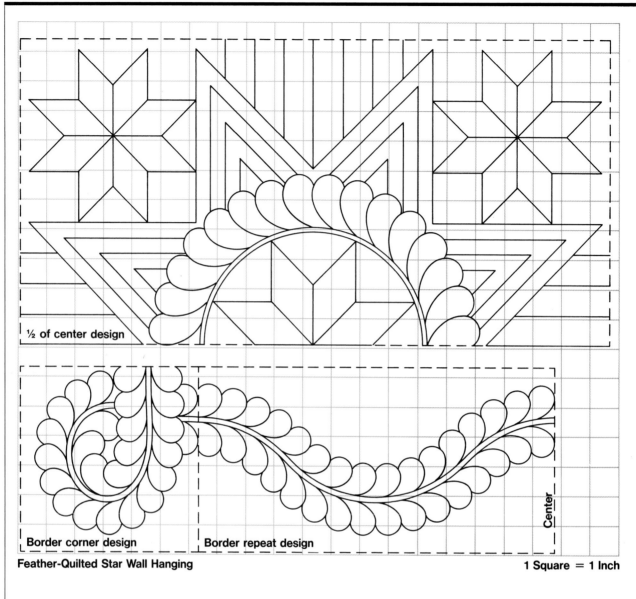

½ of center design

Border corner design   Border repeat design

Center

Feather-Quilted Star Wall Hanging

1 Square = 1 Inch

**FEATHER-QUILTED
AMISH STAR QUILT**
PAGE 224
Finished size is 37x37 inches.

Materials
1⅝ yards of pink fabric
¾ yard of burgundy fabric
1¼ yards of backing fabric
Quilt batting
Black permanent marker
Water-erasable marker

Instructions
The cutting measurements for all pieces for this project include ¼-inch seam allowances and are the exact length required.

Enlarge quilting designs, *above.* Copy designs onto tracing paper, tracing full center design and complete border with two corners. Darken quilting designs with a black marker.

To cut the pieces:
From pink fabric, cut:
One 21-inch square
Two 1¼x22½-inch middle borders
Two 1¼x24-inch middle borders
Two 6½x25½-inch outer borders
Two 6½x37½-inch outer borders

From burgundy fabric, cut:
Two 1¼x21-inch inner borders
Two 1¼x22½-inch inner borders
Two 1¼x24-inch middle borders
Two 1¼x25½-inch middle borders
Four 2½x45-inch strips (binding)

To piece the top: Sew the burgundy 1¼x21-inch borders to the top and bottom of the center square. Stitch the burgundy 1¼x22½-inch borders along the sides.

Sew the 1¼x22½-inch pink borders to the top and bottom, and the 1¼x24-inch pink borders to the sides.

Sew the 1¼x24-inch burgundy borders to the top and bottom, and the 1¼x25½-inch burgundy borders to the sides.

Finally, sew the 6½x25½-inch pink borders to the top and bottom, and the 6½x37½-inch pink borders to the sides.

To mark the quilting designs: Refer to the instructions on page 225 for marking quilting designs.

Finishing: To cut the quilt back and baste the quilt, refer to the instructions on pages 226. Quilt along all marked quilting lines.

When quilting is complete, trim the backing fabric and batting even with the quilt top.

Fold the binding strips in half lengthwise, wrong sides together, and press. Matching the raw edges of the binding to the raw edges of the quilt top, stitch a binding strip to the top and bottom of the quilt. Trim excess binding even with the quilt sides. Stitch the remaining binding strips to the quilt sides. Trim away excess, leaving about ¼ inch to turn in to finish the binding at the corners.

Turn the folded edges of the binding strips to the quilt back and stitch in place, neatly tucking in the edges of the side binding strips to finish the corners.

If you intend to hang this quilt, you may wish to add a sleeve at the top of the back.

WHOLE-CLOTH BRIDAL QUILT
PAGES 222–223 and 231
Finished size is 80x80 inches.

Materials
13 yards bleached muslin
Quilt batting
Water-erasable marker
36x60-inch cardboard sewing and cutting board, ruled in 1-inch increments

Instructions
Enlarge the quilting design, page 234. This pattern is one-fourth of the finished quilt.

To make the quilt top: Divide the fabric into four 3-yard lengths. Set two of the 3-yard lengths (backing) and the remaining yard (binding) aside.

Cut one 3-yard length in half lengthwise. Sew one narrow panel to each side of the full panel. Match the selvages; use a ½-inch seam. Trim the seams to ¼ inch; press away from the center panel.

Fold the quilt top in half lengthwise and press a lengthwise center guideline. Then fold the quilt top in half widthwise and press for a second guideline. This pressing divides the quilt top into quarters.

To mark the pattern: Lay the sewing board on a large table. Lay the quilt top over the board so that the center of the quilt (the intersection of the creases) matches one corner of the ruled grid and the creases align with the sides of the grid. Pin the cloth in place.

Using a ruler and a water-erasable marker, draw in the feathered circles. Use the grid on the sewing board to help measure accurately. Repeat to mark the other quadrants of the quilt top.

For the quilted grids, pivot the sewing board beneath the quilt top 45 degrees. Using the grid of the sewing board as a guide, and using a ruler or other straightedge, mark a 1-inch grid over the entire quilt, omitting the areas inside the four corner circles and the two side circles.

Finally, use a ruler to divide the 1-inch grid at quilt's center into a ½-inch grid. Mark a ½-inch grid in each of the remaining circles.

Finishing: Make a quilt back, following same instructions as for quilt front. Layer and baste the back, batting, and top as directed in the instructions on page 226. Quilt all marked lines as directed in the instructions on page 227.

Mark each edge with 40 scallops, if desired.

Cut 1¼-inch-wide bias strips from remaining yard of fabric and piece together to make one long strip. With raw edges together, machine-stitch binding to the quilt top. Trim away excess back, batting, and top close to the raw edge of binding. Turn binding to back of quilt; hand-stitch in place.

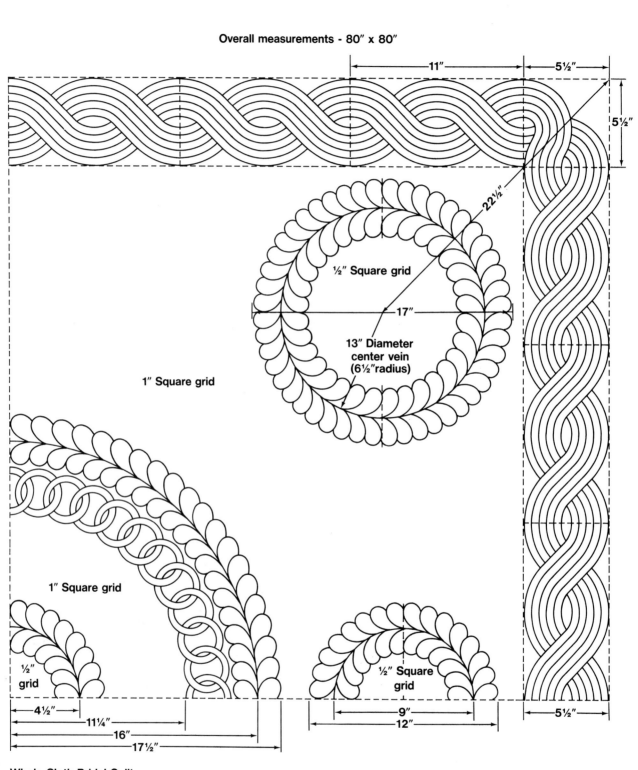

Overall measurements - 80" x 80"

11"

5½"

5½"

22½"

½" Square grid

17"

13" Diameter center vein (6½"radius)

1" Square grid

1" Square grid

½" grid

½" Square grid

4½"

11¼"

16"

17½"

9"

12"

5½"

Whole Cloth Bridal Quilt

Front neck

Back neck

Center

Quilted Collar 1 Square = 1 Inch

QUILTED COLLAR
PAGE 230

Materials
1 yard of yellow fabric
½ yard of white batiste (backing)
½ yard of 45-inch-wide
  lightweight quilt batting
¼-inch-diameter white shank-
  type button
Water-erasable marker

Instructions
Enlarge the collar pattern, *right*, and make a pattern for the collar fronts and for the full collar back. Pattern is finished size; add ¼-inch seam allowances when cutting the pieces from fabric.

Divide the yellow fabric into two ½-yard pieces. Set one piece aside for the lining. Using a water-erasable marker, draw one collar back and two collar fronts onto the remaining yellow piece, spacing the pieces at least 1 inch apart to allow for seam allowances. Fill in the space above the curve near the scallops with a ¾-inch grid of squares.

Layer the batting and batiste under the marked fabric and baste. Quilt the tulips, grid, and curved line.

After the quilting is complete, baste around the collar pieces. Cut out the pieces, adding seam allowances. Sew the shoulder seams. Cut one collar back and two collar fronts from the yellow lining fabric, adding ¼-inch seam allowances. Sew shoulder seams.

Pin collar to collar lining, right sides facing. Sew around the collar, leaving an opening for turning along one center front edge. Clip along neck edge and along scallops. Turn collar right side out through opening; sew opening closed.

Quilt around the collar ¼ inch from all edges. Sew a white button to the left collar front. Make a thread loop on the right collar front to slip over the button.

TIED QUILTS
Many kinds of quilts, including puffy comforters and large bedspreads, are suitable for tying.

Certain simple pieced patterns are so charming (such as log cabin or four- or nine-patch patterns) that quilted designs may detract from their simplicity. Other quilts assembled from wools or velvets become so thick, after batting is added, that quilting through all the thicknesses is impossible.

There are several ways to tie a quilt, and any of the natural fibers can be used, including pearl cotton, embroidery floss, or wool yarn. Quilts may be tied so that the knots show on either the top or the back.

One common way to tie a quilt is to take a single running stitch, about ¼ inch long, through all three quilt layers. Backstitch in exactly the same spot, reinserting the needle and bringing it back out through the same holes. Tie the thread ends in a tight square knot; cut ends to desired length.

JACKET WITH QUILTED YOKE

PAGES 223 and 230
*Hexagonal quilting motif is 4 ½ inches
across at widest point.*

Materials

Jacket pattern with yoke (jacket
shown is Simplicity 8177)
Peach corduroy in yardages
specified on package
1 yard light green cotton (yoke
and lining)
Quilt batting
Quilting thread to match the
jacket fabric
Water-erasable marker

Instructions

Trace the complete jacket back
and front yoke patterns onto tracing paper.

Trace the hexagonal quilting
design, *right*. Referring to the photographs, pages 223 and 230, trace
the pattern onto the back yoke
tracing. Create pattern for yoke
front pieces similarly (make one
pattern for the yoke front and reverse it). Transfer patterns to
front yoke pieces.

Cut out the jacket pieces, except yokes, chest pockets, and
pocket flaps, from peach corduroy. Trim the front facings to the
length of the jacket front pieces.

Cut two back yoke pieces and
two *each* of front yoke pieces from
light green fabric (the second pattern pieces of each shape are yoke
linings). Cut one yoke back and
two yoke fronts from batting.

Transfer quilting designs onto
all yoke pieces. Sew yoke and
yoke lining shoulder seams.

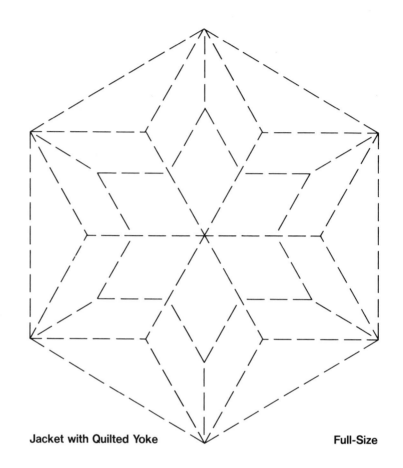

Jacket with Quilted Yoke　　　　　**Full-Size**

Baste batting to the yoke, trimming batting pieces beneath the
shoulder seam line so the edges
butt together, not overlap. Whipstitch batting together at the
shoulders.

Pin yoke and yoke lining right
sides together along center front
edges and along neck edge to collar notch. Sew center front seams
and along neck edge to the collar
notch. Trim, clip, and turn right
side out. Stay-stitch neck edge.
Baste along shoulder and bottom
edges.

Quilt the jacket yoke.

Press under ⅝-inch seam along
neck edge of collar; trim to ¼
inch. With right sides together,
stitch collar to facing, leaving

neck edge open. Trim, clip, and
turn. Topstitch collar.

Clip neck edge of yokes to stay-
stitching. Sew collar facing to
yoke neck edge, matching notches
and center back. Slip-stitch
pressed edge of collar over back
seam.

With right sides together, sew
front facing to jacket fronts. Sew
jacket fronts to side fronts, adding
pockets if desired.

Sew the jacket fronts to the
front yokes. Turn the front facings to wrong side and slip-stitch
facings over yoke seams. Complete jacket according to pattern
instructions.

ALTERING A QUILT PATTERN TO FIT YOUR BED

This scenario, alas, is familiar—you've just discovered a beautiful quilt design in a book or magazine, but the quilt pictured is twin-size and you want a queen-size one. Don't despair. There are several simple ways to fit the quilt of your dreams to the bed of your choice.

The first step is to decide exactly what size you want the finished quilt to be.

Determining quilt size: The dimensions of the new quilt will depend on the size of the bed for which it is intended (twin, full, queen, and king are the most common) *and* on how the quilt will be used. Will it be a blanket or throw? A coverlet over a dust ruffle? Or a full-length spread?

Once you've decided how you want the quilt to be displayed on the bed, consult the information below to determine a suggested length and width for the altered design.

Keep in mind that these are ideal dimensions. How closely the length and width of the finished quilt approximate the dimensions given will depend on the proportions of the original design and on the methods you use to adapt the pattern.

For a twin bed: The mattress is 39x75 inches. The size of blanket or throw is 61x86 inches; the size of a coverlet with tuck-in is 61x104 inches; the size of a bedspread is 79x110 inches.

For a full bed: The mattress is 54x75 inches. The size of a blanket or throw is 76x86 inches; the size of a coverlet with tuck-in is 76x104 inches; the size of a bedspread is 94x110 inches.

For a queen-size bed: The mattress is 60x80 inches. The size of a blanket or throw is 82x91 inches; the size of a coverlet with tuck-in is 82x109 inches. The size of a bedspread is 100x115 inches.

For a king-size bed: The mattress is 76x80 inches. The size of a blanket or throw is 98x91 inches; the size of a coverlet with tuck-in is 98x109 inches; the size of a bedspread is 116x115 inches.

Note: Measurements for "blanket or throw" allow for an 11-inch-deep overhang on the sides and at the foot of the bed. "Coverlet with tuck-in" includes an additional 15 inches in length to tuck in over the pillows at the head of the bed. "Bedspread" measurements include a full 20-inch-deep drop on sides and at the foot, plus another 15 inches in length to be wrapped over the pillows and tucked in.

Adapting the pattern: Once you've decided approximately how large you want your quilt to be, visually break the original design apart into its individual components and decide how you will deal with each portion of the design to achieve the desired overall dimensions.

There are two basic ways to adapt a quilt design: (1) Increase or decrease the number of pattern blocks; (2) alter the size and/or number of sashing strips and/or borders.

In some instances, you may find it necessary to use a combination of these two methods to achieve the desired results. Each method has advantages and each works better for certain kinds of quilt designs than for others.

As you work, sketch planned alterations on graph paper, to help you visualize how altering one component of the pattern (the number of blocks, for example) will affect the other components, such as the length of the sashing and border strips.

Altering the number of pattern blocks: Most traditional quilt patterns are composed of pieced or appliquéd pattern blocks that are stitched into horizontal and vertical rows to form the design. Usually these pattern blocks are squares, but they also may be rectangles, triangles, or hexagons.

Designs that consist of identical repeat pattern blocks are the easiest to adapt. By simply increasing or decreasing the number of blocks in each horizontal or vertical row, you can change the length or width of the quilt. If, for example, the pattern block is an 8-inch square, you can make the quilt 8, 16, or 24 inches wider or longer (or both) simply by adding one, two, or three extra rows of blocks to the sides and/or ends of the original design. (Keep in mind that sashes and borders must be lengthened accordingly.)

Certain types of repeat block designs require a little more planning. For designs in which *two* different pattern blocks (or a plain and a patterned block) alternate across the quilt creating a secondary pattern (as in Irish Chain or Ocean Waves designs), the *symmetry* of the design must be considered. In such cases, additions or subtractions must be made evenly to each side or to the top and bottom of the original design for the sake of balance. (This is also true of repeat block designs in which blocks are joined on the diagonal.)

Altering sashes and/or borders: A second simple way of adapting a quilt design is to change the width of the sashing strips—the narrow horizontal and vertical bands of fabric used to frame and separate the pattern blocks on many quilt designs. This method is a good choice if the changes you want to make in the size of the quilt are minimal. But keep in mind that the proportional relationship between sashing and blocks has much to do with the design's overall effectiveness.

Adding to, or altering the size of, borders is another simple way to adjust quilt dimensions, and this method often can be used effectively in conjunction with changes in sashing.

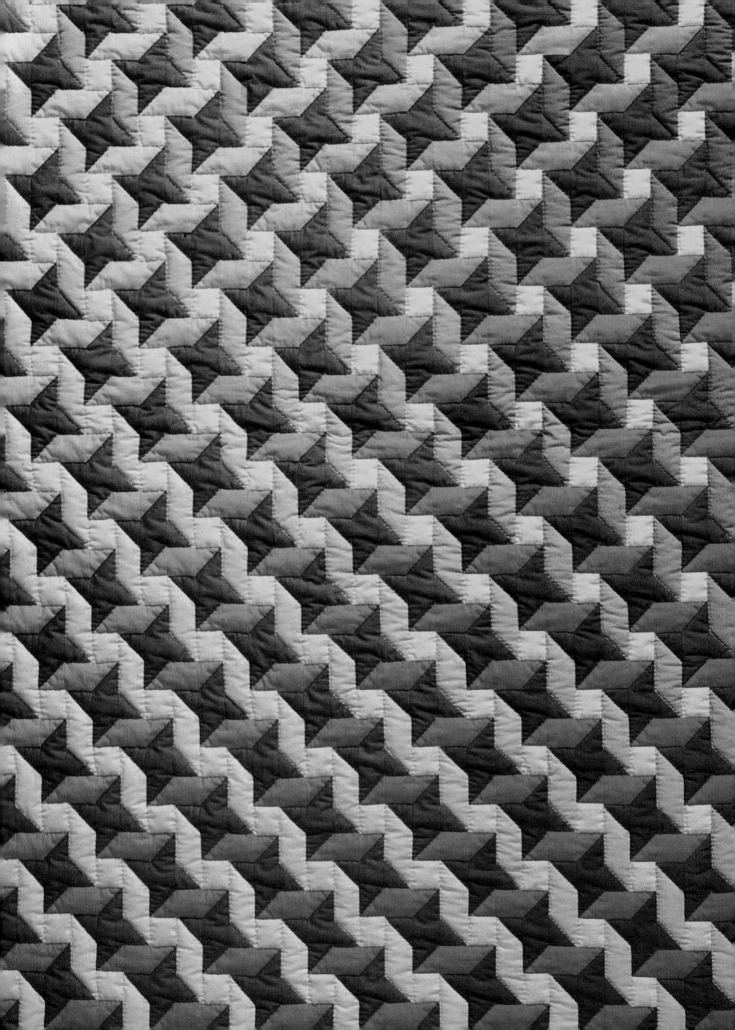